Tom Ellis

Worker and Community

SUNY Series in American Social History
Charles Stephenson and Elizabeth Pleck, Editors

Worker and Community

Response to Industrialization in a Nineteenth-Century American City, Albany, New York, 1850–1884

BRIAN GREENBERG

State University of New York Press

The map on the endsheet is from Frederick W. Beers, *Atlas of the Hudson River Valley from New York City to Troy*. New York: Watson and Co., c. 1891.

Figure 1 is from *Cities and Immigrants: A Geography of Change in Nineteenth-Century America* by David Ward. Copyright © 1971 by Oxford University Press, Inc. Reprinted by permission.

Published by
State University of New York Press, Albany

Printed in the United States of America

For information, address State University of New York Press, State University Plaza, Albany, N.Y., 12246

Library of Congress Cataloging in Publication Data

Greenberg, Brian.
Worker and community.

(SUNY series in American social history)
Bibliography: p. 211
Includes index.
1. Labor and laboring classes—New York (State)—Albany—History—19th century. 2. Albany (N.Y.)—Industries—History—19th century. 3. Industrial relations—New York (State)—Albany—History—19th century. 4. Convict labor—New York (State)—Albany—History—19th century. I. Title. II. Series.
HD8085.A43G74 1985 305.5'62'0974743 84-26774
ISBN 0-88706-046-3
ISBN 0-88706-048-X (pbk.)

To Susan, who not only made this
possible, but worthwhile

Contents

Acknowledgments ix

Introduction 1

1. Industrialization and the Awakening of Class Consciousness 9

Part I

2. Workers and Free Labor 25
3. Militancy and Consciousness: The Emergence of a Commonwealth Ideology 43
4. Labor on the Defensive 69

Part II

5. Free Labor Fraternalism: The Independent Order of Odd Fellows in Albany 89
6. The Albany Penitentiary: Model for an Orderly Society 103
7. Socialization and Acculturation: Religion, Ethnicity, and Politics in Albany 119

Part III

8. The Anti-Prison Contract Labor Movement: A Study in Albany Workers' Evolving Consciousness 143

Notes 161

Bibliography 211

Index 221

Acknowledgments

Writing history is a collaborative endeavor involving the historian with many colleagues and professionals who help him to understand the significance of those whose story he hopes to tell. Although the ultimate responsibility for what appears on these pages is mine, I am indebted to many persons for their assistance. I would like to thank the librarians at three Albany institutions: the New York State Library, especially James Corsaro and Melinda Yates; the Harmanus Bleecker Library, in particular Marguerite Mullenneaux; and the State University of New York at Albany Library, especially Jill Weinstein; and the librarians at the New York Public Library. I have also been fortunate during the past few years to be associated with the Hagley Museum and Library. I appreciate the support given me by Walter J. Heacock, and I am grateful to Richmond Williams and his able staff for all their help. Michael Nash was particularly generous in providing me with a quiet haven in which to work. I also received support for my research from the University of Delaware College of Arts and Sciences.

Throughout this study is evidence of my great debt to William E. Rowley of the State University of New York at Albany. At Princeton University both James M. McPherson and James M. Banner, Jr., gave generously of their time, interest, and advice. I have also been fortunate to receive the criticism and support of Richard Bushman, Milton Cantor, Stanley Engerman, Mark Hirsch, Bruce Laurie, Walter Licht, Glenn Porter, and Eric Schneider. An earlier version of Chapter 5 appeared in *The Maryland Historian* 8 (Fall 1977): 38–53.

Both Charles Stephenson and Harold Wechsler have been a part of this study from the outset and their wisdom and counsel have been invaluable. Without the patience and good humor of Ella Phillips, preparation of this book would have been far more difficult. I am also grateful to the staff at SUNY Press for all their assistance. Yet through it all Susan Greenberg has been my ablest critic and strongest supporter, and it is to her that I owe my greatest debt.

Introduction

In his study of shoemakers in Lynn, Massachusetts, Alan Dawley demonstrates that the relations of production essential to industrial capitalism were present long before the rise of the factory in the 1860s. In the 1820s the central shop became the basic unit of manufacture in the shoe industry. The coming of the central shop divided Lynn economically and socially. Two distinct classes emerged—the entrepreneurs who bought the raw materials, owned the critical means of production, and sold the finished products, and a much larger group, the workers who labored solely for wages. Beginning in the second quarter of the nineteenth century, not only in Lynn but in other industrializing cities, one way of life was giving way to another. Under the impact of industrial capitalism, the more personal relationship of master artisan, journeyman, and apprentice was replaced by the class relationship of employer and worker.[1]

This study focuses on the significance of industrialization in Albany, New York, between 1850 and 1884. Although destined to remain primarily a commercial city, a transmission center for people, goods, and services, Albany also developed the diversified small manufactures that still characterized the period. As the city industrialized, the economic status of its workers declined, its once independent artisans becoming solely wage earners. Yet even while industrialization was producing the objective conditions of class in Albany, workers' consciousness of class was mitigated by their attachment to the larger community.[2]

The superiority of the free labor order was assumed by most people living in the towns and smaller cities of midnineteenth-century America. The proponents of the free labor system celebrated the nation's dynamic, capitalist economy and the opportunity and dignity offered to the workingman. Ideally, class divisions should not be permanent because society's well-being required that individual ambition and industriousness be rewarded. Since all members of society presumably would benefit from economic expansion, a mutuality of interests prevailed among them. When they acted in concert, capital and labor were thought to be part of an economic process that produced prosperity for all.

The free labor ideology formed the basis of what may be called "community consciousness." The idea of community consciousness can be understood best when juxtaposed against class consciousness, its opposite. Class consciousness assumes capital and labor to be distinct social forces locked in irreconcilable conflict as a consequence of their relations to production. Community consciousness as an extension of free labor social values incorporates a belief in the mutuality of interests between capital and labor. In cities and towns throughout America, civic leaders encouraged employers and workers to develop loyalty to the community rather than to their particular class interests. Free labor values lay at the core of community order prevailing in Albany.[3]

An index to community consciousness in Albany is found in the social views expressed by the editors of the city's two leading newspapers, the *Argus* and the *Albany Evening Journal.* As the seat of New York State government, Albany was a printing and publishing center, particularly for politically engaged newspapers. Both locally and statewide throughout the nineteenth century, the editors of the *Argus* and the *Evening Journal* spoke for, respectively, the Democratic and Republican parties. Within Albany, perhaps as an extension of their political roles, the editors saw themselves as spokesmen for the interests of the community, and it is in this capacity that they responded to the social issues raised by industrialization.

Editorials in Albany's newspapers reflected the ambiguity inherent in middle-class social orthodoxy during industrialization. As free labor spokesmen, the newspaper editors believed that society had to allow for workers' upward social mobility. In this conviction they are typical of the "self-made men" Herbert Gutman has studied, who, in the smaller industrial towns, frequently supported workers in their struggles against employers.[4] Enthusiastic about economic growth, the editors nonetheless often expressed uneasiness over the social implications of large-scale industrialization. For example, they idealized the traditional master–apprentice relationship even though industrialization long since had rendered it anachronistic. Blaming an increase in the number of juvenile criminals plaguing Albany on the virtual abandonment of the apprentice system, the *Argus* called for a return to "a lengthened service and a graduation from the school of the skilled mechanic."[5] As free labor spokesmen, the newspaper editors anticipated, despite evidence to the contrary, that industrialization could proceed without a fundamental disruption in the prevailing social and economic order.

Conversely, out of their concern for Albany's industrial position, both newspapers could be very receptive to the employer's sense of what sustained his well-being. For example, as employers themselves, the editors of the *Argus* and the *Albany Evening Journal* vehemently opposed all efforts by workers to limit the workday to eight hours. Increase in the cost of production stood out among the manifold dangers they saw posed by an eight-hour system. Fearing that adoption of the eight-hour workday might make Albany a less attractive place for business, they appealed to workers not to be self-seeking but rather to consider the interests of the entire community.[6]

The *Argus* and the *Evening Journal* condemned workers' demands for an eight-hour working day as a "class position." The *Argus* recommended to workers that they recognize that "the army of Labor and Capital in hostility is war, and war is always destructive to both parties. The combination of capital with labor is peace and in its train follows plenty." Similarly, the *Evening Journal* maintained that "capital and labor are not antagonistic. They are the positive and negative elements which complete the currents and help the circuit of commerce and trade. Neither can exist without the other, and both have claims to consideration."[7] Both newspapers tried to promote what they saw as the natural harmony that should exist between all members of the community.

But what of Albany's workers? Did they adopt a community-conscious perspective and accept the notion of a mutuality of interests? Or did they instead act in accordance with their perceived class interests? Neither community nor class consciousness alone explains Albany workers' world view during industrialization. Rather, workers' perception of the social order evolved through a dialectic between the dominant free labor beliefs and the workers' own awareness of themselves as a class.

The issue of class, Walter Licht states in his review essay "Labor and Capital and the American Community," is the "distinct point of departure" for what has come to be known as the "new labor history." Within the last ten years richly detailed studies of such nineteenth-century industrial cities as Lynn, Fall River, and Lowell, Massachusetts; New York City, Troy, and Cohoes, New York; Philadelphia, Pennsylvania; and Newark, New Jersey, have been published. Emphasizing worker culture, the new labor historians focus on the rules and values that generated and guided workers' response to their newly acquired class position. In particular, these studies dramatically recreate workers' persistent efforts to resist the impositions of capitalist industrialization and their articulation of an alternative vision of the good society.[8]

The approach to worker culture by way of studying industrialization within specific communities reflects the influence of Herbert Gutman on the new labor history. David Montgomery credits Gutman with drawing our attention away from the growth of trade unions, the traditional province of labor historiography, "to the communities where workers lived and fought," and, equally important, with teaching a generation of scholars to appreciate workers as makers of their own history.[9] Gutman criticizes labor history's emphasis on trade unions because it tended to isolate American workers from "their own particular subcultures." In his major synthesis of worker culture, "Work, Culture, and Society in Industrializing America, 1815–1919," Gutman identifies the tension between preindustrial and industrial habits and values as the critical factor underlying workers' response to industrialization.[10]

Unfortunately, as Daniel Rodgers points out, Gutman's counterposing of preindustrial and industrial employs the bipolar "habit of mind" associated with modernization theory. According to modernization theorists, industrialization involved an irreversible transition from one ideal social type, traditional society, to its mirror opposite, modernity. Gutman's use of preindustrial and industrial reduces a complex historical process to the almost inevitable transition from one static and monolithic category to another. Yet worker culture during industrialization was far more diverse and involved much more than simply internalizing modern work habits.[11]

One approach that some labor historians have taken in order to break from the modernization schema and show the impact of the larger culture on workers has been to further refine the typologies of "traditional" and "modern." In their important article on working-class culture and politics in Lynn, Alan Dawley and Paul Faler distinguish "modernist" (i.e., industrial) workers as either "loyalists," those who accepted the contemporary notion that a mutuality of interests existed between capital and labor, or "rebels," those who "saw an overriding antagonism." In his study of Jacksonian Philadelphia, Bruce Laurie characterizes the loyalists as "Revivalists," as a way of indicating the influence that evangelical Protestantism had on worker culture.[12]

Although convenient for descriptive purposes, ideal types, be they those devised by Gutman, Dawley and Faler, or Laurie, inevitably stereotype workers' response to industrialization. Nineteenth-century workers, like anyone else in a complex society, were capable of holding multiple loyalties, of being simultaneously "loyalist" and "rebel." Nor were workers loyalist or rebel once and forever. Working-class culture was far more dynamic. Not surprisingly, changing economic and social conditions affected workers' ideas and behavior over time. Thus class consciousness and community consciousness should be seen not as ideal types but as poles of the spectrum of potential responses that workers could and did make to industrialization. Which response might have been salient can be explained only by reference to the specific historical circumstances.[13]

This study's three-part organization is designed to facilitate understanding of the dialectical nature of Albany workers' response to industrialization. Part I examines a range of economic actions in which the city's workers participated between 1850 and 1884—their organized strikes, labor riots, public demonstrations, and reform movements. Part II focuses on the significance of Albany's social, political, and cultural associations in the formation of workers' consciousness. Finally, as an index to Albany workers' evolving ideas, Part III surveys their long struggle in the nineteenth century against prison contract labor.

Although Albany workers' economic actions rarely have transcendent meaning themselves, as tension points they do shed light on the problems posed by the industrializing order. In these actions workers displayed elements both of free labor consciousness and of class solidarity. For example, in the 1850s Albany's printers and stove molders each raised the specter of class conflict by organizing independent trade unions. Ultimately the printers sought to resolve their grievances in an appeal to their employers to acknowledge their mutual interests; by contrast, the molders' strike in 1859 indicates the evolving class identity of these workers.

In Albany in the 1860s and 1870s workers' perception of inherent tension between the community's free labor values and their own class objectives deepened. Especially in their efforts to establish producers' cooperatives and to win an eight-hour workday, Albany workers expressed what will be called a "commonwealth consciousness." Workers' commonwealth ideals emphasized the economic and social rights they believed due them as members of the community. Although hardly socialists, Albany workers viewed reform as an alternative to ever-greater economic concentration and as an expression of the social commitment to provide for the common weal.

The 1870s found Albany workers on the defensive. They faced not only economic dislocation from the Panic of 1873 but also from the city's own economic decline. The most serious blow to workers in Albany during the decade came in 1877, with the defeat of striking stove molders. Leading to the molders' defeat was an agreement between a prominent iron founder and Sing Sing prison officials to manufacture stoves using convict labor. In response, Albany workers formed an independent political party and made prison contract labor a pivotal issue in the 1878 municipal elections. But this attempt at class-based politics failed. During the 1878 campaign Albany Democrats came out against prison contract labor. Not only did they support workers on this critical issue, but the Democrats nominated Michael N. Nolan for mayor, who, like many Albany workers, was an Irish Catholic. By directly appealing to both the class and cultural affiliations of Albany's workers, the Democratic party was able to successfully undercut their bid for independent political power. In Albany in 1878, community loyalties and not class consciousness proved the more compelling.

Their political activity in 1878 is just one reminder that workers experienced the impact of industrialization not only in their relations as employees to an employer but also as members of a community. Within their community, workers defined themselves in part through affiliation with a particular ethnic group, church, fraternal society, and/or political party. Workers' understanding of their class position, therefore, was mediated through the agencies of culture, religion, and political power in Albany. This process acquainted Albany workers with the viewpoints of other groups in the city, particularly with that of the dominant middle class, and gave them a sense of community participation that mitigated their possible alienation from the social order. Imbued with the dominant free labor values, Albany's institutions and associations helped stimulate community, rather than class, consciousness.

Albany's network of voluntary institutions functioned in other ways important to the community. Industrial capitalism challenged workers' traditional way of life and attempted to instill new rules and habits. Current research in American working-class history emphasizes the importance of the socialization of workers to the new work ethic.[14] Voluntary associations in nineteenth-century Albany exemplify one way in which the community "taught" workers the moral obligations of a "worldly asceticism" characterized by diligence, sobriety, honesty, and frugality.[15] As agencies of morality these institutions and associations helped preserve the well-being of the existing social order.

The perspective on the significance of community institutions and associations that informs this study is framed, in part, by the notion of hegemony put forth by Italian Marxist Antonio Gramsci. By hegemony Gramsci meant "an order in which a certain way of life and thought is dominant, in which one concept of reality is diffused throughout society in all its institutional and private manifestations."[16] Gramsci was particularly struck by how the dominant social group achieved the "spontaneous loyalty" of the lower orders ("subaltern classes") through a system of private ("civil") institutions in society. The concept of hegemony represents, therefore, a modification of the traditional Marxist view of the state (or government) as the sole coercive instrument of class rule.[17]

Some care should be taken in applying Gramsci's concept of hegemony to nineteenth-century America. Gramsci accepted the Marxist notion of the base, that is, the proposition that the material productive forces constituted the foundation of all other activities. If the importance of the economic structure were overemphasized, then hegemony would be understood as establishing a direct correspondence between the private institutions of society and the mode of production at a particular stage of its development. British cultural historian Raymond Williams warns against thinking of culture as determined by economic forces alone. Hegemony should not be seen as either static or omnipotent. Gramsci's concept of hegemony is pertinent in that it encourages an understanding of private institutions in terms of their social consciousness, that is, in terms of the social values that are often implicit in their ideas and practices. Through the concept of hegemony workers' culture is interpreted in relation to social structures of power, thereby avoiding the trap of seeing workers as members of an autonomous subculture.[18]

Although community institutions and associations in Albany promoted practices compatible with the existing order, workers' economic actions between 1850 and 1884 displayed their class as well as community consciousness. The alternating attraction for workers of class and free labor ideas is evident in their long struggle against prison contract labor. But as important an issue as prison contract labor would become for Albany's workers, the objective of that struggle was not to alter the economic system. By the 1880s most workers in Albany had reconciled themselves to the prevailing economic order. Few of the city's workers spoke, as they had twenty years earlier, of finding an alternative to their dependence on the wage system. The struggle against prison contract labor reveals Albany workers' acceptance of the free labor tradition along with an emerging interest-group consciousness.

This study considers, first, Albany workers' economic actions; second, their relationship to the community's social structure; and, third, the interplay of both as seen in the struggle against prison contract labor, in order to make comprehensible the complex response of Albany's workers to industrialization. Yet, even though it examines a single city in depth, it is not intended to be merely a local study. Rather, Albany provides a laboratory in which to investigate the social and cultural impact of industrialization during the middle decades of the nineteenth century. This study, then, forms an essential part of our eventual understanding of the evolution of the position of workers in American society.

1

Industrialization and the Awakening of Class Consciousness

Industrialization became a way of life for most urban Americans in the decades following the Civil War. The growth of canals and railroads and other internal improvements during the first half of the nineteenth century made possible the expansion of domestic markets and stimulated the development of American manufactures. During the twenty years before 1860, the value of manufactures quadrupled while its share of total U.S. commodity output doubled. But the greatest growth in American manufacturing lay in the decades ahead. The value of U.S. manufactured products in 1860 was still less than that for the United Kingdom, France, or Germany. By the end of the century, however, the United States not only ranked ahead of each of these countries in value of manufactures, its total nearly equaled that of all three combined. The phenomenal growth of industrial manufacturing after 1860 meant that the U.S. economy had "completed its transfer from an agricultural and commercial-mercantilist base to an industrial-capitalistic one."[1]

Between 1860 and 1910 a pattern of reduced costs, larger optimal scale of factory operation, and geographic concentration characterized industrialization in the United States. The changes that took place after 1860 in the agricultural implements and machinery industry are reasonably typical of this pattern. In 1860 the average number of workers per establishment in this industry was 7.5. After 1870 production of larger pieces of equipment replaced the manufacture of hand tools, virtually eliminating the small-scale shop as a work place. Total output per establishment increased even as the number of production units declined. As the size and scale in this industry grew, so too did the number of workers per establishment, averaging 20.4 by 1880 and 79.0 by 1910.[2]

Three recent studies of industrialization—in Lynn, Massachusetts; Philadelphia, Pennsylvania; and Newark, New Jersey—illustrate the differences in scale and scope of U.S. manufacturing in the nineteenth century. Alan Dawley shows that in 1800 shoemaking in Lynn was largely a household industry under the control of the master artisan. By 1830, however, the scale of production had expanded, and shoe manufacture was concentrated in central shops owned by merchant-manufacturers. The city's largest firms in 1830 employed fifty to one hundred people; twenty years later the average was three hundred to four hundred. With the invention of the sewing machine (1854) and the McKay stitcher (1864), the industry was fully mechanized by 1880. As a result, following the pattern noted in the agricultural implements and machinery industry, the boot and shoe industry in Lynn needed some two thousand fewer workers in 1875 to produce 7 million more shoes than it had in 1855.[3]

Unlike Lynn where a single industry, shoe manufacturing, predominated, a range of industrial settings was present in Philadelphia and Newark. Taking into account scale, level of mechanization, and market orientation, Bruce Laurie distinguishes five discrete work environments in Philadelphia in 1860: fully mechanized factories (textile and metallurgy); medium-sized nonmechanized manufacturies (building trades, printing, and shoemaking); sweatshops (tailoring); domestic outwork (shoemaking, tailoring, and weaving); and artisanal and neighborhood shops (metallurgy, shoemaking, blacksmithing, and baking). In Newark, Susan Hirsch traces eight trades through three stages in "the process of industrialization"—traditional crafts, simple human-powered machinery, and the harnessing of inanimate forms of energy to machine production. By 1860 only hatmaking, leather making, and trunk making had reached the third stage. Shoemaking was not yet mechanized, while blacksmithing and carpentry were still traditional crafts.[4]

By 1860, although concentration of production had occurred in all three cities, in Philadelphia and Newark a myriad of small producers could still be found. Looking at shoe manufacture, the one industry common to all three cities, the range in scale in 1860 was from a few small shops that still produced custom-made shoes for a local market to fully mechanized factories whose products were sold across the nation and around the world. Despite the persistence of small-scale manufacture, the trend was definitely toward larger-scale production.

The United States would not realize the full flowering of its industrial development until the 1880s. In 1869 water rather than steam still powered half of America's factories, and the average number of wage earners per establishment was 8.15. And although its share was growing, manufacturing accounted for only one-third of the goods produced in the United States in 1870. The middle decades of the nineteenth century were, therefore, a transitional phase in the development of industrial capitalism in America. During this period industrialization was not, as it later became, synonymous with big business and large-scale enterprise. Instead, these were years of experimentation and of uneven development from one industry to another.[5]

Yet even before the rise of the factory the independent artisan had begun to disappear. During industrialization a permanent wage-earning class emerged. David Montgomery calculates that by 1870 some two out of every three productively engaged Americans were wage earners. In the industrial Northeast the odds against self-employment were even greater. In Pennsylvania, in 1870, between 65 and 75 percent of the population worked for someone else; in Massachusetts the proportion was between 75 and 85 percent. By 1870 "capital" and "labor" had become recognized protagonists on the economic and social landscape, and, in many ways, a growing awareness of this fact underlay most of the political and ideological battles in the postbellum United States.[6]

Albany's prominence as an American industrial city lasted only through the transitional period. In its rise and relative decline in the nineteenth century, Albany typified the sequential and regional pattern of American industrialization described by urban geographer David Ward in his study, *Cities and Immigrants: A Geography of Change in Nineteenth-Century America.* Ward concludes that the rate and level of urban growth between 1790 and 1910 were determined by the effects of differences in regional economic development. Ward offers a three-phase model to explain the spatial organization of the national economy through the nineteenth century. In the first phase, 1790 to 1830, urban development concentrated in five seaport cities on the East Coast of the United States—Boston, New York City, Philadelphia, Baltimore, and Charleston. The American economy in these years looked outward across the Atlantic to trade with Europe. Only at the end of the Napoleonic Wars in 1815 did commerce with domestic markets become important. One major consequence of growing commercial interest in trade with the western United States was the building of the Erie Canal, completed in 1825. As the canal's eastern terminus, Albany was well placed to take advantage of the expanding commerce. The impact of the Erie Canal was such that by 1830 Albany was the second largest inland town in the United States.[7]

Between 1830 and 1870 significant improvements in land transportation, especially the spread of railroads, contributed to continued development of the domestic market and to the growth of manufactured goods as a proportion of the nation's commerce. Industrial production in these years concentrated in areas in and around the three major northeastern seaports and sections of southern New England, upstate New York, and southeastern Pennsylvania. A large part of the growth of cities like Albany during the second phase was tied to the manufacture and sale of a variety of industrial goods for the continental interior. Note on the map of urbanization in the United States (1870) Albany's central place in the economic core region.

Thereafter from 1870 through 1910 economic development concentrated in inland urban centers such as Chicago, Pittsburgh, Cleveland, and Detroit. Like other flourishing regions in this period, these cities were tied economically to large-scale manufacture and relied on a national market to support their growing populations. In contrast to the spectacular development of the western centers, cities like Albany, which proved unable to sustain viable industrial specialties on a large scale, declined precipitously during this period, particularly after 1880.

In 1860 Albany ranked roughly on a par with Chicago and Pittsburgh in terms of population and value of manufactures. (See Table 1.) But twenty years later, the growth of Chicago and Pittsburgh in both categories had far outstripped that of Albany. And by 1900, while Chicago and Pittsburgh maintained their rankings, Albany had slipped far down in the urban hierarchy.

Table 1. Rank of American Cities by Population and Manufactures

	1860		*1880*		*1900*	
City	*Population*	*Manufactures**	*Population*	*Manufactures**	*Population*	*Manufactures**
Albany	13	21	21	29	40	55
Chicago	9	16	4	3	2	3
Pittsburgh	17	14	12	10	11	10

Source: U.S. Census Office, *Statistics of United States in 1860 of the Eighth Census (Including Mortality, Property, etc.)*, (Washington, D.C., 1866), pp. xviii–xix, and *Twelfth Census of the United States. Manufactures* (Washington, D.C., 1902), part 1, pp. ccxxx–ccxxxiv.

*Based upon the value of products.

It was during the transitional period of 1830 to 1870 in American industrialization that Albany underwent its most significant economic development. Its products were typical, both in kind and in scale, of manufacturing in the rest of the country at that time. Albany kept pace relative to other urban centers through the transitional phase, but during the last quarter of the nineteenth century the city was in serious industrial

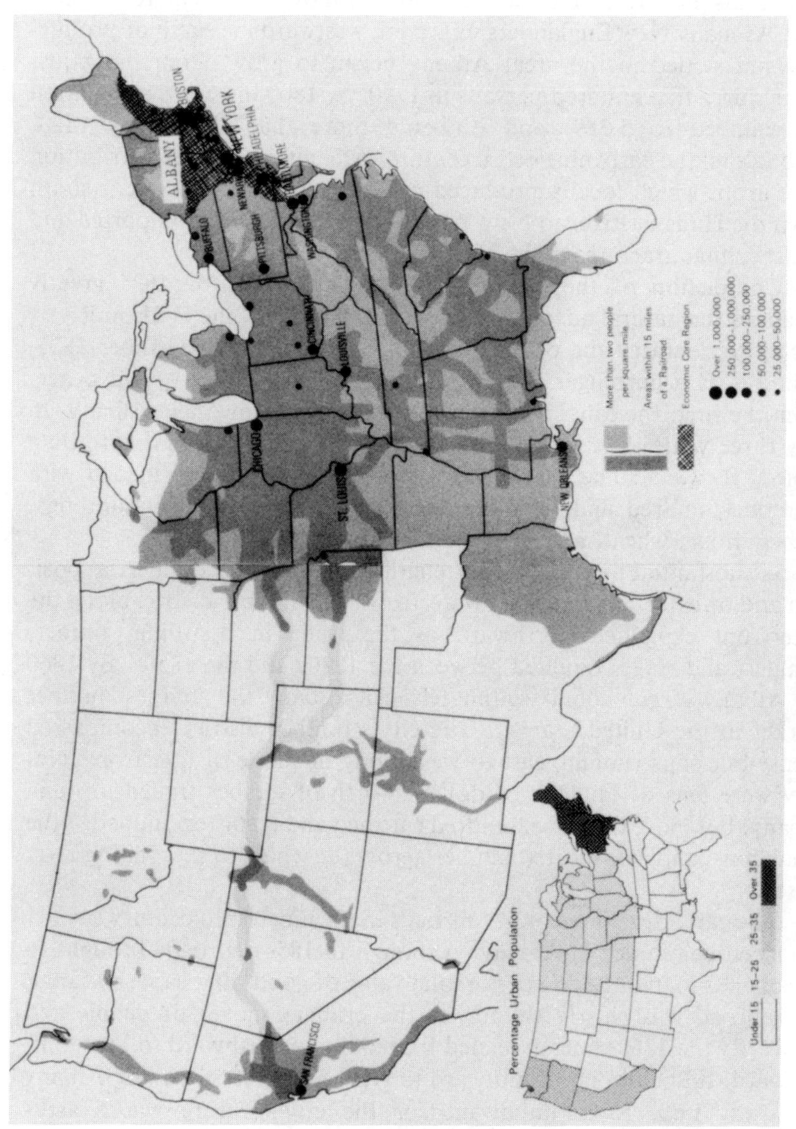

Figure 1. Urbanization in the United States, 1870.

decline. What follows is a detailed description of Albany's economy as it evolved in the nineteenth century.

Established as a fur-trading post by the Dutch in 1624, Albany remained a small frontier settlement through most of the eighteenth century. As many New Englanders migrating westward in search of productive land settled in the area, Albany began to grow. Containing just under thirty-five hundred persons in 1790, by 1800 the city's population had climbed to 5,289, and it would more than double by 1820. Throughout the early nineteenth century, Albany served as a distribution point from which locally produced agricultural goods were sent south down the Hudson River to New York City in exchange for imported and domestic manufactures.[8]

Completion of the Champlain and Erie canals by 1825 greatly enhanced the natural advantages afforded Albany by the Hudson River. The city celebrated the opening of the Erie Canal in November 1825, hailing it as a harbinger of prosperity, national solidarity, and peace. From the first, the canal quickened the pace of commerce in Albany. In only three years the number of boats using the city's docks more than tripled. By 1835 some 18,550 boats had come to Albany, loaded with over one hundred and fifty thousand tons of boards and scantlings, timber, flour, wheat, and other commodities.[9]

A substantial lumber trade strengthened Albany's commercial position and transformed the city's waterfront. The lumber district along the waterfront expanded northward as the trade in boarding, timber, shingles, and staves doubled between the 1830s and the 1850s. By 1860 the Albany *Argus* could legitimately call Albany the "largest lumber market in the United States." The city's lumber district encompassed twenty-one slips running east to west along one mile of riverfront. Not only were tens of millions of dollars worth of lumber traded through Albany, but more than one hundred cartmen and teamsters unloaded the canal boats and transported lumber across the wharf to the waiting river vessels.[10]

The early development of railroads in the nineteenth century further enhanced commerce in Albany. Although in 1854 railroads brought to Albany less than one-seventh the total value of goods that came by canal, the railroad was clearly gaining as the primary mover of people and goods. By the 1850s lines extended from Albany northward to Vermont, eastward to Boston, and southward to New York City—making Albany a railway hub. Most important for the city's future was Erastus Corning's consolidation of many short lines into the New York Central Railroad (NYCRR) in 1853.[11]

Corning was the president of the NYCRR. At his behest, in 1850 the railroad had purchased some three hundred fifty acres of mostly barren land just west of Albany in an area known as Spencerville. Here, in 1854, the NYCRR developed twenty acres of pens and loading platforms for the cattle, sheep, and hog trade and for slaughtering. Almost immediately West Albany won fame as a cattle mart. The NYCRR quickly put 700 cars to work hauling cattle from western states to the West Albany terminus to be slaughtered and sold locally or shipped on to Boston. In 1855 average monthly freight receipts at West Albany were just over $25,000; by 1861 the total was almost two and one-half times greater; and, in 1866, at the height of the cattle trade in West Albany, monthly receipts reached $75,000 as a thousand carloads of cattle arrived weekly.[12]

Improved transportation lowered the cost of moving goods, which not only stimulated commerce but led to the growth of manufacturing. Before 1825, Albany's small craft shops produced most of the goods needed by the city's residents. In 1820 Albany's manufactures consisted largely of household production of such goods as carpeting, blankets, straw and woolen hats, hollowware, solid castings for machinery, and whiskey and ale. Albany's manufactures grew steadily after 1825 due to the city's strategic location on the Hudson River and as a terminus for the Erie and Champlain canals, which gave it easy access to raw materials and to distant markets.

One of the first industries in Albany to benefit from the transportation revolution was the making of cast-iron stoves. Until 1830 the manufacture of iron stoves in Albany and elsewhere usually involved assembly by a wholesale merchant of stove plates cast directly from ore in blast furnaces located principally in Vermont, Connecticut, and eastern Pennsylvania. In 1830 Joel Rathbone, an Albany stove merchant, built one of the first cupola furnaces for stove casting. Castings made by this process were cheaper and finer, and Albany became an early center for stove production. By 1833 five Albany foundries employed about a thousand workers and remelted 2,300 tons of pig metal a year, mostly for stove plate. Before midcentury, Albany would produce 75,000 stoves annually.[13]

Albany's second most important early industry, the production of malt liquor, also owed its development to the city's access to markets and to the necessary raw materials. In 1820 the four small breweries that were operating in Albany produced only 8,500 barrels of beer. By contrast, in 1830 production from five breweries reached 42,000 barrels, 12,000 for local consumption and 30,000 for export. By 1840, nine breweries produced over 250,000 barrels.[14]

The clearest example of the interdependence of commerce and industry in Albany was the building of the NYCRR shops at West Albany. Corning decided, over the objections of Rochester and other cities along the line, to concentrate all of the NYCRR's repair work in Albany. In 1856 the company began construction on what came to be eleven buildings, including a machine and blacksmith shop, a car repair shop, a boiler house, and engine houses for passenger and freight cars. With obvious pride, the *Argus* hailed the West Albany yards as the "most extensive railway establishment in the country."[15]

The physical size of the works was impressive. The semicircular main engine house was 580 feet long around the outside and could store thirty cars. In 1862 the *Albany Evening Journal* reported that about three hundred operatives were employed at West Albany, and, the newspaper pointed out, there was the potential for hiring a thousand workers. Indeed, West Albany's shops reached their projected capacity just a few years later and, by the 1870s, had surpassed the predictions, with over fifteen hundred workers on the payroll.[16]

Although West Albany's rise is the most dramatic example of Albany's economic development after 1850, the growth of diversified manufactures—production of boots and shoes, bricks, pianos, chairs and cabinets, as well as of stoves and beer—proceeded almost as rapidly. As an expanding city Albany also supported an extensive building and construction industry. Typical of most industry in the United States at midcentury, manufacturing in Albany usually took place in a variety of small shops. By 1850 Albany had 210 manufacturing establishments, which produced over $3.6 million worth of goods in that year and employed a total of 2,728 persons. An average manufactory produced $17,500 worth of goods annually and had thirteen employees. Although both these figures are higher than the national average, over 70 percent of Albany's industrial establishments employed ten or fewer persons. In addition, only ten firms hired fifty or more workers. Discounting these firms, the average number of employees was 8.5.[17]

Among the ten firms that hired more than fifty people in 1850 were three stove foundries. Employing almost one-quarter of its work force and producing also about one-quarter of the total value of its manufactured goods, stove manufacturing continued to be Albany's most important industry. The city's three largest foundries produced $600,000 worth of stoves and employed 500 workers, or an average of 167 per establishment. Besides the leading foundries, four smaller stove factories, which together produced stoves worth $200,000, employed 132 workers.

The coexistence of small and large firms also characterized the brewing and boot and shoe industries in Albany. Unlike stove foundries, which were all powered by steam, of the fifteen Albany breweries in 1850, eight relied on manual power and seven on steam. However, the seven steam-powered breweries produced about two-thirds of the industry's total product value and employed three-quarters of its work force. In Albany's boot and shoe industry, one manufacturer, the John and Thomas Feary Company, employed fifty persons. Feary and the city's two other leading shoe manufacturers employed about half of the work force in the industry and produced half of the value of the boots and shoes made in Albany. Alongside these large shoe manufacturers, out of a total of twenty-three boot and shoe establishments in Albany, nine produced goods worth only $4,000 or less and employed a total of eighteen persons.[18]

Albany's manufacturing grew at a spectacular rate during the 1850s. By 1860, some 337 manufacturing establishments in Albany produced over two and one-half times the value of goods and employed two and one-half times more persons than in 1850. Looking at specific industries over the decade, the value of stoves produced increased by 22 percent and the number employed by 24 percent; in brewing, the increase in product value was also 22 percent, while the industry employed 47 percent more workers. The greatest increase occurred in the boot and shoe industry, where three times the number of manufacturers employed 77 percent more workers and produced 60 percent more goods. Overall, twice as many firms hired fifty or more persons in 1860 than in 1850. But many small manufactories persisted. Once again discounting the industrial enterprises employing fifty persons, the average size of the remaining manufacturing establishments in Albany was only slightly above that for the nation.[19]

Twenty years later, in 1880, Albany had over eight hundred manufactories, more than doubling the total of 1860 and producing about two times the value of goods as well. Iron making, including stove manufacture, continued to account for most of the firms with fifty or more workers, employing an average of 79.1. Although still an important part of the local economy, the industry now employed only 20 percent of the city's work force, compared to 25 percent in 1850, and produced 12 percent of the total value of goods, as compared with 25 percent in 1850. Of Albany's other leading industries, brewing averaged twenty-seven workers per establishment (totaling 815 employed), printing, forty workers per shop (690 employed), and boot and shoe manufacturing, thirty workers (1,677 employed). Overall, the average size of each Albany firm remained slightly above that for the nation.[20]

The tendency of particular firms to dominate their industries persisted. In stove manufacturing, one firm, Perry and Company, turned out 1,000 tons of stoves in 1860; twenty years later it was annually producing 9,500 tons, or 90,000 stoves. In the 1860s, Rathbone and Sard, then Albany's biggest stove manufacturer, produced in two molding rooms 300 stoves per day at capacity and employed an average of 300 men (500 men at capacity) in its foundry, which covered some two and one-half acres. By the mid-1880s this company melted 90 tons of iron daily and produced 75,000 stoves annually in three large molding shops (there were nine buildings in all). Rathbone and Sard also sold some 50,000 patterns for stoves each year.[21]

In the boot and shoe industry factory production continued to replace custom work, and large firms continued to displace smaller ones. While some small firms, such as M. W. Dodge and W. B. Bellows, which hired only sixty and twenty-five workers, respectively, survived, Feary and Sons (formerly the John and Thomas Feary Company) increased its work force from fifty workers in 1850 to some six hundred operatives in the 1880s. As the largest boot and shoe manufacturer in Albany, Feary and Sons, in addition to one shop for custom work, had three fully mechanized factories, which produced "medium-grade goods for the masses."[22] When working at capacity this company turned out 2,000 pairs of shoes a day. Another large manufacturer, the East New York Boot and Shoe Manufactory, employed about four hundred workers at its Albany branch factory.[23]

Yet, as already noted, by 1880 Albany and similar intermediate-size cities in the Northeast had begun to decline. Despite West Albany's considerable growth, the city never developed the resources for long-term economic progress. Although the size of the rail shops and the number of workers collected under one roof were impressive by contemporary standards, the shops did not foster fundamental change in the manufacturing process. Many skilled workers—painters, carpenters, machinists—repaired the railroad cars at West Albany. But the major breakthrough for Albany industry would have been construction of entire railroad cars at West Albany. Manufacture of railway cars was suggested when the shops were being built, but it was never introduced, and Albany missed an opportunity to develop large-scale industry.[24]

That innovation did not occur at West Albany may have been a consequence of Corning's and Albany's loss of control over the NYCRR. Following a dispute between the NYCRR and the Hudson River Railroad over a freight exchange deal in 1867, Commodore Vanderbilt, president of the Hudson River line, successfully seized control of the NYCRR. The New York Central would remain a mainstay of Albany's economy for many years, but the city's businessmen had lost their voice in its management. It was far less likely that with Vanderbilt as president of the NYCRR Albany would receive the special consideration it had during Corning's tenure.

No single factor explains Albany's decline. Yet that the change in ownership of the NYCRR did have far-reaching consequences for Albany can be seen by looking at the importance of railroads in Chicago. While Albany declined after 1860, Chicago experienced a period of spectacular growth. Prominent among the industries in Chicago that boomed in these years was slaughtering and meat packing. Expansion in this industry as well as in other Chicago industries was largely due to the competitive advantage provided the city by its rail and terminal facilities. Chicago's rail facilities lowered ton-mile costs to its customers, encouraging large-scale production, industrial concentration, and urban growth.

In 1860 slaughtering and meat packing had also been an important industry in Albany, an industry that benefited from Corning's patronage. Under Corning, the NYCRR required that all livestock carried by the railroad be unshipped and fed at Albany. It may have been that there was nothing Corning could have done to offset Chicago's competitive advantages. Nevertheless, perhaps it is not coincidence that just after Vanderbilt's takeover of the NYCRR the cattle trade at West Albany began to diminish. What is clear is that Albany did not achieve the kind of multiplier benefits from its rail facilities that Chicago did. In the 1880s Albany's newspapers sadly recorded the arrival of "dressed beef" in refrigerated cars from Chicago and acknowledged that this form of "meat for the millions" represented yet another blow to the city's economy.[25]

From 1850 to 1884, the period under study here, Albany manufactures expanded, and each of her leading industries came to be dominated by a few powerful firms. However, the city failed to generate truly large-scale manufacturing, and by the 1880s important segments of Albany's economy were under great pressure from competing cities. Albany was a city, therefore, that reflected the local, small-scale character of American industrialization in the transitional period. Albany had benefited from early industrial expansion but was left behind as the locus and scale of industry shifted.

Although the main focus of this study is on Albany after 1850, the city had begun to experience significant economic and social changes before then. The response of workers to early industrialization in Albany as elsewhere was complex, encompassing, as English social and cultural historian Raymond Williams points out, residual and emergent elements. Workers both retained traditional values characteristic of preindustrial culture and took on values more consonant with industrialization. However, even among those workers who accepted industrialization, there were many who, from the beginning, hoped for a more organically bound community than one based on competitive capitalist individualism.[26] American workers first began to express a coherent critique of industrialization and its accompanying class differences during the Jacksonian era in America, the late 1820s and the 1830s.

The class consciousness of workers during the Jacksonian era took primarily two forms: (1) development of worker societies, specifically of trade unions, and (2) participation in political reform movements (which also included members of other classes) that sought basic changes in American society. Underlying the Jacksonian labor movement was the nagging fear, especially among skilled workers, that concentration of wealth and monopoly of privilege were inevitable consequences of industrialization. Frequently sounding like the pamphleteers of the American Revolution who had raised the alarm over the undemocratic excesses of the British aristocracy, radical Jacksonian workers marched under the banner of "Equal Rights" and vilified those "rapacious tyrants" who were corrupting the system by their greed. They drew a sharp distinction between producers, those like themselves whose labor had tangible utility, and nonproducers, or monopolists, those who lived off the wealth that others created.[27]

Workingmen's political parties began organizing in the industrializing cities of the Northeast in 1828, initially as a protest against unemployment and in an effort to secure a ten-hour workday. Although strongest in New York City and Philadelphia, workingmen's parties were also active in many upstate New York communities, including Albany. The workingmen's movement in New York attracted a coalition of insurgent forces opposed to the leadership of the Democratic party, which they dubbed the "Albany Regency." Typically, the motto of the Albany Workingmen's party (organized in 1829) declared it to be "anti-Aristocracy" as well as "anti-Regency." In common with the national movement, the Albany Workingmen's party advocated a reform agenda that expressed a broad range of social and political grievances.[28]

Appearing in the party's campaign newspaper, the *Farmers', Mechanics', and Workingmen's Advocate* (its name alone indicates how fluid class lines remained in the 1820s), the platform of the Albany Workingmen's party identified those conditions that workers felt threatened their position in society. The party cited ten reform goals: public education for "every child"; abolition of imprisonment for debt; abolition of the militia system; "a less expensive and more common sense system of laws and practice"; restriction on monopolies; reduction of salaries for public offices; "security of industrious mechanics against fraudulent employers" (a mechanics' lien law); "equal taxation on property"; revision of all election districts "nearer the people"; and "election of all officers of government immediately, by the people, in all practicable cases." Together, these reforms represent a catalogue of republican grievances against concentrated power and wealth as well as a plea to sustain equality.[29]

The republicanism of Albany workers is particularly evident in their emphasis on the platform resolution concerning public education. Most educational institutions in Albany were private; only the Lancaster School provided an education for children whose families could not pay tuition. During the 1828–29 winter session of the New York State legislature, impelled by the city's then-nascent Workingmen's party, "a very numerous and highly respectable portion" of the people of Albany presented a petition to the legislature and to the Albany Common Council calling for school aid to be distributed in the city's wards for use by common schools. The petition explained that many parents refused to send their children to the Lancaster School because "children cannot be admitted . . . without a direct or implied acknowledgment that they are objects of public charity." In order to end such social discrimination between the rich and the poor, Albany needed a school system where no one had to pay, a "mechanic" wrote to the *Argus.* Education was a right that should be enjoyed by all citizens equally.[30]

The legislature sent the petition to Azariah C. Flagg, a powerful member of the Albany Regency who was New York secretary of state and superintendent of common schools. Flagg, despite widespread support for public education in Albany, opposed the proposed change, and the Senate voted to kill the measure. The following winter (1829–30), workers revived the petition, and this time their efforts met with success. In 1830 the legislature passed a bill authorizing each of Albany's wards to create common schools to be supported by state aid. In the years that followed, the city opened four schools—the foundation of free public education in Albany.

The failure of leading Democrats to support them on so fundamental an issue as public education reinforced workers' suspicions that the Albany Regency was a party of wealth and privilege. The *Advocate* chastised local Regency leaders for proclaiming their "zeal for the public good" while in reality showing concern only for "power and personal emolument." The newspaper specifically accused Edwin Croswell, editor of the Albany *Argus* and a leading figure in the local Regency, of benefiting from the suffering of the poor. As state printer, Croswell published legal notices of debtors' bankruptcies in the *Argus.* The workingmen attacked Croswell for growing rich on the bankruptcy of poor debtors.[31]

Convinced of the need for political action, reform-minded citizens, including many workingmen, held meetings in the spring of 1830 to nominate candidates for the county elections in May. They claimed an initial victory when their candidates beat Regency-supported opponents in two wards. In September the Albany Workingmen's party announced a slate of candidates for the upcoming statewide elections. Among the party's nominees was a descendent of a Dutch patroon family, Stephen

Van Rensselaer, Jr., who was running for alderman in Albany's Fifth Ward. Workingmen's party candidates defeated Regency-supported candidates in thirteen of the twenty aldermanic elections in Albany. Although they hailed these victories as a "revolution," the Workingmen's party, lacking any real unity or party machinery, soon disintegrated.[32]

A recent study of the Albany Workingmen's party reveals that its membership was more representative of the lower- and middle-class occupations than any other political party in the city. Even so, the party chose Van Rensselaer and other well-to-do persons as its leaders and candidates. A leading contemporary Albany reform journal, the *Microscope*, criticized the Workingmen's party on just these grounds. According to the *Microscope*, by nominating for public office "certain haughty, purse-proud aristocrats, who have not a single feeling in common with them," party leaders had been "blind to their own interests." As if to confirm this judgment, on January 1, 1831, the Workingmen's party–dominated Albany Common Council selected as mayor Francis Bloodgood, a successful merchant and president of the State Bank and of the Albany Insurance Company. Yet despite his background, Bloodgood proved his commitment to the workingmen's political goals. One of his first acts as mayor was to go to the Albany jail and release all debtors.[33]

The labor reform movement of the 1820s and 1830s in Albany and elsewhere reflected the growing sense of inequality that animated workers during the early years of industrialization. Yet at no point did workers articulate a coherent explanation of the economic causes of their plight. The workingmen's movement in Albany appears to have been especially cautious. The Albany *Advocate* disavowed what it saw as the more radical views associated with such leaders of the New York Workingmen's party as Fanny Wright and Robert Dale Owen. Albany workingmen, it said, were "neither infidels or agrarians . . . but rather honest men seeking their rights." These rights, according to the *Advocate*, obviously did not include an open attack on private property.[34]

Many of the reform objectives articulated in the workingmen's platform were meant to keep open the avenues for social advance. Such acceptance of the success ethic reflects the continuing attraction for workers of the bourgeois values present in the larger culture. At the same time, workers were increasingly aware of the depredations of capitalist industrialization. There was, then, a tension in workers' consciousness between their class experience and the values of the dominant culture. This tension could only intensify as the pace of industrialization in Albany picked up. The next three chapters focus on the response of Albany's workers to these economic changes.

Part I

2

Workers and Free Labor

The free labor ideology as an expression of community consciousness conditioned the local response to industrialization in Albany. One index to this process in the 1850s is the editorial comments of the city's leading newspapers. Both the *Argus* and the *Albany Evening Journal* attempted to reconcile the changes wrought by industrialization with their commitment to the presumed harmony of interests between capital and labor. However, newspaper editorials were not the only way that the community expressed its social values. Many public events became opportunities for the city's diverse peoples and classes to affirm shared values and to encourage community loyalty.[1] In the midnineteenth century such public events as a dinner honoring Edward Gilbert, former printer, or the day-long festivities marking completion of the transatlantic telegraph cable can be understood as free labor rituals, occasions for celebrating the superiority of the free labor social order.

Perceiving themselves to be members of the community, workers actively participated in Albany's public events. Yet the evidence of their participation does not mean that they had adopted the free labor world view. The degree to which they subscribed to the notion that a mutuality of interests existed between labor and capital can be measured by examining the broad spectrum of their activities in the 1850s. Their responses ranged from that of the laborers on the city's waterworks, who emerged as the group most dependent on the community, to that of the printers, who organized a trade union but still expressed free labor sentiments, to that of the stove molders, who seem to have been the most sensitive to evolving class differences. When added to the public events, these labor activities, along with the reaction to them by the city's middle class, help define the hold that free labor ideas had in Albany in the period.

In February 1850, a committee of Albany printers and nearly one hundred other leading "citizens" invited Edward Gilbert to return to the city for a public dinner in his honor. In the short time since the *Argus* compositor had left Albany to fight in the Mexican War, he had accomplished much. Settling in California after the war, Gilbert began his own newspaper, and, in 1850, he was awaiting his entry into the U.S. Congress, pending California's admission into the Union, as a representative from the new state. His recent "attainments," the committee wrote Gilbert, were "but another proof" of the "honorable aspirations and sterling qualities" that he had shown while living in Albany.[2] But the dinner would be more than just a chance to recognize the particular achievements of a native son. The participants celebrated Gilbert as a symbol of the success possible in a free labor society. The dinner honoring Gilbert is one example of how, by the 1850s, the success ethic had become a widely shared secular creed in Albany.

The Gilbert dinner was held on June 5. After enjoying a lavish meal, the participants got to the "business" of the evening, a long series of elaborate toasts. Mayor Franklin Townsend, who presided, set the tone. He praised "Our Honored Guest" for encompassing the qualities of "the intelligent citizen, the adventurous pioneer, the skillful artisan, and the young patriot soldier." Gilbert's career served as "a bright example of the reward which the combination of industry, enterprise and integrity always commands." In a similar vein, Thurlow Weed, editor of the *Evening Journal*, hailed Gilbert as "a printer, soldier and statesman—rewarded for his industry, patriotism and virtue, with prosperity, distinction and happiness."[3]

Both Townsend and Weed regarded Gilbert as the quintessential self-made man, an individual who by dint of his industry and strength of character had made his way upward in the world. Gilbert's success had come, another dinner guest put it, "Unaided by affluence or aristocratic blood; all his superior accomplishments he obtained by his own industry." In his career Gilbert was following in the footsteps of that archetypical successful printer, Benjamin Franklin. A leader in the recent organizing of a printers' union, John Nafew, drew just such a connection between the two men and then toasted Franklin, "May his success prompt some brother of the craft to emulate his fame, and gather laurels as rich as Prometheus." By becoming self-employed, Gilbert, like Franklin, had achieved the free labor goal of economic independence.[4]

Because they saw self-employment as the end to which all purposeful effort should be directed, free labor adherents extolled the dignity of all toil. In their invitation to Gilbert, Albany's printers had addressed him as their "fellow-craftsman," and he had responded in kind. Whatever "fame or good I have achieved," he wrote them, was due to his training as a printer: "It is to the *case* and the *composing-stick* I am indebted—they were my tutor and my college."[5] Many of those toasting Gilbert during the dinner also referred to his early career as a working printer and to this experience as a significant part of his education. For example, H. J. Hastings, editor of the *Knickerbocker*, claimed that printing "had graduated more useful members of society, had brought out more talent, intellect and turned it into practical, useful channels . . . than many of the Literary Colleges." Gilbert was clearly still another "worthy graduate of the Poor Boys' College, the Printing office."

In crediting Gilbert's success to his experience as a craftsman, the dinner guests celebrated a society that they believed continued to value the dignity of labor. Gilbert's career reflected the most cherished aspirations of the free labor outlook: economic progress, social mobility, and political democracy.[6] To the workers and "other citizens" who honored him, Gilbert's individual accomplishments confirmed the social progress made possible under the free labor order.

In 1858 the citizens of Albany gathered again to celebrate a symbol of progress, this time not an individual but a technological achievement, the transatlantic cable. Albany's "jubilee" on September 1, 1858, was part of national and international festivities marking the commencement of telegraphic communications between the United States and Great Britain. In announcing plans for the day, Albany's mayor, Eli Perry, observed that it was "eminently fitting that the Capitol of this Great State, whose interests are so various and widely extended, shall rejoice in this magnificent success." For Perry and many others, the cable ("this great work") was one example of the marvels of "the scientific history of the present century. . . . The men of Commerce, the Cultivators of the Useful or the Elegant Arts, all who love peace among mankind and all who exult in the triumphs of science or the diffusion of knowledge, may here have a common theme for admiration."[7] By invoking the cable as a symbol of progress and harmony among diverse interests, Perry articulated a theme that would be repeated throughout the day-long celebration.

The day's events included daytime and evening parades. In the evening 1,500 firemen led a torchlight procession. The parade during the day took over three hours for the marchers to complete. Flags and banners adorned many of the businesses and residences along the parade route. The most striking feature of the parade was the illumination of some of these buildings with transparencies, which, like the banners, carried "mottoes" to commemorate the great event. Two such transparencies, illuminating the mayor's house, paid homage to "Labor Triumphant" and "American Enterprise Triumphant."[8] The cable was saluted as an international cooperative achievement, which, it was hoped, would inaugurate an era of greater harmony and peaceful understanding among nations. Draped across Washington Hall was a banner proclaiming "The Old World and the New—Mother and Son, through electricity united in one."[9] That all progress depended on such cooperative effort, was assumed.

The cable as a symbol of the progress possible through united effort, among the city's diverse interests as among nations, was not lost on those who planned the day's events. In order to assure the widest participation, Mayor Perry asked that all normal business be suspended for the day. The parade during the day was made up of detachments from many of Albany's businesses—manufacturers and mechanics marching together behind wagons that either displayed examples of the firms' products or carried machinery producing them. The "feature of the procession," according to the *Argus*, was a display by Emery Brothers, a manufacturer of agricultural implements, that used a portion of the "genuine Atlantic cable" itself. In a tribute to labor, a "Jack Tar" from one of the ships that had laid the cable rode on an Emery Brothers wagon. The mechanics' band from Wheeler, Melick and Company Nail Works marched in the parade, as did the 110 members of the Rathbone Guards, a volunteer military corps composed of workers at Rathbone and Company stove foundry. No other "Jubilee" in the city's history, the *Argus* exclaimed, had been "so generally participated in" as the celebration of "the great event of the Nineteenth Century," completion of the transatlantic cable.

In further commenting on the day, the *Argus* stated, "We like such exhibitions. They exercise a happy influence on human nature and social life." The opportunity for "the mechanic, the manufacturer, the laborer, the merchant, the artist—all occupations and all interests" to participate "in displaying the triumphs of their skill, industry and enterprise, and in mingling together" made the festivities a "gala day." The parades, like the cable, caused "the general heart to thrill with happiness and creates a community of feeling and pleasure, which makes us really a homogeneous people." The "happy influence" of the day's events that especially pleased the *Argus* was in the fraternal feelings that it excited in Albany.

The jubilee for the transatlantic cable, like the public dinner for Edward Gilbert, was a communitywide celebration of the free labor order. But industrialization also brought with it social changes that challenged the free labor ideals accepted in Albany, especially the citizens' belief in themselves as members of a homogeneous community. Many of the laborers and skilled workers who came to work in factories and shops in Albany and other U.S. cities were immigrants. In the mid-1850s public reaction to the growing presence of these new arrivals led to an outbreak of nativism across the nation. Nativism as a political force in Albany will be discussed in Chapter 7. But nativism can also be examined here for what it reveals about the Albany community's free labor social objectives.

As spokesmen for different political parties, the *Argus* and the *Evening Journal* predictably disagreed over a number of economic issues. Yet despite their differences, both newspapers accepted the basic premises of the free labor ideology, and both praised immigration as a boon to the free labor order. The *Argus* called immigrants "an army of laborers constructing the avenues of trade . . . [and] at the same time, the army of consumers, which constitutes the home market."[10] Trying to make political capital out of the *Argus*'s statement, the *Evening Journal* charged that its rival saw immigrants only as a source of "CHEAP LABOR." Yet virtually repeating the *Argus*'s sentiments, the *Evening Journal* saluted immigrants as "passengers who come to subdue our wilderness lands, to cultivate our soil, to multiply our products, to enrich our country."[11] The editors of both newspapers favored immigration because it would stimulate American economic growth and progress.

As nativism became a more potent force in Albany, the *Argus* and the *Evening Journal* spoke out against it. In rejecting nativism they emphasized the contribution that immigrants made to the free labor system. The effect of immigrant labor in the North, the *Argus* claimed, was "to elevate our native population to a great extent above the mere drudgery of physical labor . . . to make them employers instead of employed." Without immigrant labor the North would be forced, like the South, to rely on slave labor. In place of "involuntary servitude," immigrants bring to America "a gradual and safe extension of a system of free and enterprising labor."[12] The *Evening Journal* expressed a similar point of view: "In the future, Economy will have to appraise that element of value in the Immigrant, derivable for his influence in making the United States Government a REPUBLICAN Government, instead of an oligarchy of slaveholders.''[13] As part of a free rather than slave labor system, the immigrant became, for Albany's newspaper editors and many other opinion makers in the North, the cornerstone of the antebellum social order.[14]

At the core of the free labor ideology was the belief in the mutuality of interests between capital and labor. Progress necessarily followed from the general acceptance of society's interdependent nature. Yet free labor capitalism had generated a competitive relationship whereby employer and employee were bound solely by wages. Associations like the Wheeler, Melick mechanics' band and the Rathbone Guards, which marched in the cable parade, represent an effort to form nonpecuniary bonds between owners and workers. Other important Albany firms in the 1850s, such as Boardmen and Grey and Company (piano manufacture), Van Benthuysen (printing), Perry and Company (stove manufacturing), and S. H. Ransom and Company (stove manufacturing) also sponsored volunteer corps among their employees. These employer-sponsored associations sought to recreate a system of reciprocal obligations that at one time was thought to have united masters and journeymen, but which had been severed with industrialization. Employers clearly expected that creating bonds of good fellowship with workers could lead to harmonious relations and prosperity for the firm.

The main activity of each volunteer corps was an annual excursion, usually taking place near year's end. Generally these excursions featured a target-shooting competition with guns for a long list of prizes, followed by an elaborate dinner. The cost of this largesse seems to have been taken on by the employer.[15] In 1850 the *Argus* reported on two excursions, in November by the Corning Corps and in December by the Perry Volunteers. Prizes awarded by the Corning Corps included such expensive items as a gold watch, a silver goblet, and a gold pen-and-pencil set, as well as the target itself.[16]

In October 1855, three years before the cable celebration, the Rathbone Guards visited Cohoes, New York, for their annual target exercise. There were two sets of awards, ''gift prizes'' donated personally by the employers, their wives, and other Albany employers, and ''company prizes.'' Typically, the prizes included such costly items as a gold watch, two suits of clothes, a marble case clock, and a gold breast pin bearing the emblem of the iron molders' profession. After the shooting match, the participants went to dinner at the Wilkens' Cohoes Hotel.[17] One month later, the guard corps of Boardmen and Grey visited Waterford, New York, for their excursion. According to the *Argus*, the men anticipated ''a jolly time,'' and they were not disappointed. Due to ''the liberality of their employers,'' the members secured ''every hoped for advantage." Returning to Albany with their "well-riddled" target, the men sat down to a "Collation" arranged for them by the company.[18]

Workers' reasons for joining these volunteer corps and participating in the excursions were complex and likely to have involved matters unrelated to their employers' motivations. The evidence suggests that while these associations were intended to encourage a sense of camaraderie between employer and employed, they may have become for the workers an economic benefit that they considered their due. In November 1856, the *Argus* commented that the company excursions had "grown into disrepute of late. . . . They are expensive, and aside from an hour's pleasure, make no return."[19] Clearly, the *Argus*'s editor questioned whether the outings fulfilled their intended social purposes or had become just a holiday. His concerns may have been widely shared, but employer-sponsored associations and excursions continued at least into the early 1880s.[20]

Whatever may have been their motives for participating in the company-sponsored volunteer corps, workers in Albany initiated some activities that do indicate their wish to reciprocate expressions of good fellowship by their employers and foremen. On numerous occasions workers would give an expensive gift to an employer or foreman in a "presentation." In one instance, when Erastus Corning returned home in August 1856 from a tour of Europe, New York Central Railroad employees all along the line turned out to welcome him. In Albany, the workers greeted Corning at his home and "presented" him with an elaborate wooden coat of arms carved by two local stove molders. "In this, as in other instances," the *Argus* claimed, "the employees have exhibited in a spirited and happy manner their appreciation of and attachment to their employers."[21]

The salute to Corning was not an isolated event. During the two weeks at the end of 1855 and beginning of 1856, stove mounters at Eagle Furnace presented their foreman with a diamond breast pin; workers in Eagle Furnace's pattern and carpentry department gave their foreman a gold pen-and-pencil case; NYCRR workers presented a gold watch to a freight agent; and employees of S. Young and Server, boot and shoe manufacturer, presented each of their employers with a silver cake knife "as a token of esteem and respect." Employers often returned the compliment by providing a sumptuous dinner to commemorate the occasion. Pointing out that most Young and Server workers had been employed by the firm from seven to fifteen years and that it had taken "the premium on boots and shoes last fall," the *Argus* saw a lesson for all its readers in this event. For the *Argus*, it proved that when employers and workers recognize their mutual interests, both prosper.[22]

From their participation in the Gilbert dinner, the transatlantic cable jubilee, the volunteer corps, the presentations, and other such activities, it would appear that many workers in Albany agreed with the *Argus.* However, experiencing a decline in their economic well-being in the 1850s led workers also to challenge the free labor notion of a mutuality of interests. Instead, they saw an inherent antagonism arising between employers and themselves during industrialization. During the 1850s the economic actions of the waterworks laborers, printers, and stove molders illustrate the varying degrees to which workers in Albany subscribed to free labor values in the years leading to the Civil War.

As examples of labor and capital in disharmony, strikes would seem to represent the limits of the free labor ideology. Yet such was not always the case. During (and after) the 1850s, certain strikes in Albany, especially those by unorganized laborers, engaged middle-class members of the community in a kind of public collective bargaining with workers. These "negotiations" symbolized the community's commitment to the free labor order. As long as the laborers conducted their strike "responsibly" (nonviolently), and their employers were shown to be treating them unjustly, the workers could expect and did receive the larger community's support.

One characteristic "free labor" strike took place in June 1851 and involved laborers on Albany's waterworks. The contractors for the new waterworks, promising wages of one dollar per ten-hour workday, had advertised as far away as one hundred miles for workers to dig and lay pipe. These notices drew many laborers to Albany, and the contractors, hoping to take advantage of the temporary oversupply, cut wages to eighty-seven cents for a twelve-hour workday. Angered, the laborers on the project decided not to work for less than what they had been promised.

A public meeting of "laborers and friends" was held on June 21, 1851, in front of City Hall. There being no formal organization of waterworks laborers, the meeting selected leaders from among those attending. Chosen as chairman was an attorney, John Costigan, and as secretary, Alderman Joseph Clinton. Clearly, by designating these men of standing as officers, the waterworks laborers sought to involve the middle class in their dispute and thereby apply broad public pressure on the contractors.

Many of the speakers acknowledged the legitimacy of the laborers' grievances. Nevertheless, they cautioned the workers to "violate no law, insult or abuse neither laborer or contractor." Costigan expressed the desire that they press their demands "in a proper way, upon the parties that oppressed them." Only in this way, he insisted, could they hope to "enlist and secure the good feelings of the American community in their favor, and ultimately accomplish what they proposed viz.: *a fair remuneration for their labor*."[23] The middle-class speakers also reproved the heartless contractors and endorsed the laborers' cause.

In addition to members of Albany's middle class, striking laborers enlisted the support of working-class leaders. At one point "loud calls" rang out for James Kilbourn, the "Orator Carpenter," to address the meeting. Kilbourn depicted the laborers' hardships, especially their inadequate compensation, "in glowing colors." He echoed Costigan's call for "obedience to the laws," coupled with a "firm stand for the rights of labor."[24] Following other speeches, the meeting appointed a committee to confer with the city's water commissioners and the waterworks' contractor and to report to another public assembly to be held at the same place on the following Monday evening. Patrick Grady, David Mahoney, and Edward Grimes, who appear to have been workers, and Isaac Neville, a grocer, were selected to serve on the committee along with Costigan, Clinton, and Kilbourn.[25]

The committee met with the contractor, James McDonald, in the office of Alderman Eggleston, and reported on the negotiations at the Monday public meeting. After discussing the reciprocal rights and duties of employers and employees, the committee and McDonald had reached a compromise. Laborers who dug and filled trenches for ten hours would be paid eighty-seven cents per day while those who worked for twelve hours would receive one dollar per day. They also agreed that all circumstances being equal, resident Albany laborers would be given priority in employment. Although the compromise was not all the laborers sought, they accepted it and unanimously thanked the committee for its efforts. In concluding the meeting, Kilbourn advised the laborers to continue to pursue the same peaceable, steady, orderly course of conduct that had marked their present "turn-out."[26]

The strike by Albany's waterworks laborers was a practical demonstration of the obligations imposed by belief in a mutuality of interests. The laborers had met peacefully and had sought out and deferred to a largely middle-class leadership. In turn, their chosen leaders had accepted the inevitability and propriety of this arrangement. Acting from a commitment to free labor values, middle-class leaders felt an obligation to intercede on the laborers' behalf and ensure that the dignity of labor be protected. Here was one strike in the 1850s in which the much-heralded communitywide reciprocal relations appear to have been in force. But rather than rely on middle-class sympathy for their cause, other workers in the 1850s in Albany, especially printers and molders, preferred to organize unions for their self-protection.

On the evening of May 23, 1850, twenty-eight printers in Albany gathered at the Clinton Hotel to organize a union. What had brought them together was a pervasive fear that industrialization threatened to diminish the value of their skill, thereby undermining their position in society. A "Typographical Association" was necessary, according to Myron H. Rooker, a leader of the movement, in order "to stay the present downward tendency of the profession—to advance and preserve the character of the Art of Arts."[27] Four days after their meeting the printers met again to elect officers and adopt a constitution. Reiterating Rooker's assertion, the constitution pronounced "the objects" of the union to be "the maintenance of a fair rate of wages, the encouragement of good workmen, and to use every means which may tend to the elevation of printers in the scales of social life."[28] Albany printers intended their union to be an agency that would protect their economic well-being by upholding craft traditions.

The printers initiated their campaign to fulfill the union's constitutional objectives by forming a committee to review the state of the printing trade in Albany. What they found confirmed their anxieties. Surveying the city's fourteen printing offices, the committee reported that among approximately one hundred ninety workers not much more than half were journeymen, the rest were boys (and some girls). The ratio of boys employed to men employed was one of the worst features of the trade in Albany. Some printing offices, the committee claimed, were run principally by boys. Newspaper offices especially were "turning-out" what the printers called "two-thirders," partially trained boys who were then hired as journeymen and paid at two-thirds the standard wages for fully trained journeymen. The union had to end this "evil" if it was ever "to preserve the Art on a respectable footing."[29]

The printers felt they could protect their craft by establishing apprentice regulations. Apprentices were "the rising generation." They had to be trained to be good workmen, to become "men of principle, and in consequence, give the trade its dignity, honor and justice." The committee recommended that a ratio of two apprentices to eight journeymen in newspaper rooms and of three to nine in book offices be established.

Complicating the threat posed by the "two-thirders," according to the committee, was "an unjustified system of underbidding competition" among employers in Albany. Whereas Jacksonian workers in the 1830s had honored the producers and vilified the monopolists, the committee of printers now distinguished between the "honorable" offices and the dishonest "mongrel" offices with which they were forced to compete. Such competition forced journeymen's wages down to the lowest common denominator. To remedy this condition, the committee proposed that Albany printers seek a uniform scale of prices for their work.

In identifying the "two-thirders" and the growing price competition as the major threats to their craft, Albany printers ignored the implications of contemporary changes in printing technology. Their anxiety over industrialization derived less from the introduction of the machine than from a perceived shift in values held by their employers.[30] Printers believed that their bosses were beginning to view their labor as just another commodity, to be obtained as cheaply as possible. They predicted that if the "employers' only interest was profit, if they sought the greatest income from the smallest outlay, then they would continue to fill offices with boys, two-thirders and young men." Employers who viewed labor as something to be purchased at the lowest possible cost ignored the reciprocal obligatons imposed by the free labor order.

Albany printers rejected independent action by the union as a response to the ills afflicting their trade. In its report, the committee conceded that it was at a loss as to how the printers might ameliorate these unsatisfactory conditions. Yet they specifically condemned strikes: "On the contrary, we deprecate all violent measures. Our weapon must be moral suasion and combined vigorous action by ourselves and for ourselves." Clearly the printers had to organize, but the committee were still "of the opinion that many of the grievances which the Trade at present labors under, might be partially removed by a respectful and reasonable remonstrance to the employers. . . . *If they wish good to themselves, let them come up with us and help us.*"[31] A reform and remedy, they concluded, "will at once suggest itself" to every employer who either values his honor "or has humanity enough to consider the rights and interests of workmen." Like the waterworks laborers, the printers put their faith in their employers' willingness to respond to a communitywide standard of justice. Although committed to worker organization, Albany printers were not yet liberated from the free labor ideal of a mutuality of interest between capital and labor.[32]

During the 1850s the city's iron molders also formed a union. However, the molders of Albany, unlike the printers, chose to protect their interests by confronting their employers. Much as the printers had, Albany molders in the 1850s found that their labor "had become something impersonal to be obtained as cheaply as possible."[33] During this decade, iron founders in the Albany and Troy area tried to corner the national market for iron stoves by underselling their competitors. To accomplish this they reduced profit margins and cut costs. Throughout the decade Albany molders continually faced efforts by the iron founders to lower the cost of their labor.

In 1852 Messrs. Jagger, Treadwell, and Perry, owners of Eagle Furnace, proposed a change in the way they paid molders. Workers who had been paid weekly were now to be paid on the Saturday nearest the 15th; in addition, the employer would withhold two weeks' wages until the end of the molding season.[34] Before the year's seasonal layoff, workers protested the new system, successfully, they believed. But when the molders returned to work in April 1852, they discovered that the company had not rescinded the proposed changes, and they went out on strike.[35]

To call attention to their grievances against Eagle Furnace, the molders, like the waterworks laborers a year earlier, held a public meeting. Once again leading citizens of Albany attended and spoke in "defense of the working men." But the molders at the meeting chose officers from among themselves, unlike the waterworks laborers. The striking molders specifically rejected any appeal to "the sympathy of the man of wealth, or those who have grown fat on the sweat and toil of the mechanic and laborer." They would rely instead on the "encouragement and sympathy of our fellow mechanics and workingmen, who can properly understand the many injuries the 'new system' will inflict upon us."[36]

A "large and enthusiastic meeting of molders and workingmen" on April 8 adopted a resolution endorsing the strike. They agreed that Albany molders would neither "seek nor take employment" at Eagle Furnace and would prevent "by all legal means" others from so doing. A committee of three molders from each local foundry was to be appointed to solicit contributions in support of the strikers.[37]

Unfortunately, Albany newspapers did not record the outcome of the 1852 strike. However it was resolved, there is no doubt that the iron founders retained their desire to cut costs. In 1859, iron founders in Albany, hoping to capitalize on labor's weakness after the Panic of 1857, advanced an even more fundamental reorganization plan for the industry. Agreeing to stand together, they organized a founders' league and proposed that molding be done solely by piecework, each molder producing one part of, rather than an entire, stove. The employers also sought to introduce the unrestricted hiring of helpers, or "berkshires"; the rental of molding floors; the payment of workers in "truck"; and contracts wherein workers forfeited the right to recover damages for injury.[38]

In March 1859 stove workers formed the Albany Iron Moulders' Union to combat these "odious rules and obnoxious conditions." Like Albany's printers who had been alarmed by the hiring of boys, Albany's molders feared the impact of the helpers. By making molders responsible for supervising and paying a number of helpers, the system would, in effect, transform them into employers. Equally offensive, the berkshire system would produce an unlimited supply of partially trained workers (like the two-thirders in printing) with whom skilled molders would have to compete for work. To fight this system the newly organized molders' union forbade its members to hire helpers in any foundry where it had a majority and exhorted them to exert their "influence to prevent others from so doing." The union also resolved to try to enforce a ratio of one apprentice to every fifteen molders, with the term of apprenticeship to be a minimum of three years.[39]

In April a committee representing the workers presented their demands to a leading Albany stove firm (probably Treadwell, Perry, and Norton). The company immediately fired the committee members and told them to inform the molders on the floor that any other union members among them should leave as well.[40] The founders' league had devised a plan to battle the molders' union. Its members agreed not to employ union molders and to close their shops at the first sign of union "movement." Thus the morning after the union committee presented its demands, the owners closed all stove foundries in Albany. Notices in the local newspapers announced that "[no members of the] Moulder's Association would be employed by any of the manufacturers, unless they ceased to be members of the said association."[41]

The Albany lockout (which molders referred to as a strike) became a battleground in the drive to establish a national molders' union. In July 1859, in Philadelphia, iron molders held their first national convention. Representatives from the Albany union attended, and the strike took center stage in the convention's proceedings. Affirming that the conditions imposed by the "Foundrymen of Albany . . . clearly demonstrates that tyranny begins with the capitalist, who invariably claims the lion's share of that wealth which labor produces," the convention resolved that the molders could not submit "without degrading themselves as American mechanics." After declaring the Albany strike to be entirely proper, the delegates announced, "We consider the cause of the Moulders of Albany, the Cause of our craft at large."[42] As a sign of solidarity, the convention appealed to union members to support the striking molders, and money poured into Albany from throughout the United States. Believing that voluntary contributions were not enough, Albany's brother local, in Troy, began assessing its members one dollar per week. This local also expelled two Troy men who were charged with working in Albany as scabs, and notified all molders' unions of its action.[43]

The Albany molders held firm, and after two months, the founders' league offered a "compromise." The proprietors agreed to abolish "store orders" and to pay workers the wages that had existed in each foundry before the Panic of 1857. The iron founders continued to demand, however, that there be no interference with the right of each molder to use a helper. Although agreeing to rehire any man who had left work because of the strike, the founders made it clear that they would not recognize the union.[44] The strikers apparently rejected this compromise, for on June 25 the founders advertised in the newspapers for molders. The advertisements announced the proprietors' willingness to employ, at good prices, several hundred molders. Members of the iron molders' union would not be hired, although preference would be given to all former workmen who had withdrawn from the union.

The iron founders believed that "the question between the employers and employees *is not one* of price, but of control."[45] By control, the employers meant their presumed right to run the foundries free from interference by a union of their workers. The editor of the *Daily Wisconsin*, visiting Albany at this time, wrote to his paper that the molders were striking "not merely for an increase of wages, but to introduce certain regulations into the foundries which the proprietors naturally resist, as an interference with the details of their business." Such interference, he continued, "must impair the individuality of enterprise, and is so far an injury to every interest."[46]

An especially "injurious" regulation concerned union shop committees. According to the constitution of the molders' union, the responsibility of the shop committee was "to see that the laws of the association are enforced [against their own members] in their respective shops."[47] The owners, according to D. G. Littlefield, an employer although not a founders' league member, regarded such committees as well as the union rules that they would enforce as a serious affront. The iron founders would not permit workers to tell them how to run their businesses and they were resolved to destroy the shop committees and the union.

Almost inevitably the long strike produced violence. Throughout the summer of 1859, striking molders abused, threatened, and assaulted scabs. In September, events came to a head. One working molder was shot at through his window at home and in another shooting a scab was wounded in the leg. Albany's mayor, Eli Perry (probably no relation to foundry owner John S. Perry), called a special meeting of the Common Council to consider "taking some decided action . . . in reference to the recent attempts at assassination of peaceable and unoffending citizens."[48] Alderman Albion Ransom (probably not a member of the founders' organization) complained that "the police offered no protection" and demanded that action be taken against the union molders.[49]

Ransom asked that the mayor be authorized both to hire special police to protect the few men who were working and to offer a reward for the apprehension and conviction of those guilty of the "outrages." After a lengthy debate over the effectiveness of the police, the Common Council agreed to authorize the mayor at his discretion to appoint a special police force of up to fifty men to deal with the problem and to offer up to $1,000 as a reward.

According to the *Argus*, three to four hundred men applied to join the special police force, but no one was ever appointed. Possibly the threat of such a force was enough to quiet the situation. At its next regular meeting, the council, aware that the incidents had stopped, rescinded its previous resolutions on the matter.[50]

Once again the local newspapers do not report the end of the strike. But sometime in September Treadwell, Perry, and Norton's Eagle Furnace failed, and its successor, Treadwell and Perry, reopened as a "union shop." Albany's other foundries appear to have quickly followed suit.

Albany's printers and molders in the 1850s organized unions to protect and advance their interests as members of a craft. Developing industrial capitalism had made it difficult for both groups of workers to maintain their position in society as skilled workers; in particular, they saw the value of their skill being eroded by a profusion of partially trained workers. Both groups believed that their employers were increasingly seeing their labor as just another commodity to be bought. Yet, for the printers their union offered the opportunity to reaffirm their commitment to cooperation with their employers "for the protection and advancement of their mutual interest." The molders, on the other hand, held no such illusions about the founders. In their readiness to do battle over the helper and apprentice issues, molders exhibited a heightened awareness of emerging class differences and directly challenged accepted notions of the free labor order.[51]

It might be expected that the formation of trade unions by printers and molders would raise the specter of class conflict for Albany's middle-class newspaper editors. Workers organized among themselves would seem to be antithetical to the free labor ideal of a mutuality of interests between employer and employed. Yet even in the instance where the editors were also the employers, as when the printers organized, they did not perceive unionization per se as a threat to the free labor social order. According to the *Argus*, workers' societies, "if founded on the right principles, and managed in a judicious manner, are productive of good. . . . May the Printers' Union of Albany be eminently successful in all those aims and objects which tend to the welfare of themselves and others.''[52] The *Evening Journal*, declaring the union's aims to be praiseworthy and important, observed, ''This organization will bring [printers] oftener together, and tend to a kindlier feeling amongst those whose interest are identical. . . . We cordially unite in the organization, and shall cheerfully cooperate in whatever shall be deemed necessary to promote the interest of our fellow-craftsmen.''[53]

There were no confrontations with their own employees to test these newspaper editors' sympathies in the 1850s. In fact, in 1859 the editors expressed reluctance even to comment on the molders' strike. The editor of the *Evening Journal* declined to interfere because, as he stated, the strike was ''a business affair between employers and employés, which the Press and Public might wisely let alone, since they could embitter such a controversy by taking part in it.''[54] Both newspapers, however, overcame these scruples once the molders' struggle erupted in violence, and they severely condemned the violent acts as coercion.

In the editors' view, the molders' violence was coercive and inimical to the free labor system in Albany because it prevented the individual worker from disposing of his labor as he saw fit. When unions physically restrained nonmembers from working they became more than just associations for mutual support; such unions were, in the words of the *Argus*, ''conspiracies, punishable by indictment, and morally as well as legally wrong. To deprive a laborer of his right to work is to do him and do society the highest injury.''[55] Similarly, the *Evening Journal* pronounced that to ''admit for a moment the right of any Union to dictate the action of those who do not belong to it, is to strike a death blow at the independence of the Workingman.''[56]

When they condemned workers' violence as coercion, the newspapers were not merely parroting the employers' narrow individualism—they were acknowledging the free labor idea that workers had property rights too. A worker's right to ''own'' his labor sanctioned his efforts against unfair or evil regulations. The *Evening Journal* commented that it would be authorizing ''the grossest tyranny to allow a Proprietor to compel workmen to submit to his regulations.''[57] And the *Argus* sought to make clear that when ''the employers threaten, and attempt by violence or fear to coerce, they too, are conspirators, and may be punishable as criminals.''[58]

Several years after the 1859 molders' strike, one iron founder, not a league member, wrote that the true cost of the strike was that it engendered ''a disposition to bad feelings between [the workers] and the employers, which ought never to exist.'' Most unfortunately, it had become ''a part of the education of a molder to look upon an employer as being filled with a disposition to rob him at every turn.''[59] Clearly,

Albany's newspaper editors feared just such divisiveness. They believed that the well-being of the community rested with capital and labor recognizing their mutual interests. According to the *Argus*, "conciliation, the abandonment of prejudices and irritations, on the side both of the employers and the workmen" was all that was necessary to restore the natural harmony of interests. And, the *Argus* concluded, "it is in the interest of all good citizens to aid in producing such a result."[60]

Inherent in the free labor ideology espoused by the city's newspaper editors were the ambivalent feelings of Albany's middle class toward the changing economic order. Concerned about the social status of labor, the editors accepted the right of workers to organize to protect themselves and to gain better wages. But they considered strikes to be in general harmful to the community. The solution they proposed in order to avoid strikes—indeed in order to avoid all economic conflict—was for capital and labor to recognize their mutual interests.

The years from 1850 to the Civil War saw the emergence of permanent trade unions among Albany's printers and molders. Although both groups of workers in many respects shared a common perception of the problems they faced as skilled workers in a changing economic world, they reacted to industrialization in markedly different ways. These differences illustrate the dialectic of class and free labor community consciousness among organized workers in Albany. In the Albany of the 1860s and 1870s, workers' perception of tension between free labor community values and class objectives would broaden, resulting in many different kinds of labor organization.

3

Militancy and Consciousness: The Emergence of a Commonwealth Ideology

At the end of the third year of the Civil War, in April 1864, Michael Cassidy, a union molder from Albany, addressed a rally of striking textile workers in nearby Cohoes, New York. Identifying the workers' main grievance, he asserted that while the manufacturers' profits had risen because of higher prices for textile goods, the workers' wages had not. "As a general thing," he told the crowd, "the proprietors have got rich by the war, while the employees are compelled to resort to so-called 'strikes' in order to obtain anything like their rights." Cassidy denied that he had come to Cohoes to create "any feelings of animosity between employer and employees . . . to array one against the other." Indeed, he believed that "good feelings and a sense of mutual interest" should exist between workers and their bosses. But, he asked, how could a man live on the wages being paid in Cohoes when "greed and the desire for large profits" overwhelmed "generosity and reason."[1]

Over the next ten years the sentiments expressed by Cassidy would be repeated many times in Albany and across the nation. For many workers their experiences during industrialization cast doubt on the promise of dignity and opportunity claimed for the free labor system. Aware that their status as wage earners was becoming permanent, workers more actively organized for themselves. Yet their heightened sense of the wrongs caused them by the industrializing order also led workers, in the decade after the Civil War, to seek fundamental reform.

Only through organization and reform could workers be certain that their rights would be secure.

In the 1860s and early 1870s workers in almost every trade in Albany belonged to either a union or a labor association. Uniting on behalf of their general interests, the city's unions in 1864 organized themselves into a citywide trades assembly. Albany workers were also prominent in the formation of national unions in their specific trades and in the founding of the New York State Workingmen's Assembly in 1865.[2] Workers in Albany eagerly turned to unionism after 1860 in self-defense against further exploitation by their employers.

But despite their enthusiasm for organization, in the decade after the Civil War, Albany's workers began to look beyond the immediate protection that unions offered them. They found hard-won gains extracted from reluctant employers continually challenged, and often lost. As an alternative to never-ending conflict and in order to prevent further erosion of their condition, Albany's workers started consumer and producer cooperatives and tried to secure the eight-hour workday. Cooperatives and eight hours of work would permanently reform the free labor order, they believed.

In Albany, as elsewhere, the reform movement of the immediate postbellum years arose from workers' deep discontent with economic and social conditions associated with the industrializing free labor order. Workers turned to reform as a means of securing the economic and social rights they believed due them as members of the community. In free labor capitalism, the determination of wages, and thereby of workers' standard of living, was left to the laws of supply and demand that governed the marketplace. Through reform, workers could modify this process by introducing a different calculation, economic justice. The reform movement of the 1860s and early 1870s reflects workers' "commonwealth" values. Although they did not speak in terms of a "just price," as had eighteenth-century food rioters in England and France, American workers nevertheless insisted that they be able to maintain a decent standard of living through a fair return on their labor. Workers in Albany, increasingly distrustful of the promises of open opportunity proclaimed by proponents of the free labor order, sought from the community assurance of a social commitment to the commonweal.[3]

The reform movement represents Albany workers' hopes for an alternative to the social system emerging with capitalist industrialization. Unfortunately, little of lasting significance came from the reform movement, and the lack of tangible reward suggests the limits of the commonwealth ideology. Although increasingly more conscious of their class interests, Albany workers never embraced class struggle to achieve class goals. Workers in Albany were not socialists; they did not abandon free labor principles altogether. As they searched for a degree of independence from the wage system, workers still recognized the legitimacy of private property. However determined they might be to alter the bleak future that they envisioned for themselves, Albany workers were unable to devise an effective strategy to fundamentally change it.[4]

The proponents of the free labor order, although they continued to voice support for the idea of the dignity of labor, felt threatened by workers' militant reform activities. Their ambivalent response to workers' postwar struggle for change reveals the limits imposed on the ideology by its inherent contradictions and by the community's economic dependence on employers.[5] Still, their ambivalence did not mean that the largely middle-class spokesmen for Albany's community consciousness automatically sided with capital.[6] In the face of growing class conflict, the middle-class community in Albany strove to minimize the class behavior of both capital and labor by insisting on their essential mutuality of interests.

While most of Albany's workers detected a seemingly inexorable decline in their economic well-being, the city's unorganized laborers were the first group of workers to seek a remedy. The early Civil War years had been quiet ones on Albany's labor front. Many workers had volunteered for service in the Union Army, and their absence made organizing trade unions and sustaining strikes difficult. However, the North's hoped-for quick victory proved elusive, and, as the war dragged on, veterans returned home to find soaring prices and stagnant wages. Like Michael Cassidy, many workers in Albany attributed the Civil War–induced inflation to their employers' greedy desire for profit. In mid-1863, workers' frustration over their declining economic fortunes precipitated a virtual general strike among the city's day laborers. It began on June 13, 1863, a Saturday, when dock laborers who loaded and unloaded river craft at Albany's Hudson River pier walked off their jobs demanding an immediate 25 percent pay increase. The strike has been called "the most formidable strike" in the city's history.[7]

On the following Monday morning, gangs of striking longshoremen marched through the city. They stopped work by hod carriers at a grain elevator under construction for the New York Central Railroad as well as work at the New York Central's freight houses in West Albany. Eventually, laborers at Albany's gasworks and at businesses such as Boyd and Brothers' brewery and S. H. Ransom and Company's foundry joined the strike.[8]

Some employers quickly met the laborers' wage demands. But the

NYCRR offered only a ten-shilling increase (the laborers sought twelve shillings), and its laborers remained at the forefront of the strike. On Wednesday morning some four hundred striking laborers surrounded one hundred to two hundred railway freightmen who sought to return to work. Mayor Eli Perry, Chief of Police G. B. Johnson, and about fifty policemen were also present. Harsh words and threats soon erupted into a flash of clubs, a hail of stones, and a concerted attack by the strikers against the scabs. But the police, wielding their own clubs, thwarted the initial charge. Some twenty minutes later a laborer attempting to lead a second charge against the scabs was arrested. On his way to the stationhouse the strikers tried to free their comrade. In response the police fired on the demonstrators, hitting one in the face. Even this did not break up the crowd, which milled around the stationhouse for some time but did not again attempt to free the man.

After the dinner hour, a great crowd assembled at the freight houses. But by then, following an appeal by an unidentified citizens' group, New York's governor had called out three companies of the state militia's Thirty-fourth Regiment. One company was then stationed in Albany's Capitol Park and one at the arsenal; the third relieved the police at the West Albany freight houses. In addition, Albany's sheriff had asked the Twenty-fifth Regiment to stand by. Mayor Perry spoke to the workers gathering in West Albany and informed them that Erastus Corning, the railroad's president, had returned to Albany.[9] Faced by the determined show of official force, the crowd peaceably dispersed after deciding to confront Corning directly.

The next morning the NYCRR's laborers marched to Corning's home, and a committee of the strikers met with him. Corning is reported to have told the committee that once the strikers returned to work he would notify them, through their respective foremen, of the company's response to their demands. The laborers appear to have accepted this arrangement even though it broke their momentum, and they called off the strike. Shortly thereafter, the railroad informed the laborers that it would meet their wage demands. But two weeks later an item appeared in the *Argus* claiming that, because of a "decrease" in freight business, the NYCRR would have to reduce wages to ten shillings—the railroad's original offer. There is no record of any protest by laborers over this action.[10]

The struggle initiated by the city's unorganized laborers to raise wages seriously eroded by inflation would soon be taken up by Albany's skilled workers. In December 1863, the city's coach makers, complaining of the "many encroachments" that had been made "upon our rights," organized a union. Only in unity could they "prevent this unfairness and

. . . maintain the prices of labor in accordance with the times and the prices of the necessaries of life.''[11] Shortly thereafter, a revitalized iron molders' union, numbering about three hundred fifty members, easily won a 15 percent wage increase.[12] By 1865 workers in at least twenty of the city's trades had organized their own unions. Invoking the city's Dutch heritage and legends, workers spoke of ''waking up'' and opening their eyes to find that they had ''slept too long.''[13]

Many Albany workers supported the efforts to organize national unions. In February 1865, members of the city's reorganized tin, copper, and sheet-iron workers' union tried to promote the formation of their national union. The president of the Albany union, G. B. Green, stated flatly, ''It is essentially necessary that we should have a grand head, and all united under the same, if we expect to perfect the objects for which we first organized.''[14] Self-protection alone dictated that Albany workers unite with brother workers outside the city. They increasingly came to see themselves as participants in a general movement of workers.

Within Albany, workers from twenty ''bona fide'' trade unions issued a call in February 1864 for a citywide trades assembly.[15] As one union member in Albany noted, it was easy to see that twenty-five hundred were stronger than twenty-five, and since the workingman was not earning what he was entitled to, ''He *must* better his condition by *some* means, or submit to be still further reduced in the social scale.''[16] The constitution of the ''Trades' Assembly of the City of Albany and Vicinity'' offered the organization's support to any union numbering at least twenty-five members that sent delegates to the assembly.[17] Its members anticipated that the solidarity expressed through the trades assembly would strengthen workers' bargaining power. In one of its first actions the assembly published a list of ''unfair employers'' in Albany in order to inform workingmen and public alike of those bosses who did not pay ''a fair and living'' wage.[18]

The resurgence of unions in Albany in the early 1860s was part of a widespread movement throughout New York State. Opposition to these developments surfaced in the state legislature in March 1864 when Frederick R. Hastings of Rensselaer introduced a ''Conspiracy Bill'' in the Senate. The bill would have made punishable as a conspiracy any interference with employees going to work, coercion of an individual to join a union, or levying of fines against anyone for breaking union rules. Workers throughout the state protested the proposed legislation. In Albany local unions convened on April 20, 1864, a ''mass meeting of indignation'' against the ''Strike Bill.'' In response to the formidable opposition to his bill statewide, Hastings allowed it to die in committee.[19]

Buoyed by their success against the conspiracy bill, members of

Albany's trades assembly pushed for organization of a statewide trades assembly. To this end, representatives from the Albany and Troy assemblies met in March 1865. Insisting that "under the present State law the mechanical labor of the State is not properly protected," the two cities' trades assemblies issued a call for a state convention. Jonathan Fincher, the editor of the leading labor paper in the nation, *Fincher's Trades Review*, congratulated the Albany and Troy assemblies for commencing "the work of vibrating public sentiment, until it settle down upon the conviction that workingmen ask nothing but what is right and just."[20]

Representatives from unions across New York met in Albany in September 1865 to formally organize a state trades assembly. The statewide assembly would act primarily as a lobby for labor reform. After each annual convention committees from the assembly would present its resolutions to state legislators for action. But Albany's workers, although active in these meetings, concentrated on local labor issues.

Facing an increasingly militant and organized labor force, employers in Albany mounted a counteroffensive. In the postwar period, stove manufacturers united to form employer associations to oppose trade unions. In March 1866 iron founders from throughout the country gathered at Albany's Delevan House. The founders ascribed their meeting to the "present aggressions and exorbitant demands" of the molders' unions, which threatened "the relations which naturally exist between employer and employee."[21] They singled out as particularly offensive the national union's rules limiting the number of apprentices, restricting employment to union members, and authorizing local unions to form shop committees to screen prospective employees and enforce union rules in the foundries. To represent their interests, the founders at the Albany meeting established the National Organization of the Iron Founders and Stove Manufacturers of the United States.

The assembled iron founders denied that they sought either to array capital against labor or to "denigrate the mechanic." Instead, they claimed they were emancipating "the working man from those arbitrary restrictions upon his manhood, to which he had been subjugated by the moulders' union, a device of selfish men." Through organization the founders would restore their natural rights, that is, "the right to control and direct our own businesses, as our own directions may dictate, and the right to make our contracts for labor, and with whomsoever we may deem proper."[22]

Events surrounding the national confrontation between the iron founders and the molders in 1866 very nearly replicated what had happened in Albany seven years earlier. Once again founders posted "obnoxious notices" announcing their intention to "introduce into our shops all the apprentices or helpers we deem advisable" and to ban union shop committees.[23] As before, molders responded by walking out of the foundries. However, at this point, William Sylvis, president of the Iron Moulders' International Union, stepped in. Having decided that it was unwise to shut down every shop and take on the founders nationwide, Sylvis sought to confine the strike to Albany, Troy, and Cincinnati. Working molders in other cities would be called on to support those on strike. Success against the employers in these three centers, Sylvis projected, would likely smash the national founders' organization.[24] By March 21, 1866, all of the foundries in Albany were closed.[25]

The molders had two objectives in striking. First, they sought to hold onto their union, and, second, they hoped to keep in force their hard-won rules on helpers and apprentices. They heartily agreed with Fincher, who saw the iron founders' association as "the entering wedge . . . designed to split our trade organizations in twain, and scatter them in impotent fragments."[26]

While Sylvis developed the national union's strategy, the local molders' unions in Albany, Troy, and Cincinnati assumed the burden of the strike. In Albany, the local union appointed a committee to answer all "false" charges made against them. In a "Card to the Public," the committee responded to the iron founders' assertion that the union enforced arbitrary and coercive rules. Union shop committees were merely "a part of the machinery of our organization to look after our financial affairs and do the business between the Union and its members."[27] The real difficulty, the molders countercharged, was the employers' resolve to introduce unlimited numbers of apprentices and helpers.

In a letter printed in the *Argus* during the strike, "Honest Labor" voiced the molders' concern over the issues of apprentices and helpers. Prior to the adoption of union rules in 1859 it was common for molders to employ helpers. The result was to double the number of molders every two or three years. The partially trained men worked for less than experienced molders, which drove down the scale of wages in the trade. Nor had union rules caused a hardship for the iron founders. Since 1859, according to "Honest Labor," there had been no scarcity of molders in Albany. He realized that a long strike could drive the trade from the city. But "every true Albanian," he hoped, would understand and lend a helping hand when a "few narrowminded capitalists conspire . . . to mould the workmen to their will, which in years gone by was little better than slavery."[28]

Sylvis's strategy worked. Concentrating union resistance ultimately broke the iron founders' unity. In the strike settlement, the founders agreed to hire helpers only with the journeymen's consent and not to increase the number of apprentices as long as the supply of molders adequately met the demands of the trade.[29] They also agreed that union shop committees could continue to operate in the foundries as before. These terms, which included a wage increase as well, represented "a complete victory," Sylvis justly boasted.[30]

Unions and union-imposed rules in their industries motivated other employers in Albany besides the iron founders to organize themselves. In May 1869, building trades employers in the city formed the Boss Builders' Board of Trade. There does not appear to have been an immediate confrontation between the builders and their employees. However, the following year, boss masons and carpenters announced a wage cut. The reduction was justified, they claimed, because the industry was experiencing its "dullest season" in years, and there had been generally a drop in the cost of living.[31] Both the local Bricklayers', Masons', and Plasterers' Union (BMPU) and the Carpenters' and Joiners' Union refused to work for the dollar a day less that was offered.[32]

Ostensibly a dispute over wages, the real issue for the boss builders, as it had been for the iron founders, was control. The builders declared that as employers they refused to be governed any longer by arbitrary union rules. "In the future," they stated, "[we shall] manage our own affairs according to such just rules as we may deem proper, taking such apprentices as we think necessary, and in fact exercising the same control over our private business as merchants and others enjoy."[33]

Workers in the building trades understood what the bosses wanted. Like the molders, they realized that their employers sought to restore preunion conditions. Before the unions, every boss builder could employ from three to fifteen apprentices. Many of these boys stayed only one season before moving on to work for lower wages than fully trained workmen. "And that is what this combination wants now," the unions declared. If the unions had allowed the builders to hire as many apprentices as "they seem fit to employ," the wage issue would never have been raised.[34]

The Carpenters' and Joiners' Union stood "shoulder to shoulder" with the BMPU in defense of their collective "rights." The carpenters, who had accepted a wage cut the previous spring, resolved now to fight the boss builders as a test of their union. Fully trained carpenters required a long time to learn the trade, and they purchased their costly tools. Rather than accept what amounted to "laborers' wages," the Carpenters' and Joiners' Union and the BMPU went out on strike.[35] The strike ended after three months with the unions victorious, their rules intact and wages unchanged. It had been a "sharp dispute," one Albany worker observed, but the victory was decisive.[36] Indeed, after the strike the Boss Builders' Board of Trade faded out of existence.[37]

In May 1870, coopers in Albany affiliated with the Coopers' International Union of North America. Boss coopers in the city responded by trying to promote an employer-sponsored union, the Mechanics' and Manufacturers' Albany Coopers Union. The bosses claimed that the international union was a "secret society" requiring a secret oath. The "not secret" goal of the proposed mechanics' and manufacturers' union was to encourage "the mutual interest of employer and employed in matters relating to the trade in an open, just and lawful manner" and "to obtain and give by mutual agreement a fair remuneration for labor."[38] Union coopers were unimpressed, and the bosses' union proved short-lived.[39]

By the early 1870s employers and workers in Albany had both organized along class lines. For free labor advocates, to have capital and labor in the city arrayed against each other posed a danger to the well-being of the community. They accepted the need for employers and workers to form separate associations to promote their particular interests, but the relations between them should remain harmonious.

Throughout the 1860s and early 1870s the editors of Albany's leading newspapers frequently expressed their views on the respective rights of capital and labor. In 1864, both the *Argus* and the *Albany Evening Journal* used the debate over the conspiracy bill to comment on the right of workers to combine.[40] The *Argus* criticized the bill for inventing, "under the vague phrase of 'molesting or obstructing,' a new and ill-defined crime." Because it proposed punishing only the workmen and not employers, the legislation was, the newspaper concluded, "unworthy of the age and the times, unless indeed we are confessedly retrograding to the era of favoritism, class-oppression, and force."[41] The *Albany Evening Journal* expressed similar sentiments. Workers had too few advantages and opportunities, according to the *Evening Journal*, and because "capital is in its very nature selfish and oppressive, . . . the [workers'] League often affords the only immunity from positive injustice."[42] Both newspapers accepted unions as necessary to workers' self-defense.

A few months after its expressions of warm support for unions, the *Argus* found itself in a dispute with Albany Typographical Union No. 4. The union struck the newspaper over the employment of a "rat"—a printer working below the recognized "scale of prices"—as well as over management support of a foreman who had fired a union member. Expressing reservations about the demands of "workingmen's combinations," the *Argus* refused to dismiss the foreman as the union demanded. In an editorial the newspaper presented its case: "Several of the men have grown up from boys in our employ, and we entertain the kindliest interest in their welfare. But the demand which they and their associates made of us was unreasonable, and one which no proprietors, with proper regard for their own interests, or with becoming self-respect, could concede.''[43]

Nevertheless, the printers and the newspaper soon reached an accord, and the strike ended. The ''rat'' the union complained of was let go, but although opposition to the foreman remained, he appears to have kept his job. The *Argus* granted its workers a large wage increase. Using the pseudonym ''S. Pica,'' a member of the typographers' union in Albany later wrote to *Fincher's Trades Review*, ''The whole affair was carried out in the most sociable manner, and gives evidence of an increasing good feeling between the employer and employee.''[44]

But what was the real basis for this ''good feeling''? In commenting on the settlement, the *Argus* expressed a paternalism that reveals how little room unions really had to maneuver in the free labor system. The newspaper described itself as pleased to have had the chance ''to deal directly with our employees—to understand their wants and wishes, and to express to them our own—and to settle our relations by mutual consultation.'' Such a reasonable course, the *Argus* believed, would ''enable employers and employees to feel more interest in each other, and will better promote their mutual prosperity, than any compulsory regulation of their relations by outside organizations.''[45] The settlement represented a natural adjustment of the relations of labor and capital.[46] The free labor system imposed reciprocal obligations on both employers and workers. Ideally, they should meet as individuals. Trade combinations implied class awareness and, too often, produced class behavior.

The *Argus* expressed its concern about the iron molders' and founders' organizations during the 1866 strike. The strike ''cannot but prove injurious to all interests concerned,'' the *Argus* lamented, ''more so now than ever before, because the parties stand pledged to act in concert, if need be, the one class against the other.'' The newspaper reiterated that the only way to resolve class conflict was for employer and employee to recognize ''a common interest . . . and that interest can best be consulted and profited by mutual forebearance and concessions.''[47] The *Albany Evening Journal* echoed these sentiments. In 1870 it commented on the boss builders' association: ''All are organized. . . . It is in the main a bad sign, as if Justice and Charity had taken wings, and none dare to enter for the selfish combat single-handed.''[48] For both newspapers, when employer and employee combined to oppose each other they threatened to undermine the free labor order. Only if capital and labor recognized and acted in accord with their mutual interests would the community prosper.

For their part, workers in Albany also worried over the seemingly endless warfare between labor and capital. But, unlike the newspaper editors, workers had little faith that appeals to employers would help them. They saw combination among themselves as the key to their self-defense. Yet trade unionism by itself was inadequate to stop the erosion of their position in society. Writing to the *Iron Moulders' International Journal*, a molder signing himself "Co-operation" explained: "A successful strike is but temporary relief; year after year the programme must be gone over, and anything tending to give us a permanent peace, even at a small sacrifice of a couple of years, is far preferable to the present continued warfare between capital and labor."[49] This world view, that capital and labor were at war, as well as the desire to find some alternative to the conflict, sustained Albany's labor reform movement during the 1860s and early 1870s. Not all workers supported each reform, but the commitment to reform was widespread. By promoting such reforms as consumers' cooperatives, producers' cooperatives, and an eight-hour workday, workers in Albany hoped to alter permanently the relations of capital and labor.[50]

In September 1864, the city trades assembly launched the Workingmen's Co-operative Association of Albany. Because the goods that they purchased passed through so many hands, workers supported "in ease and luxury an idle horde of speculators." Cooperation among workers as consumers would "emancipate the working classes from these oppressing evils" by overcoming the disadvantages of "making their purchases alone."[51] Workers could achieve together, united in cooperation, what they could not as individuals. Cooperative buying was to be a strike against monopoly.

A few months after forming the cooperative, its members resolved to stop purchasing butter, deeming its price to be too high. "To lessen the demand" was, they insisted, "the best way of bringing the middlemen and speculators to terms."[52] In its boycott of butter, as in its other actions, the workingmen's cooperative association was invoking notions of a moral economy similar to those motivating the eighteenth-century English and French rioters who demanded that food be sold at a "just price."[53]

The association formulated guidelines to ensure that the cooperative fulfilled its twin goals of checking monopoly and discountenancing "anything having a tendency to enrich the few at the expense of the many." No member could purchase more than five shares (which cost $5 each), and shares were not transferable. The association justified such rules because it was likely that without safeguards the shares "would soon all be in the hands of a few, and the store become just like any other store, where one or two proprietors get rich off the profits on articles bought by workingmen." The association also proposed to divide dividends in proportion to the amount of goods purchased at the cooperative's store rather than "upon shares." By adopting this system the cooperators hoped to avoid rewarding the large shareholder with more of the profit just because he had the most capital. Unless the cooperative profited those who had shown the greatest need, the association would be guilty of perpetuating one of the "worst evils" of the competitive system.[54] Workers turned to consumer cooperation as a way of assuring a more equitable distribution of the goods they purchased.[55] For at least the next five years the Albany Co-operative Union Store appears to have been able to operate on these principles.[56]

While consumer cooperatives benefited workers as purchasers, cooperatives in production brought workers together as producers. Workers felt that the amounts that they received in wages belied their role as producer. It was clear "to every thinking mind," the Albany workingmen's assembly maintained, that only through producer cooperation could workers "enjoy all the profits of their own labor."[57] By cooperation workers would get "rich on their own earnings."[58] Under the present system the profits from their toil flowed like "thousands of little streams . . . into the pockets of a few men." Cooperatives would liberate workers "from that power which compelled us to toil eternally without a recompense."[59] The cooperative system rewarded the worker as producer and as investor; he received a share of the profits, in addition to his wages. Cooperation would guarantee workers what they were denied under capitalism, the full fruits of their labor.

Among Albany's workers the city's iron molders came closest to realizing the cooperative ideal. The molders had expressed interest in opening a cooperative foundry during their 1866 strike. In March 1866, reporting on the strike, the *National Trades Review* noted that in both Albany and Troy "the great principle of 'self-help' [cooperation] will be practically applied."[60] By December of that year Albany's molders had formed the Union Foundry Association (UFA). The association created a stock company, to raise $50,000 in capital by selling 500 shares at $100 each, and elected company officers. Michael Cassidy, an active union member, was chosen to be foundry superintendent. The association bought a local foundry in Albany on Broadway formerly owned by Vose and Company and announced that it would go into operation in February 1867 on the cooperative plan.[61]

In early January 1867 a notice in the city's newspapers heralded the opening of the Albany Co-operative Foundry for the manufacture of stoves, hollowware, and all kinds of castings. The UFA assured the public of "prompt and faithful attention" to all work entrusted to the new foundry.[62] One month later Albany Moulders' Union No. 8 reported in the *Iron Moulders' International Journal* that the cooperative foundry had taken off its "first heat. Everyone is pleased. So far it is a success."[63] The foundry grew, and by the end of its first year the UFA was able to declare an 80 percent dividend.[64] Most of the casting done by the Albany Co-operative Foundry was under contract from other foundries rather than directly for the market.[65]

Success inspired emulation. In August 1868 the Capital Co-operative Foundry Association was also incorporated in Albany, "for the purpose of uniting our labor, capital and patronage" in the manufacture of iron castings. Individuals became association members by paying "in good faith" 10 percent in cash of the $100 that each share cost. Most members took only one or two shares and paid only $10 a share. A few shareholders paid in coal and sand instead of cash.[66] As a result, at the time of incorporation the cooperative foundry's real capital was less than a third of the $10,000 officially subscribed.

Raising sufficient capital was an ongoing problem for most cooperative enterprises in the nineteenth century. Nevertheless, the two Albany foundries flourished as long as they had contracts for work. In mid-March 1870 a credit investigator for R. G. Dun and Company reported that the Albany Co-operative Foundry was handling all the casting it could for three Troy foundries and was "giving satisfaction."[67] The annual report of the Capital Co-operative Foundry Association for 1870 stated that the foundry was "flourishing." During the previous two years the company had declared an average annual dividend of 15 percent. In June 1872 the *Argus* reported that the company had added a number of buildings since opening and that its yearly receipts ranged between $60,000 and $70,000.[68]

Conscious of "the seriousness of the present conflict between capital and labor," Albany's molders embraced cooperation primarily as an alternative to ever-greater concentration of ownership and as a means of assuring a republican system of manufactures.[69] Worker-owned cooperatives eliminated at once the nonproducers and the wage system. The rules governing the molders' cooperatives also protected republican values within the evolving industrial order. For much the same reason that the city workingmen's assembly had regulated shareholding in the cooperative union store, the molders limited the number of shares in the foundries that any one person could own. Initially all shareholders worked in the cooperative foundry and each had only one vote. Management—the association's officers (including the foundry superintendent) as well as its board of directors—was selected by the owner/operators.[70] In a report in 1868 to the national iron molders' union membership, William Sylvis called the cooperative shops in Albany and Troy "the beginning of a new era in our trade."[71] Sylvis and the molders in both cities agreed that only by cooperation could they assure that property was distributed widely.[72]

Out of the same hope of finding a "permanent peace" in their eternal war with capital, which led them to consumer and producer cooperatives, workers in Albany took part in the movement to establish an eight-hour workday. Prior to 1863 the ten-hour day and the sixty-hour week were standard for most piece work and day laborers.[73] Extending far beyond Albany, the eight-hour movement covered two phases. In the first, from 1865 to 1867, workers, especially those in New York State, lobbied to win public support for and legislative enactment of an eight-hour law. The second phase, which followed passage of an eight-hour law in New York in 1867, encompassed the workers' struggles, both through electoral politics and through strikes, to gain enforcement of the law. Albany workers were highly visible participants in both phases of the eight-hour movement.

The eight-hour reform was prominent in the labor agenda adopted by the New York State Workingmen's Assembly. In 1865, at its first convention, the delegates resolved to ask the state's workers to hold public rallies and to promote discussion in the press on behalf of an eight-hour law. Only when they felt that the public understood the eight-hour question fully should workers push for legislation.[74]

Workers in Albany moved swiftly to fulfill the mandate of the Workingmen's Assembly. A few weeks after the workingmen's state assembly had adjourned, the city trades assembly organized an eight-hour league to coordinate local efforts to build public support. Among its local activities the league passed a resolution asking the Albany Common Council to incorporate an eight-hour clause in all future city contracts. The league also wrote to all candidates for the state legislature from Albany, soliciting their support for a state eight-hour law.[75] When J. F. Crawford, who was running for the State Assembly from the city's Fourth District, did not respond to its letter, the league inserted a notice in the newspapers advising workers to assume that Crawford opposed the law and to act accordingly. Subsequently, Crawford announced his support for the eight-hour workday, and the league told workers to vote as they wanted.[76]

The eight-hour movement in Albany and elsewhere originated in workers' increased awareness of the need to sustain economic justice in the evolving industrial order. Albany's eight-hour league held that the system as it stood made "the rich richer, and the poor poorer" and in so doing was contrary "to the spirit of our national institutions, which propose to treat all men as equal." The league insisted that barriers be erected against the "downward tendency on the part of the vast majority of the people," a tendency caused by the "insane hope of individual elevation at the sacrifice of the many."[77] Workers had to unite "in a solid phalanx" behind the eight-hour workday in order to achieve "a more just and equitable division of time and remuneration."[78] Beyond the immediate benefits, the eight-hour law became for workers a symbol of the community's commitment to uphold the dignity and opportunity promised by the free labor system.[79]

Indeed, a "solid phalanx" of New York State workers for eight hours did manage to win approval in 1867 of an eight-hour law. The law that passed, however, did not provide penalties for violators, and New York's Governor Reuben Fenton admitted that nothing would be done to promote observance when he signed it. By its clause preserving full "freedom of contract," the law essentially left the question of hours where it had been, as an issue to be decided between employer and employee. New York's legislature had officially recognized the eight-hour workday as a reform important to the state's workers, but it left them to their own devices in terms of enforcement.[80] After 1867 workers shifted their attention from the political sphere and demanded that their employers institute the eight-hour workday. Not surprisingly, most often the result was a strike.

In the spring of 1868, workers at the West Albany shops of the New York Central Railroad struck for the eight-hour workday with full pay. Shortly before the strike, the New York Central had granted shop workers the eight-hour workday but coupled it with a 20 percent cut in wages. In March the company notified workers that not only would the shops be returning to a ten-hour workday but only half of the wage cut was to be restored. The next morning the workers in the shops met and voted against accepting these changes. When Vice-president Torrence of the NYCRR refused to meet with them, the workers walked out. They demanded eight hours as a "legal day's work," and in addition the restoration of the full 20 percent cut from their wages.[81]

The evidence suggests that NYCRR shop workers in Albany thought of themselves as the vanguard of a larger movement for the eight-hour workday. Shop workers in other cities along the NYCRR line, and at the East Albany shops of the Harlem and Hudson River Railroad eventually did join the strike. But the shop workers' hopes that the train workers (engineers, brakemen, and switchmen) of the NYCRR as well as workers in other trades in Albany would join their protest went unfulfilled.

Their failure to ignite a general movement undermined the shop workers' strike. Two days into the strike, Commodore Vanderbilt, on behalf of the New York Central and the Harlem and Hudson railroads, offered a compromise of ten hours of work with full pay. Vanderbilt was reported to be firmly against the eight-hour workday; nevertheless, West Albany workers wanted to hold out, and rejected the offer. But at this point the reform thrust of the strike was blunted by issues not connected to the desire for an eight-hour workday. Brakemen on the New York Central organized a union and demanded a wage increase without reduction of work to eight hours. Railway engineers and switchmen followed suit. The company quickly met the train workers' wage demands. The shop workers condemned the train workers for exploiting their strike for the eight-hour "principle."[82]

The final blow to the cause of the West Albany shop workers was the move by their counterparts in other cities and in East Albany to accept Vanderbilt's offer of ten hours with full pay. This, too, the shop workers stated, undercut the justification of their strike as one for the eight-hour principle and not simply for raising wages. The failure of the other trades in the city to support the strike also disappointed the West Albany workers. The shopmen criticized these workers for standing "aloof in this contest of principle."[83] Only the carpenters' union seems to have offered the shop workers any moral and material aid.[84]

The machinations of the train workers, the absence of assistance from workers in other trades, and the willingness of brother shop workers to compromise on eight hours ultimately broke the strike at the West Albany yards. Although acknowledging its "mistake" in not restoring full wages when it returned the shops to ten hours, the NYCRR flatly refused to permit the eight-hour workday. After striking for a week, the West Albany shop workers voted to allow those who wished to go back to work to do so. With great bitterness they declared that if dollars and cents ruled other workers, then it would have to do for them as well.[85]

But the effort to introduce the eight-hour workday continued on a number of labor fronts. During the summer of 1868, New York City bricklayers engaged in a long, angry strike for the eight-hour workday. In August, representatives from Albany unions met and resolved to hold a rally in support of the New York City bricklayers and the eight-hour movement. On September 8, a procession stretching over half a mile filled Albany's streets. Escorted by the Townsend Zoaves, a military guard company, and Shreiber's Band, thousands paraded under banners proclaiming "Eight Hours A Legal Day's Work—The Workingman must have his Rights." When the marchers arrived at the State Capitol, they chose officers from among participating trade union leaders and other community members. The crowd then approved resolutions supporting the bricklayers' strike and calling on state authorities to enforce the existing eight-hour law: "The progressive tendency of the institutions of this nation demand that all citizens shall be participators in all the blessings and benefits to be derived from an advanced and enlightened form of government." After three cheers for the eight-hour cause, the ralliers dispersed.[86]

Despite their best efforts Albany workers seemed unable to find a means to secure the eight-hour reform. Confronted with their employers' absolute refusal to accept the eight-hour workday and with their elected officials' unwillingness to see the eight-hour law enforced, a few union leaders, principally from the city's workingmen's assembly, decided that workers might make more headway if they launched an independent labor party. But the new party could barely field a ticket and garnered few votes in the 1870 spring municipal and fall statewide elections. Most Albany workers, at least at this point, restricted their political activities to lobbying and, occasionally, threatening political leaders on behalf of labor's reform agenda. Six years later, when prison contract labor presented an immediate threat to their livelihoods, Albany workers revived the idea of an independent political party.[87]

In 1872 the eight-hour movement heated up. Between May and August 1872, more than one hundred thousand workers participated in a strike for the eight-hour workday in New York City.[88] In Albany in June 1872, NYCRR workers once again struck for an eight-hour workday.

The 1872 strike against the New York Central had much in common with the one four years earlier. As in 1868, West Albany's shop workers asked fellow workers along the rail line to join their strike—only shop workers at Schenectady and Utica agreed.[89] Again, strikers' committees exhorted all machine shop workers in Albany to join them, but only one shop's employees did so. And, as before, only the carpenters' among the city's unions publicly endorsed the railroad shop workers' action.[90]

But the two strikes also differed. By 1872, shop workers were better prepared. Realizing the need for more effective leadership, they had organized a new "Eight Hour League" to coordinate and control the strike.[91] The league held public meetings and rallies daily and agreed that all communication with the NYCRR should be in writing, "so that no bartering could be made between any one man and the company."[92] The league appointed committees to handle specific tasks during the strike. For example, a twenty-member police committee was created to "curb the overzealous and prevent lawlessness.''[93] Although not sympathetic to the NYCRR workers' cause, the *Argus* admired their groundwork, calling the strike ''the most deliberately planned combination or conspiracy (whatever its friends or enemies choose to style it) which had been entered into.''[94]

Better organization was not the only difference between the 1868 and 1872 strikes. The intervening years had been especially frustrating for the workers as all peaceful efforts at securing the eight-hour workday proved fruitless. The sentiments expressed at the daily rallies suggest workers' growing sense of grievance and anger. Although some workers still spoke of eight-hour reform as necessary to allow workingmen sufficient time ''to cultivate their minds,'' more frequently they depicted the strike as ''an attempt by workingmen to free themselves from slave holders. Labor was sold at an unjust price, and the men did not get a fair share of the profits resulting from it, and it was time that the nation arose and shook off that oppression.''[95] Of course, by slaveholders the speaker was referring to capital, ''the one-fifth of the entire population who did no labor.''[96] Yet as a consequence of the wage system just such nonlaborers could determine workers' standard of living. John Fehrenbatch, president of the Machinists' and Blacksmiths' International Union, explained to rallying strikers that ''the man who has nothing but his labor has the price put upon it by those who buy his labor.''[97] The eight-hour workday, if adopted, a local strike leader asserted, ''would have the tendency to equalize both labor and the wealth of the country.''[98] Eight-hour reform answered workers' needs less because it shortened their workday by two hours than because it gave them a means by which they could impose their will on the emerging industrial order.

By the 1870s workers had become convinced that economic power was concentrated in the hands of capital. Another rally speaker sarcastically referred to ''a man'' in Albany earning a yearly salary of $5,000 who claimed that a worker was not worth ''more than $1.25 a day.''[99] Presumably, workers could best respond to such spurious claims by seeking simply to raise their wages. But this would only ''postpone the matter'' because they would then have to pay higher prices for the goods that they purchased. Instead, ''the object in view'' was to effect a more permanent reform, ''to equalize the price of products and labor,'' and this could be achieved better through an eight-hour workday than an advance in wages.[100] If workers persisted in the struggle for eight hours, their victory would force the capitalists to grant them their ''just due.''[101] If successful, labor would have overcome the determined opposition to the eight-hour workday by both employers and elected officials. Such a victory would make workers independent of the forces constraining them, and would enable labor to "regulate itself."[102] Like their purpose in forming consumer and producer cooperatives, the impetus behind workers' agitation for the eight-hour workday was to make economic justice a necessary calculation in determining how the wealth of the country would be distributed.

A militant spirit animated the NYCRR strikers in 1872. At one point more than five hundred workers paraded through the streets of Albany, their banners proclaiming, "Eight Hours: No Compromise."[103] At the strike's peak more than thirteen hundred workers, including machinists, blacksmiths, carpenters, and painters, participated.[104] But despite this solidarity, the strike failed. The company's absolute refusal to consider the eight-hour workday for the shops proved to be an insurmountable obstacle. For many workers in Albany and across the nation the eight-hour workday would remain a much sought after but largely unattainable goal through the rest of the nineteenth century.

In responding to Albany workers' cooperative and eight-hour labor reform movements between 1863 and 1873, both the *Argus* and the *Evening Journal* tried, in their view, to reconcile the competing social claims of labor and capital. Each newspaper, as already noted, endorsed the right of workers to organize, as long as they respected the equally valid right of the individual to contract for his labor. But any movement that encouraged enmity between capital and labor alarmed the newspapers. What was best for labor and the whole community, they believed, was when workers and employers acknowledged their mutual interests.

During the molders' strike in 1866, the *Argus* and the *Evening Journal* commented on the molders' decision to open a cooperative foundry. Although both newspapers questioned the practicality of cooperative ventures, they did not follow *Hunt's Merchant Magazine* in denouncing worker-owned enterprise as "fallacies" that neutralized the "principles of individual energy." In fact, one historian considers contemporary public characterization of cooperatives as "Frenchy theories of communism," with their "infidel and leveling" ideas, as the cause of their failure in the nineteenth century.[105] Yet neither of the Albany newspapers saw cooperatives as a threat to the free labor system.[106] While expressing its preference for "the individual system," the *Argus* could still concede that the cooperative system had potential: "Let the experiment be tried but fairly and fully."[107]

Although somewhat skeptical about the future of the molders' cooperative, the newspapers nevertheless celebrated its completion. "Our citizens generally rejoice at the success of this [cooperative] enterprise," the *Argus* observed.[108] The *Evening Journal* now regarded cooperation as "a rational and philosophical solution of questions affecting the relations of capital and labor.''[109] For both newspapers, producers' cooperatives, far from interfering with the free labor system, became mechanisms for preserving it.

In the free labor order no figure ranked higher than the small independent entrepreneur. Their belief that society had to provide the opportunity to become self-employed made free labor spokesmen suspicious of economic concentration.[110] ''Does labor consume the fruit it gathers?'' the *Argus* asked. ''Or rather does not a system of monopoly and privilege turn the swelling volume of wealth into the hands of a small perferred class, and leave the masses to unrewarded toil!''[111]The *Evening Journal* also distrusted the way in which the industrializing order distributed the products of labor. It saw cooperation as a remedy. Cooperatives did not injure the community; on the contrary, they ''profited'' it. Through cooperatives workers would ''become more independent and self-reliant,'' the *Evening Journal* predicted.[112] Workers' cooperatives sustained the free labor ideal of a worker's trade as the first step to his self-employment.[113] To these middle-class spokesmen cooperatives helped to perpetuate a society of individual entrepreneurs.[114]

The dignity of labor was a constant theme among free labor adherents, and they could be sharply critical of employers whose actions appeared arbitrary or unfair. Endorsing the workers' right to combine for fair wages, the *Evening Journal*, like the *Argus*, had been impressed by ''the calmness, the good temper, the moderation'' of the NYCRR shop workers during the 1868 strike.[115] Although two years earlier the *Evening Journal* had condemned the ''arbitrary impositions'' of the molders' union, in 1868 the newspaper reacted just as harshly when the NYCRR returned the shops to the ten-hour workday without restoring the wage cut. While deprecating strikes, the *Evening Journal* admitted that sometimes labor was left with no alternative. The laborer should never be regarded ''simply as a tool or adjunct—through which certain processes in the machinery of the community are to be carried forward,'' the newspaper declared, ''without reviving in effect the spirit of Slavery.'' To have given in to the railroad's order without a struggle would have meant ''a loss of independent manhood'' by NYCRR workers.[116]

However the *Argus* and the *Evening Journal* might sympathize with the shop workers' just grievances, both newspapers discounted their demand for an eight-hour workday. According to the *Evening Journal* and the *Argus*, what the workmen wanted was higher wages. Their demand for eight hours was merely a bargaining tool to force the New York Central to restore in full the 20 percent reduction in wages. The *Evening Journal* insisted that the strike was hardly a great question involving the relations of capital and labor.[117] All that was required to resolve the dispute was a practical adjustment based on fixed business principles.

The more militant strike by NYCRR workers in 1872 led both newspapers to warn workers against the potential damage the movement for eight hours could cause Albany. During the previous year 1,500 NYCRR freight cars and 75 locomotives had been repaired elswhere, and, the *Evening Journal* reasoned, strikes and other inconveniences would only lead to a more serious loss of jobs and revenue. The newspaper appealed to the workers to consider these consequences "for their own sakes, for the sake of their families, for the sake of the city in which they live," before they continue the strike.[118] The *Argus* too cautioned the workers that increases in cost of production caused by an eight-hour workday might lead the NYCRR to consider transferring even more work to other cities. This fact of economic life made the eight-hour movement "a danger that menaces the workingmen as well as the rest of the community."[119] Like that of any city, Albany's economic health was in part tied to local employers' feeling that the city provided a good environment for business. Middle-class spokesmen's awareness of this "fact" of economic life mitigated their support for the workers' cause.

Yet in opposing the eight-hour workday the newspapers were not simply expressing narrow economic self-interest. The eight-hour workday, they believed, violated fundamental principles of the free labor system. According to the *Argus*, any combination to diminish the volume of production was "a crime against society, an obstruction of the law of progress, and abdication of man's highest prerogatives as an inventor and discoverer, and as controller of the forces of man."[120] The eight-hour doctrine stood convicted as false in the eyes of the *Evening Journal* because "no action of the laborers can reverse the immutable law of supply and demand, or change the economic principle that capital must have its fair profit as well as labor its just reward."[121] In contrast to the workers, both newspapers accepted as inevitable the capitalist principles that governed the free labor economy.

The newspapers ridiculed workers' attempts to alter economic principles by legislative fiat. To remove the decision over hours from the marketplace threatened hallowed tenets of free labor capitalism. The *Argus* predicted that the eight-hour law or any "schemes got up by politicians" would not be much of a boon for the workingman. The law covered only one-twentieth of the state's workers; more important, "The causes of distress among the laboring classes lie deeper than the statutes regulating the hours of occupation can reach," the *Argus* concluded.[122]

When the 1872 railroad workers' strike ended, both the *Argus* and the *Evening Journal* reflected on how best to improve the condition of the workingman. The newspapers assumed that the dynamic expansion of the free labor economy benefited all members of the community.[123] In the *Argus*'s view, the true "theory" of society sought "to increase all activities of industry and trade, to multiply machinery, to add to the varieties of employment, and by constantly increasing the volume of production to allow each individual member of society a large share."[124] Legislation that "fosters industry" and places the workingman "upon a higher scale than his brother in the Old World" protects the workingman, the *Evening Journal* asserted.[125] The editors' optimistic faith in progress frequently overwhelmed any qualms that they may have had about the social and economic consequences of industrialization.

Both newspapers saw themselves serving the general interests of the community by minimizing any tendancy toward a division of society into classes. Employers and employed might each organize to press their demands. But, the *Evening Journal* reminded its readers, neither should ever forget that

> Capital and labor are not antagonistic. They are the positive and negative elements which complete the currents and keep up the circuits of commerce and trade. Neither can exist without the other; and both have claims to consideration. The effort and study on all sides should therefore be to adjust and harmonize the balances as between employer and employed, so that both shall secure the best advantages from their relations.[126]

The *Argus* agreed. "The army of Labor and Capital in hostility is war, and war is destructive to both parties. The combination of capital with labor is peace, and in its train follows plenty."[127] Neither newspaper ever questioned that a mutuality of interests existed between capital and labor. For them this was the most "immutable" economic principle.

In his work on class and status the sociologist Max Weber defined the social order as the way "social honor is distributed in a community between the typical groups participating in this distribution."[128] At least until the early 1870s, "social honor" in Albany was distributed in such a way that concern for the social position of workers was part of the community's consciousness. It was not yet accepted in Albany that workers were merely a factor of production. Nor were the city's industrialists, at this time, able to translate their economic power into political and social domination.

Nevertheless, workers in Albany during the 1860s and early 1870s felt their social honor imperiled by their eroding economic condition. Discontented, the workers sought an alternative to the unceasing war with capital. In the tradition of earlier labor reform campaigns, Albany workers opposed monopoly and aristocratic privilege, denouncing the growing class of capitalists who exchanged and lived off wealth but did nothing to produce it. As the producers, workers saw themselves being denied the full fruits of their toil.[129]

The cooperative and eight-hour reform activities of workers in Albany are measures of the degree to which the concentration of capital under industrialization alienated them from free labor capitalism. They could assure an equitable division of the joint profits of capital and labor only if they could fundamentally change how those profits were distributed. Workers expressed a commonwealth ethic whereby they would be guaranteed a fair return on their labor and a decent standard of living. By assuring workers' well-being, cooperatives and the eight-hour workday would contribute to a just economy under industrialization.

Yet despite widespread support for cooperation and the eight-hour workday, these reforms remained more an ideal than a reality in the 1860s. Except for producers' cooperatives in nearby Troy, attempts to emulate the example of molders in Albany were rarely successful. Even the cooperatives in these two cities flourished for only a short time. A credit agent for R. G. Dun and Company reported the Albany foundry, organized by the UFA, to be in trouble in early March 1870. Although the cooperative revived after negotiating three new contracts, by April 1871 he found that it was "pretty hard up," and the following year the UFA went bankrupt.[130] More successful, the Capital Co-operative Foundry in Albany nevertheless had reorganized by 1874 as a private stock company.[131]

The cooperatives, which workers began in an attempt to eliminate the capitalist, foundered in part because they never really solved the problem of securing adequate financing. Neither of the two cooperative foundries in Albany was able to raise sufficient capital under the guidelines they established for their operation. For example, when the UFA opened its foundry it had no capital reserves outside the property and fixtures. Of necessity, the cooperative had to rely on the local iron founders for whom they did work to supply iron and other basic materials. The cancellation of one contract forced the UFA to take out a mortgage in order to purchase the moulds the foundry had been using.[132] Ironically, cooperation may have made Albany's molders more, rather than less, dependent on capital.

Whatever their aspirations for cooperation, the initial efforts of workers to form both consumer and producer cooperatives were hardly the linchpin of a mass movement. The industrial cooperative movement was quite limited in comparison with that led by populist farmers in the South and West in the 1880s and 1890s. Beginning with the Farmers'

Alliance in the 1880s, populists in many states had come to share a sense of common identity. The farmers supported their own system of over one thousand insurgent newspapers and a revivalistic lecture circuit. The populists' cooperatives evolved into a "schoolroom" of a "movement culture for democratic reform." Populists fashioned the organizational, institutional, and political forms to challenge capitalism.[133]

At no point did the post–Civil War cooperative movement approximate the national movement forged by the populists later in the century. By 1869 there were fourteen cooperative foundries in the United States, including those in Albany. But the Iron Moulders' International Union's attempt to launch a cooperative in Pittsburgh in 1867 ended in dismal failure. Members balked when Sylvis tried to introduce a per capita tax in order to raise capital for the venture. In 1868 the molders' international union adopted a plan to raise funds for cooperatives through voluntary subscription by individual molders to "coöperative stock" funds. These funds would be invested in local foundries under the supervision of an international union board of seven directors. Not a single group of union members took advantage of this plan. By 1870, after the death of Sylvis a year earlier, molders' interest in producer cooperation had waned.[134]

Workers' world view in the 1860s and 1870s reflects Robert Wiebe's notion that in the midnineteenth century local autonomy was "the heart of American democracy."[135] Even the unions that workers organized after the Civil War remained strongest at the local level. Few unions in this period developed the administrative mechanisms necessary to become aggressive national organizations.[136] Workers were not yet ready to generate a mass movement to challenge forthrightly the existing order.

Neither the cooperative nor the eight-hour reform movement became class oriented. As David Montgomery correctly points out, in lobbying for eight-hour legislation workers remained content to demand from government "just laws." Their conception of eight-hour reform was broad enough to permit the coexistence of a "legal working day" and "free contract" in the same statute.[137] In Albany in 1868 when the New York Central shop workers tried to arouse the general effort they so clearly desired, they found other workers too willing to let "dollars and cents" rule their actions. A commitment to the prevailing free labor ethos worked against class action for either the "eight hour principle" or any other significant reforms.

The years between 1863 and 1873 were part of a transitional period in American industrialization. Albany workers' struggles for reform in these years demonstrate their evolving awareness of the social and economic impact that industrialization was having on their lives.

Workers' commonwealth ideals reveal a deepening understanding of the way society distributed wealth and a greater awareness of themselves as a class than had their earlier labor activities. But few workers were ready to move beyond this understanding, few were ready to engage in class struggle to achieve class goals. Convinced that their position in society was threatened, workers struggled for an alternative future in which the dignity and opportunities America offered them would be preserved.

4

Labor on the Defensive

With the observation that the "bubble['s] bursting," Albany newspapers announced in September 1873 the onset of the Panic of 1873. Vastly overextended, the banking house of Jay Cooke and Company had collapsed, precipitating other commercial failures and the closing of the New York Stock Exchange.[1] Although serious, financial panic was by no means an uncommon event in the nineteenth century. "Money panics," as William Sylvis observed in 1869, were a fact of life for American workers. Labor made headway when times were good only to lose out during hard times. About every ten years, "ever since we have been a nation," the "same operation [has been] repeated over again."[2]

At least initially, Albany's newspapers looked upon the 1873 panic as a familiar occurrence. The *Albany Evening Journal* recommended that everyone "Keep Cool!" There was nothing in "the character of this particular crisis" that should extend it beyond the realm of the "speculators into the domain of general business."[3] In fact, if the panic swept away "doubtful enterprises" then, according to the *Albany Daily Evening Times*, it would serve as a necessary "chastisement," cooling off an economy overheated by rampant speculation.[4]

But the economic depression that came on the heels of the 1873 financial crisis overwhelmed "legitimate business" as well as speculators. Lasting until the latter part of 1878, this industrial depression was far worse than any that had preceded it.[5] Unemployment figures for the depression of the 1870s vary widely yet clearly indicate its severity. For example, estimates for Massachusetts alone range from a high of three hundred thousand unemployed to a claim by the chief of the State Bureau of Labor Statistics that just under twenty-nine thousand were unemployed in 1878.[6] For Albany the closest to an unemployment figure during this depression is the claim made at a public rally in 1877 that two thousand persons (or slightly more than one-fifth of the adult male work force) were without jobs. Whatever the specific figures, it was generally acknowledged that "hard times" left many in the city in "desperate circumstances."[7]

Workers in Albany had reason to expect some relief from the harsh conditions that came with the depression. Typically in times of extreme hardship caused by a natural disaster or an economic downturn, community leaders from Albany's middle class (including government officials, administrators of the city's religious voluntary associations, and philanthropic citizens) distributed temporary aid to those in need. Starting with the first winter of the depression, the Albany community rallied to provide free food, clothing, and other provisions on a limited basis. But after two years, as the depression persisted, the inadequacy of traditional relief measures became self-evident to Albany's middle-class civic leaders. The city's workers, as well, began to ask that the community go beyond its usual almsgiving.

During the winter of 1876–77 workers held large public rallies in Albany demanding "Bread or Work."[8] Visibly impatient with existing voluntary efforts, workers insisted that the city underwrite public works projects to provide employment for those out of work. All types of workers, skilled and day labor, gathered at these demonstrations. Nevertheless, it seems to have been generally accepted in Albany that the unemployed—those who would be the primary beneficiaries of the public works projects—were the city's unskilled day laborers. Albany's middle-class leaders, because they believed work was better than charity, responded sympathetically to the clamor for public works projects. Since midcentury, Albany's laborers had engaged the larger community repeatedly in a kind of collective bargaining that evoked the free labor ideal of a community of interests. Thus by meeting the laborers' demands for public works jobs, civic leaders in Albany sustained a tradition of social authority marked by the acknowledgment of reciprocal obligations binding all members of the community.

If unskilled day laborers were the core of Albany's unemployed, what was the depression's impact on the rest of the city's workers? Apparently many skilled workers remained at least partially employed; yet they did suffer. For example, by 1877 NYCRR shop workers had seen their wages cut by at least half. Indeed, the city's carpenters, as well as other skilled workers, offered more than once to accept lower wages in order to protect their jobs.[9]

But confrontation did eventually occur over the conditions generated by the depression. The city's stove molders, as they had in the past, led the way. In late 1876, molders in Albany once again faced a challenge from the city's iron founders, who hoped to take advantage of the hard times in order to smash the molders' union. And, the following year, shop workers at West Albany joined fellow railroad workers across the nation in refusing to accept another cut in their wages.

The struggles of Albany workers during the 1870s depression signal their shift away from the commonwealth ideals of the previous decade. The reform movement of the 1860s and early 1870s had taken place during a period of economic expansion. Confronted by very different conditions in the mid-1870s, workers in Albany became more defensive. The strikes by the city's molders and railroad shop workers as well as the public works demonstrations arose more from an effort merely to survive than from an organized campaign to change the system. The circumstances workers faced in the mid-1870s led them to reassert free labor ideals.

"Hard times" hit Albany even before the 1873 financial crisis. The winter of 1872–73 was one of "great destitution," according to the city official in charge of poor relief. Many laborers came every year to the city to work on the Erie Canal and Hudson River docks. In 1872 they found themselves stranded in Albany because such casual jobs had become scarce.[10] With the panic, conditions quickly worsened. Laborers roamed the city offering to work for board alone, the *Argus* reported in December 1873, and still they found no jobs.[11] Two months earlier, Perry and Company stove works had dismissed forty workers. In the same month, the men at the NYCRR yards in West Albany saw their pay cut by 10 percent. A few weeks later the central shops cut back on hours as well.[12]

Albany's leading citizens did not have to see official reports or precise unemployment figures to realize that many people in the city needed help. In November 1873, the city's police reported that the number of people applying to sleep overnight at the station house was so great that they were assigning three and four persons to each cell. Calling for some action to "lessen the calamity" of these destitute persons, the *Albany Evening Journal* suggested that the community hold the winter's usual social functions or "amusements" more frequently than in other years and donate their proceeds to benefit "the poor."[13]

The first group to answer the *Evening Journal*'s call was the Albany Burgess Corps (ABC), one of the city's oldest independent voluntary military organizations. Many prominent merchants and professionals in Albany, a number of whom also held political office, belonged to the corps. "In appreciation of the wants, and in many instances severe destitution," of the unemployed, the ABC proposed to devote the proceeds from its annual George Washington's Birthday ball to the relief of the city's poor.[14]

Thomas W. Olcott, president of the city's Mechanics and Farmers

Bank, chaired the ABC charity committee sponsoring the ball. In December 1873, Olcott, along with a number of other leading businessmen, had organized a private relief committee which offered assistance to those who found themselves unemployed "for the first time" and unable to provide for their families. The ABC donated its receipts from the ball, totaling $2,304, to aid this relief effort.[15] Over the next five years many of Albany's voluntary associations held balls, sponsored lectures, ran musical entertainments, and arranged other social functions to bolster similar private relief groups.

Various ethnic benefit societies, fraternal societies, and religious charity societies contributed to Albany's efforts at poor relief. Such ethnic organizations as the St. George's Society (English), the St. Andrew's Society (Scottish), and (for Irish-Americans) the newly formed United Irishmen of America and the older Hibernian Provident Society devoted part of their treasuries to relieving the needs of their "Brothers." Founded in Albany in 1803 by wealthy persons of Scottish descent, the St. Andrew's Society had nearly ninety members by the 1870s. Its purpose was to aid those Scots natives or their sons or grandsons in Albany who found themselves in want. In 1873 this society spent $525 assisting 125 persons.[16]

Early in 1873, local St. George's societies throughout New York organized the North American St. George's Union to aid English emigrants who were moving either from state to state or between the United States and Canada or England in search of work. According to the *Argus*, the St. George's Benevolent Society of Albany was very active in the city in procuring employment for its members. By the end of its first year of such service this society reported having provided about $600 in relief for 183 persons, found suitable work for 25 persons, and "passed" 15 others on to "friends" elsewhere. By 1877, 100 prosperous citizens of English background in Albany maintained a permanent fund of $4,000 through their society.[17]

Fraternal societies, such as the Free and Accepted Masons and the Independent Order of Odd Fellows (IOOF), had long been popular in America, in part for their benefit features. The depression of 1873 motivated these societies to broaden their relief activities. The IOOF, for example, spent over $700,000 on its relief programs in New York State between 1873 and 1878. In Albany alone, Odd Fellows distributed relief benefits in 1875 that were more than four times the amount they had spent in 1870.[18] Under a charter granted in 1871 by the New York State Grand Lodge, Albany's masonic lodges had appointed a relief committee to ascertain and then ameliorate the needs of its members, including, if possible, finding work for them. In its first five and one-half years the Albany Masonic Relief Association paid $15,000 in benefits.[19]

To be sure, attending to the wants of the needy was still thought to be the peculiar province of religious charity societies. Even the relief committee formed in 1873 by Thomas Olcott had been instituted, it was soon revealed, at the behest of Bishop William Croswell Doane of All Saints Cathedral (Episcopal). In December 1873, Doane helped to organize the wives of many of Albany's prominent men into the Ladies Industrial Society. The society provided poor women with the opportunity to earn money by doing needlework.[20] Society members raised funds by selling the items produced by poor women and by holding private theatricals. Bishop Doane reported that the society during its first winter had given work to 150 women, who had made 3,300 garments. The women were paid "a fair wage," Doane stated, adding that the largest proportion of those helped were Roman Catholic.[21]

Like the ethnic benefit associations, religious societies extended their usual efforts to help the city's needy during the depression. The Ladies Protestant Union Aid Society, established in 1866 to aid the worthy Protestant poor, received support from the collections of each Protestant church in the city. In 1877, the Union Aid Society reported having assisted some 259 families, distributing $1,480 worth of provisions and $1,798 in cash. In the society's annual report the secretary noted that, under normal circumstances, "We reach . . . the class who have not been improvident, but whose wages or salaries have been just sufficient to keep the wolf from the door in prosperity." During the depression, "when adversity overtakes them . . . from no fault of their own, it becomes a dire necessity to them either to suffer or to accept alms." Nor was the Union Aid Society's almsgiving merely altruistic. "We save society many an added criminal," she concluded.[22]

Religious aid societies in Albany censured sentimental almsgiving. To be effective, charity had to be systematic. Led by ladies in the community with the "highest most respected standing," the Union Aid Society withheld aid until one of its members had visited the home of a prospective recipient.[23] Home visiting guaranteed that only those individuals whose condition was a consequence of external circumstances and not inner moral decay would receive assistance.[24] The Ladies Industrial Society, at the insistence of Bishop Doane, also required that a visiting committee in each ward "look up" any case referred to it. In the Industrial Society's first few months its members visited most of the more than five hundred applicants for aid. Of these, the society gave assistance to 280, found 118 to be "unworthy," and provided help for the rest through other means.[25]

The desire among religious charity associations for more efficient almsgiving seems to have accelerated a trend toward Protestant ecumenicalism in Albany. The Protestant Union Aid Society criticized efforts by local church groups as "too diffuse" and advocated a joint treasury in order to reach greater numbers.[26] The Albany City Tract and Missionary Society (ACTMS) instituted the most ambitious interdenominational Protestant relief effort. Organized in 1835 to "promote the interests of evangelical religion and sound morality by the circulation of religious tracts," the ACTMS at first merely cooperated in the general temporary relief efforts of the early 1870s.[27] However, it did itself sponsor one special event that won wide community support, a "poor children's excursion," in August 1874. The ACTMS provided fifteen hundred children with a holiday that included a boat trip, a picnic, and games and prizes. After all, the *Argus* explained, children need fun as well as bread and soup "to make their hearts lighter." Revealing the serious social purpose behind this holiday, the newspaper noted that poor children see about them "respectably dressed children," and this could confirm for them that there was a "wall or separation" between them. That would be very unfortunate because, "It makes the poor child the enemy; and the boy is but father of the man." Asking "who would like to give these children a day of pleasure, and thus strengthen the securities of society?" the *Argus* appealed for contributions to support the excursion.[28]

But by May 1874 the ACTMS had decided that the time had come for it to unite behind a project that would have evangelical as well as moral consequences. Rather than continue its "scattered and random efforts," the society's board of managers declared that "there should be a concentration of the forces of the Society in some particular locality of the city."[29] The board proposed that the ACTMS build a new mission, which would be "a nucleus for many kinds of benevolent work among the masses for whom the work is to be done."[30] After conducting a careful religious census, the ACTMS found that the lower portion of the city had the highest proportion of nonchurchgoers. Since "no other area of Albany presented such claims," the society decided to build its new mission there.[31]

The ACTMS opened its new three-story mission in December 1877. "To bring people to a personal, saving knowledge of the gospel of Christ" was the "whole work" of the society. Hence an "audience room" occupied the entire first floor. Those facilities that the society believed made the building more than an "ordinary mission" were on the basement floor. Here the ACTMS installed a "temperance coffee room" as well as "bath rooms" and "laundry rooms" for the use of the poor whose own homes had "no such conveniences." These facilities made the mission a "practical charity." The ACTMS hoped that the example the mission provided might "educate" the poor to make "a tidier home" and from there that they might "take another step . . . toward saving the pennies which find their way to the rum shop, from this to better associations, eventually bringing the family to a knowledge of the blessed Lord Jesus."[32] The mission had been built without a "churchly appearance . . . it looks like a bank or business house." That was what the society had intended; the mission was "a business house for God's work in saving men."[33]

The relief work furnished by religious societies in Albany followed preexisting divisions among the city's Protestants and Catholics. From its founding in the late 1840s, the Diocese of Albany had created Catholic religious and social institutions that paralleled existing Protestant agencies and eventually set Albany's largely Irish Catholic population off as "a distinct community, if not a separate city."[34] Through the years the diocese had established its own parochial schools, orphan asylums, and charitable societies. Like their Protestant counterparts, individual Catholic church societies supplemented diocesan relief efforts, spearheaded by the Society of St. Vincent de Paul and the Little Sisters of the Poor, during the depression of the 1870s.[35]

Private voluntary relief efforts merged with public programs. At the outset of the 1873 panic, Albany's Common Council empowered George W. Hoxie, the city's overseer of the poor, to work with private relief agencies. Hoxie relied on the support of these private benevolent societies and on the generosity of individual donors to help him maintain the city's outdoor relief programs through the depression years.[36] For example, donations from local merchants, bankers, and businessmen, as well as the proceeds of numerous entertainments and other social events, supplemented the public funds Hoxie used in the first winter of the depression to start a "soup house," which gave at least one good meal a day to those in need. In April 1874, Hoxie reported having spent nearly $2,200 for provisions to make over seventy-six thousand meals of soup and bread.[37]

By early 1876 conditions in Albany compelled the city's Republican mayor, Edmund L. Judson, to issue a special appeal to "charitably disposed citizens" to help promote greater relief efforts; otherwise, Judson said, "the result will be starvation."[38] Citizen response to the mayor's plea was immediate and came from a broad social spectrum. Contributors to a Citizens Relief Fund included such diverse individuals and groups as the Lew Benedict Post No. 5 of the Grand Army of the Republic, members and employees of the city fire department, employees of the Craft, Wilson, and Gross dry goods store, and the United Irishmen of America. Most gave money, but the fund also received 1,000 bushels of heating coke from the Albany Gas Light Company and 2,250 loaves of bread from Henry Howell.[39]

Feeling the need to better coordinate the now larger relief effort in

Albany, Mayor Judson appointed the Citizens Relief Committee. This committee opened a relief depot, a store that stocked provisions that could be "bought" by persons in need. Payment at the depot was made by vouchers of one to three dollars. These vouchers had been distributed to those reported to the mayor as in need and whose claims had been verified by the police.[40] During one three-week period (January 24 to February 12, 1876), some two thousand families were said to have been assisted through the relief depot.[41] In March 1876, in recognition of the relief committee's success, the Albany Common Council appropriated $2,000 to help maintain the store.[42]

The depot helped to make relief assistance in Albany more systematic. But the intent of all relief activities in the city remained, as always, provision of temporary assistance during unusually trying times. Forty years earler Albany's Mayor Francis Bloodgood had supported the opening of "soup houses" in the city, and, during a period of hard times in the late 1850s, a citizens relief committee had also helped coordinate temporary relief efforts. But confronted by the prolonged depressed conditions of the 1870s, the ACTMS had come to believe that any plan that just "feeds and clothes the idle," although it might "alleviate present distress," will not work permanent reform. By 1876 the society concluded that the times required "work instead of open hand giving," and called on the city government to consider this problem.[43]

Overseer of the Poor Hoxie agreed with the ACTMS. In November 1875 he asked Albany's Common Council to institute a public works program in place of home relief. Hoxie believed that relief through work on public projects would make its recipients "independent and save them from the stigma which they consider attaches if they should accept money or fuel without giving an equivalent."[44] Partly in response to Hoxie, the council decided at its first session in January 1876 to have construction start immediately on a reservoir already authorized for Albany's new water supply system. It was unusual for construction projects to be carried out during the winter, but the council wanted to provide work for "many of our suffering mechanics and laborers" without delay. A week later, the council authorized the city's park commissioners to begin work on a new park boulevard and passed a $37,000 bond issue to support this improvement. Finally, the council set up three committees to investigate what other projects might be initiated to help furnish work for the unemployed.[45]

The growing consensus among Albany's middle-class leaders in support of public works projects may have had its origin in the actions of Albany's unemployed. By 1876 conditions had deteriorated beyond the reach of the city's usual relief efforts. At well-attended public rallies, participants demanded "Bread or Work" from the city. Yet even though the Common Council had agreed to the projects, construction did not actually begin until the spring. Punctuated by repeated popular demonstrations, a frustrating "pattern of negotiations" developed each winter between workers and city officials. These negotiations effectively nullified the Common Council's promise of immediate public works jobs.

"Bread or Work" demonstrations in Albany were not of the magnitude of New York City's Tompkins Square riots or Chicago's parade of twenty thousand unemployed.[46] But demonstrations by the unemployed did become a fact of life in Albany during the winters of 1876–77 and 1877–78. Notices in the city's newspapers (and presumably other places as well) would announce each demonstration, and hundreds of unemployed workers would gather near City Hall. At each rally the participants chose a delegation to call on the mayor and other city officials in order to push for the immediate start of promised public works projects. On meeting with the delegates, the mayor usually expressed his support for the Common Council's actions, as well as his concern for the plight of the unemployed, and promised to intensify the city's relief efforts. The delegates then reported this "progress" to still another assembly of unemployed workers. But time and again each winter, objections from the city engineer or the Board of Contract and Appropriation to any work being done while the ground was frozen delayed construction on the projects until warmer weather.[47]

The negotiations surrounding the demonstrations for public works jobs provide evidence for assuming that, in most instances, during the depression Albany's "unemployed" or "poor" were unskilled day laborers. Although most of the demonstrators are unknown, newspaper accounts do name those persons who were chosen to be delegates or officers. Of forty such "leaders," eighteen (45 percent) can be identified as laborers, fifteen (37½ percent) as skilled workers, four (10 percent) as small businessmen, and three (7 percent) as clerks. Among the skilled workers, eight were either iron molders or stonemasons.[48]

Skilled workers and laborers appear to have shared leadership roles almost equally. Yet an account of a meeting between the unemployed workers' delegation and Mayor Judson in January 1876 reveals that each group of workers might have had different reasons for participating in the demonstrations. During the meeting, Judson "interrogated" delegation members concerning their personal needs. John Hopkins, a molder at Rathbone's foundry who headed the delegation, stated that he was serving on the committee at the request of "some of the men." He was not, he added, in need himself. Nor was Michael Kelly, a saloonkeeper on the committee. Invariably, only the laborers on the delegation were unemployed and looking for assistance.[49]

Albany's skilled workers did not see themselves as the subjects of the city's relief efforts. Skilled workers joined the "Bread or Work" rallies and accepted positions of worker-designated authority more out of a spirit of solidarity with their fellow workers than from self-interest. In fact in January 1876 Mayor Judson expressed resentment at the presence on the delegation of persons not out of work themselves. Albany's skilled workers (in particular, molders and stonemasons) had by their attempt to mediate between the distressed laborers and the community power structure appropriated a role that middle-class leaders assumed to be exclusively their own. Members of Albany's middle-class community expected the city's laborers to defer to their authority, not to form a class alliance with their fellow workers.

In July 1876, in response to a situation reminiscent of what had happened to Albany's waterworks laborers in 1851, laborers on the new reservoir appealed to city officials for justice. The contractor for the reservoir was trying to take advantage of the depressed economy by paying laborers less than the Common Council had authorized. The laborers struck for the higher rate. Representatives of the strikers met with city officials, asking them to intervene on their behalf. After a brief confrontation in which the contractor tried to break the strike, the mayor and the chief of police arranged a compromise settlement.[50]

The manner in which the Albany community reacted to the laborers' strike for the higher wage indicates the social meaning that informed the city's relief movement. For the middle-class community, whatever the specific mechanisms of relief, the process had to encompass the features that, according to Gareth Stedman Jones, define all charitable gift giving—voluntary sacrifice, prestige, subordination, and obligation. The giving of charity must involve a reciprocal relationship, one that accords prestige to the giver and imposes an obligation on the receiver.[51] An event like the poor children's excursion exhibited these features. What society needed, the *Argus* stated, was to "bind" the poor to it "by common sympathies." The children's excursion served this end, according to the *Argus*, because the young recipients realized that "they are considered children of a common community."[52] In a letter read at a "Bread or Work" public rally, former mayor of Albany Eli Perry reminded "mechanics" and "men of wealth" alike that "all are dependent upon each other. . . . A combination must exist where we can all be beneficial to each other that we may be prosperous alike."[53] To Perry and other civic leaders in Albany, such a combination would only exist when all members of the community acknowledged their reciprocal obligations.

The expected social benefits from interaction between the giver and receiver in a charitable exchange underlay a controversy arising in February 1876 over the use of the police to investigate claims for relief.

The Pastor's Association of Albany questioned the propriety of this arrangement and expressed concern that favoritism might influence policemen to aid only those who lived in their wards. The poor should be visited by "respectable citizens," rather than by the police. The clergymen recommended that Albany's mayor appoint unpaid citizen visitors and a board of overseers. According to the pastors, such a system was being used in Elberfield, Germany, to great advantage.[54]

In Albany as elsewhere religious charity organizations visited the needy at home not merely as protection against "imposition" by the "unworthy," but also to enable the city's respectable citizens to satisfy their obligations as moral stewards in the community. The ACTMS continually reminded the wealthy of their duty to be involved in Christian enterprise, "They are judged in this world as the next for their stewardship."[55] Almsgiving only fulfilled its central social purpose of maintaining authority when it established human ties across barriers of class, religion, and nationality. The critical relationship was the bond forged between those in need and the general community.[56]

Despite the evidence of cooperation between skilled and unskilled workers, the public works demonstrations in the 1870s did not testify to an emerging class-conscious movement in Albany. In September 1875, laborers helped to organize a "Workingmen's Independent Association," which would ameliorate "the present depressed and alarming condition of the working classes" by forming a political party.[57] But the association faded quickly, without nominating any candidates for public office. Repudiating class politics Albany's laborers also never turned to violence. Work was especially scarce during the winters and the need for help greatest then. Yet despite the numerous frustrating delays, the public demonstrations for "Bread or Work" remained peaceful.

The rallies in favor of public works projects represent the laborers' desperate appeals for assistance to survive the depression. When 1877 promised a repeat of the previous year's pattern of negotiations, workers reiterated their need for work lest they be forced to "depend on the poor master or the poor house" to feed their families. They implored Albany's mayor and aldermen "in the name of humanity, and by the love that they cherish for their own wives and helpless children, to provide work for us temporarily at least."[58] But once again, construction on public works projects was delayed until the spring. The laborers, left with no alternative, acquiesced to the one dollar per day wage that they had rejected a year earlier.[59]

Under the circumstances imposed by the depression, laborers could show little of the independence that Albany's workers had aspired to during the previous decade. They were constrained, however, not simply by absolute economic need but by their consequent dependence on the middle-class community for relief. During a rally in early 1876, middle-class participants praised the unemployed workingmen, who, by being "orderly and respectful" had enlisted "the sympathies of our citizens in general."[60] The "Bread or Work" demonstrations reflect Albany laborers' understanding of their dependence on the middle-class community's willingness to recognize its obligations to them.

Although Albany's skilled workers continued to have jobs, they felt the impact of the depression in shortened employment "seasons" and reduced hours and wages. For example, the West Albany shops of the NYCRR, although open, ran at reduced time during the winter.[61] Even so, some of the "most experienced and skillful artisans" working in the shops had to be laid off, reported the *Argus* in November 1874.[62] Reports from Albany Moulders' Union No. 8 to the *Iron Moulders' International Journal* depicted Albany's stove trade as "dull" and union members as "idle."[63] Nevertheless, shop workers and molders probably found work for at least part of each year. During the depression the foundries ran about eight and a half months a year, and at times in West Albany the vast majority of men, perhaps over a thousand, were working.[64]

The depression exacerbated the local stove industry's problems, caused by increased competition from western stove-making centers. Eastern iron founders blamed their difficulties on union wage demands that forced them to cede a competitive edge to the western founders.[65] By the winter of 1876–77, Albany's iron founders (and Troy's as well) seem to have become even more determined to break the molders' union. In February 1876, Mayor Judson asked that the Rathbone, Sard, and Company foundries be opened earlier than usual. The founders' reply indicated that trouble was brewing. The company stated that because there was a large stock of stoves on hand it could open the foundry sooner only if the molders accepted lower wages. To reinforce its point, the company added that it was considering doing certain "classes of work" outside Albany where wage "reductions had already been made."[66] As intended, the threat contained in the company's answer was clear to both the molders and the city officials.

During the winter of 1875–76, molders at one small Albany foundry struck over wages. But all the other foundries in the city stayed open through the year, and molders received the same wages they had been paid the previous year. At one point during 1876 at least one foundry was even reported to be open overtime; its workers could take only fifteen minutes for dinner.[67] In retrospect, it appears that Albany's iron founders were stockpiling stoves in anticipation of implementing the Rathbone, Sard, and Company threat.[68]

In 1876, just after the normal December close of the molding season, Rathbone, Sard posted a circular "To Our Moulders," in which the company declared that it would reopen the foundry only when these four conditions were met: (1) the price (meaning wages) of molding was reduced; (2) the company could have as many apprentices or boys as it deemed best; (3) the company could employ anyone at its discretion; and (4) the company could set wage scales with each individual worker. Two weeks later Perry and Company posted a similar notice in its foundry. Both companies set deadlines for the molders to accept these terms or "their places would be filled by other men." Sure that union molders would reject these terms, the founders were in effect locking them out.[69]

Since employers in Troy took the same steps as those in Albany, it is evident that the iron founders were acting in concert, even though they had no formal organization.[70] As they had before, they insisted that they were merely defending management's prerogatives, especially as to the hiring of helpers. John Perry told local newspapers that the real issue was not wages but the freedom of employers to hire "as many boys or helpers as we choose, and whenever they are capable of earning moulder's wages—no matter if it is in a month—to pay them full wages."[71] Thus the substance of the founders' position in this dispute, which came at the height of the depression, was not very different from their stance in all the seventeen years since the molders had unionized.

What did distinguish the 1876–77 struggle was the sense of urgency that informed the iron founders' commitment to destroy the molders' union. Perry claimed that the founders risked "ruining" themselves unless they regained control over their businesses. Rather than have the work driven away from Albany and Troy, Perry called for "*free trade* in molding and mounting stoves" in the two cities, as there was in the West. According to Perry, only after employers had rid themselves of all union interference would there be "no lack of work in our foundries."[72] Obviously, the founders felt that the depression had given them the upper hand.

The molders considered the hiring of boys as helpers to be the key issue in the struggle. They claimed that if each molder hired a helper, at least one-third more molders would be idle. "The employer seeks to go too far," they argued, "when he desires to compel a molder to hire boys and pay them out of their own wages."[73] Union members repeatedly charged the founders with seeking to reinstate the conditions that prevailed in the industry before 1859, the year the molders had organized.[74]

Realizing that Albany molders would not agree to their demands, the iron founders, from the very beginning of the lockout, made every effort to bring other molders down from Canada to replace the strikers. Albany newspapers reported that Rathbone, Sard had armed the molders who were working for the company with Smith and Wesson revolvers. Inevitably violence flared. Union molders continually threatened and sometimes attacked scabs on their way to the foundries. On February 1, 1877, union molders allegedly shot at five working nonunion molders who had been playing cards in the back of a bar. At least officially the union disassociated itself from this and similar violent incidents.[75]

The Albany iron founders' determination to break the union during the 1876–77 lockout can be seen in a spectacular move undertaken by Perry. In late March, local Albany newspapers disclosed that Perry and Company had signed a contract with officials at Sing Sing prison in Ossining, New York, to open a branch foundry at the institution. The initial contract specified that Perry would employ 150 prisoners. If the arrangement proved satisfactory to both parties, then as many as 800 prisoners would be hired to make stoves. The newspapers also reported that Rathbone, Sard, and Company was negotiating with Ohio prison authorities for a similar contract.[76]

Against the iron founders' committed opposition to the union and with the national union's inability to assist its locals in Albany and Troy, workers found sustaining their organized resistance difficult. Unable to stay out longer than five months, molders began returning to work by late May 1877. But rather than be thought to have capitulated, the union decided to suspend its rules for six months, which allowed members to go back to work without appearing to be strikebreakers. How conditions in the foundries may have been affected by the lockout is uncertain, but clearly the union had suffered a defeat. Perry and Company renewed its contract with Sing Sing, and by 1881 some nine hundred prisoners were working at stove making.[77]

The difficulties Albany molders experienced in 1876 and 1877 did not originate in the depression. Yet while they had withstood all previous attempts by the iron founders to weaken or destroy their union, molders had to give up their strike in 1877. According to the *Argus,* the union was unable to hold a meeting in early June. However, Albany Union No. 8 continued its monthly reports to the *Iron Moulders' International Journal.* Two years later, with the depression ended, the union struck at both Perry and Company and Rathbone, Sard.[78]

Unlike the 1877 lockout, which was the culmination of conflict that went back to the formation of the molders' union, the "great upheaval" among railroad workers' in 1877 was directly caused by the depression. The strike broke out first in July 1877 in Martinsburg, West Virginia, when the Baltimore and Ohio Railroad announced its third cut in pay that year. From there the strike spread, without national or even local leadership, to other rail centers in what is often called "the climactic event of the depression."[79]

As the rail strikes spread across the nation, Albany's newspapers dispatched reporters to the city's rail yards to assess the prospects for difficulties there. The newspapers found everything quiet, which seemed to justify the employers' confidence that Albany might avoid the strike.[80] Albany remained quiet even as the strike reached Buffalo and Rochester. When the strike finally did erupt in Albany, the workers were organized even though no union was officially in charge. On the evening of July 23, 1877, NYCRR workers met in West Albany and agreed to seek a 25 percent wage increase. A public rally the following day reaffirmed that figure as representing the wishes of all railroad workers in Albany. The demonstrators appointed a committee to present their demand to William H. Vanderbilt, the president of the NYCRR, who happened to be summering just north of Albany in Saratoga.[81]

In contrast to the chaotic violence that marked the 1877 strike elsewhere, in Albany railroad workers initially chose to disrupt service in an unusual manner. They gathered their families along either side of the NYCRR's tracks and picnicked, raced the hand cars, and sang songs, presenting a "picturesque appearance," according to one account. But when Vanderbilt rejected their demand for the 25 percent increase, striking workers marched to West Albany, stopped work in the shops, and forced switchmen to lock the switches in order to prevent more freight trains from entering the yards.[82]

Given the bloody path of the 1877 rail strikes, New York and Albany authorities were prepared to act at the first sign that events might get out of hand. Once workers disrupted freight traffic, the state militia quickly established itself at key points in West Albany. But Albany's middle-class leaders hoped, like the city's workers, to avoid an open confrontation. In a show of sympathy for the rail workers, Mayor A. Bleecker Banks, Chief of Police John Maloy, the commander of the Grand Army of the Republic, Colonel R. K. Oliver, the superintendent of the ACTMS mission, Charles E. Reynolds, and other prominent Albanians attended a rally of strikers. They next led a drive to collect the signatures of influential citizens endorsing the workers' request that Vanderbilt rescind the most recent 10 percent wage cut. The West Albany shop workers accepted the intervention of community leaders in the strike and agreed to return to work while they awaited Vanderbilt's answer.[83]

Vanderbilt refused the petitioners' request. Yet, one month later, he directed that $100,000 be distributed among company employees as bounties "in recognition of the [workers'] loyalty and faithfulness."[84] Having established the company's authority, Vanderbilt was willing to be generous.

In *Strike!* Jeremy Brecher designates the 1877 national railroad uprising the "first great American mass strike." To Brecher the concept of a mass strike encompasses more than a single act, it marks "a whole period of class struggle."[85] Yet the battles of the NYCRR workers, at least in Albany, as well as the protests by other workers in the city during the 1870s depression, hardly suggest the intensity of class struggle that Brecher claims for the rail strike. The activities of Albany workers after 1873, although important to their well-being, indicate more their defensive-mindedness than their commitment to class conflict. The depression tempered the aggressive spirit that had animated the cooperative and eight-hour-workday movements of the previous decade. Surviving the depression became the most important consideration.

By 1877 the depression's hold on the community had deepened. Temporary relief clearly would not adequately ease the plight of the city's unemployed. Conditions had worsened even for workers who were employed. The wages paid workers at West Albany by 1877 had been cut back to only $1.44 per day; blacksmith helpers and other unskilled laborers worked for a mere 80 cents per day.[86] The molders, who had been relatively effective in resisting wage cuts, faced the possible loss of the protections they had won as early as 1859.

Compounding the serious impact of the depression in Albany was the city's declining economic fortunes. By the 1870s, Albany faced stiff competition from new and expanding industrial centers. The city's future welfare, the *Argus* insisted, depended on "the growth of local manufactures." "Where is the body of men who will organize a revival of enterprise, energy and public spirit in Albany?" the *Argus* asked. "Let some of her practical men speak out."[87]

Under these circumstances, Albany workers realistically narrowed their vision of the possible. Yet their militancy did not fade altogether. Labor's answer to Perry's 1877 contract with Sing Sing, which had so seriously undermined the molders' strike, was to launch an independent political party. Prison contract labor became the pivotal issue in Albany's municipal elections in 1878. Over the next six years, Albany's workers, along with their allies across New York State, would force the prison contract labor issue into the center of the political arena until, in 1884, the system was ended.

Despite the fervor with which Albany workers struggled against prison labor, in the end the nature of their opposition demonstrates the hold that free labor ideas had on them. During the 1860s and early 1870s, the city's workers had framed their demands for reform in terms of altering the economic system. As significant as the abolition of prison labor became for them, the issue represents a particular grievance, in this instance, against one employer, and not a fundamental reform of the free labor order. In fact, the movement against prison labor eventually united workers with the larger community, including employers, in opposition to this practice. Apparently reconciled to free labor capitalism, Albany workers reveal in the 1880s an emerging interest-group consciousness.

In Albany a dialectic between the dominant middle-class free labor world view and workers' class consciousness had persisted from the 1850s. The more defensive nature of workers' ideas in the 1880s and the reinvigoration of their free labor social views were not, therefore, simply consequences of the depression. Throughout the nineteenth century, Albany workers saw themselves as an integral part of the community's social fabric. Workers in the city formed interclass as well as intraclass ties, and in so doing came to participate in what Christopher Lasch has called America's "cultural consensus," "the heart of which was a common stake in capitalism and a common tradition of patriarchal authority." According to Lasch, this cultural consensus persisted throughout the nineteenth century, despite the weakness of "agencies of social cohesion (church, state, family, class)" in the United States.[88]

But in Albany, local community institutions effectively provided the cohesiveness that Lasch finds missing in the nation. The shared consciousness revealed in the community's response to workers' struggles since 1850 also pervaded Albany's institutional and social structure. Along with the city's public agencies, a network of voluntary associations generated a social policy and promoted a civic identity that contributed to Albany's social cohesion. Civic identity, or community consciousness, in Albany encompassed the basic values of the free labor order. Imbued with the dominant free labor social values, the Albany institutional and associational network stimulated the formation of community, rather than class, loyalty.

Class, as Eric Hobsbawm reminds us, "defines not a group of people in isolation, but a system of relations, both vertical and horizontal."[89] To comprehend working-class consciousness in the Albany community over time, all of the relations forged by the city's workers need examination. To this end, Chapters 5 through 7 look at the social role of the Independent Order of Odd Fellows, the Albany Penitentiary, and the city's religious, ethnic, and political structure.

Part II

5

Free Labor Fraternalism: The Independent Order of Odd Fellows in Albany

When the need arose to accomplish some project of general importance in the nineteenth century, Americans most likely formed an association rather than assign the responsibility to government. This feature of "civil life" in America attracted the attention of Alexis de Tocqueville as he traveled through the United States in the 1830s. "Americans," he observed,

> make associations to give entertainments, to found seminaries, to build inns, to construct churches, to diffuse books, to send missionaries to the antipodes; in this manner they found hospitals, prisons and schools. If it is proposed to inculcate some truth or foster some feeling by the encouragement of a great example, they form a society.[1]

The fraternal order was a particularly popular form of voluntary association that flourished in the nineteenth century. Primarily social and recreational organizations, these societies also served benevolent, philanthropic, reform, and other purposes. One of the largest fraternal societies in nineteenth-century America, the Independent Order of Odd Fellows (IOOF), was especially active in Albany.

Odd Fellowship was typical of a range of voluntary associations in Albany that brought workers together with individuals from other social classes. Men from all occupations in the city joined local lodges and met as "brothers" in every rank within the order. This fraternal relationship helped integrate workers into the community. Tocqueville had been particularly struck by the "reciprocal influence of men upon one another" that was accomplished by voluntary associations in the United States.[2] Workers' participation in the IOOF in Albany encouraged them to feel that they were members of a common community.

Like any voluntary association, the IOOF "educated" members to its particular values. By the middle decades of the nineteenth century the IOOF embodied the social values of the free labor order. Odd Fellowship celebrated the ideal of an open-class, harmonious, society in which all members acknowledged their mutual obligations. The symbolic "lessons" of the order's ritual also taught members the moral obligations of diligence, sobriety, honesty, industriousness, and frugality—qualities essential to an industrial work ethic. Thus the IOOF functioned as one institution that reinforced continuity, stability, and control in Albany. Acting as a moral policing agency, Odd Fellowship conveyed to its members values necessary to industrial society. In its symbols and ritual the order transmitted the prevailing free labor social values.

Only a few thousand men belonged to fraternal organizations in America at the beginning of the nineteenth century, primarily as members of the Free and Accepted Masons. But by the end of the century, some seventy-eight fraternal orders existed, with over six million members. One study of fraternal societies in the United States claims that lodges outnumbered churches in all the large cities.[3]

Although they differ over the specifics, the order's official historians agree that Odd Fellowship originated in England in the eighteenth century. English workingmen are said to have organized the society for social purposes and to aid brethren and help unemployed brothers find work. The formal organization of the Manchester Unity in 1814 officially launched the Independent Order of Odd Fellows as a social, or "convivial," society. In March 1819 at a meeting over a Baltimore tavern, a recent emigrant from England, Thomas Wildey, established the first Odd Fellow lodge in the United States.[4]

During its early years, American Odd Fellowship spread slowly. Lodges were concentrated in the port cities of Boston, New York, and Philadelphia. By 1830, however, some one hundred lodges had been chartered, with 6,743 members. Of seven Odd Fellow lodges in New York State at this time, six were in Albany; the first, Hope Lodge No. 3, dated from 1826. Firmly established in four states and the District of Columbia by 1830, Odd Fellowship had "passed its period of probation. . . . already an army had been enlisted in the service of the cause of Friendship, Love, and Truth."[5]

The order structured its government as a "fraternal republican

Union." Control over the IOOF resided with the national body, the Sovereign Grand Lodge (SGL). Each state had a State Grand Lodge; local, or subordinate, lodges carried on the work of the order in the cities and towns.

The SGL maintained "supreme jurisdiction in the general laws and usages of the Order, the lectures, charges and unwritten work, and [was] a court of final appeal, and . . . the National Legislature of the Order."[6] The Sovereign Grand Lodge furnished the IOOF's "written" (nonsecret) work to the State Grand and subordinate lodges; only the Grand Secretary of the SGL had access to the order's "unwritten" work, in which was kept the secret journals of diagrams.[7] Odd Fellowship expected all state and local bodies to enforce strict adherence to its ritual. It explicitly enjoined them to "neither adopt nor use, or suffer to be adopted or used, any Charges, Lectures of Ceremonies, Forms of Installation or Regalia [other] than those prescribed by the S.G.L."[8] Thus the national body mandated and controlled the symbolic language and rituals of Odd Fellowship. As the Odd Fellows' manual stated, "The Signs, Grips and Passwords of the order are designed to speak one universal language to the initiated of every nationality the world over."[9]

The order expected each subordinate lodge to formulate bylaws and rules of conduct that would regulate the local work of Odd Fellowship. The local lodge elected its own officers and maintained the order's beneficial relief features.[10] In addition, the subordinate lodge controlled the process of becoming an Odd Fellow, which involved four steps, known as degrees, each having appropriate emblems, regalia, and lessons. Within the lodge the "Priestly Order" was the highest, the Scarlet Degree.[11]

The most important function of the subordinate lodge was to perpetuate and extend Odd Fellowship through the initiation of new members. The order restricted membership to white males over twenty-one who believed in the Supreme Being and were of good health and moral character.[12] Although the specific procedures governing initiation were left to the subordinate lodges, the order urged them to test the honesty and sincerity of proposed new members "at the threshold."[13]

Descriptions of the social composition of Odd Fellow membership during the nineteenth century vary. One of the order's historians, Theodore Ross, claimed that it was composed of the "great middle, industrial classes almost exclusively."[14] Wildey described the membership of the Grand Lodge of New York (in 1830) as mainly English and Scottish mechanics and tavernkeepers. But by 1840, according to another official historian of Odd Fellowship, the order had extended its reach to include members from every "department of business, . . . men of every sphere of life, . . . men of character, influence and power."[15]

Only a few records for Albany's Odd Fellow lodges have survived, particularly a list of all members in 1845 and membership lists for certain lodges in 1850, 1872, and 1882. Nevertheless, from the names on these records and the names on constructed lists from the records of New York's State Grand Lodge, some general conclusions about who became an Odd Fellow in Albany in the nineteenth century are possible.[16]

Was Odd Fellow membership representative of Albany's social composition, and did it function as a mediator between workers and nonworkers in the community? That workers became Odd Fellows is easily confirmed. A check of the 1845 list of Odd Fellows in Albany for their occupation in the city directory reveals that many members in each lodge could be classified as workers. In addition, membership lists, which were divided by degree attained, show that in every Albany lodge workers were present in each degree, including the Scarlet, and among the "Past Grands." Most of these individuals were skilled workers—carpenters, printers, stonecutters, coach makers, painters, and masons are most commonly noted. The directories identify only a few members as laborers.[17]

Every lodge had members with diverse occupations. Among professionals who became Odd Fellows, attorneys were the most prominent. Many of these men were important civic leaders in Albany. Most attorneys who belonged had joined the city's oldest lodge, Hope Lodge No. 3.[18] In every lodge, men involved in commerce comprised the largest group of members. Wholesalers, retailers, and owners of dry goods stores, as well as greengrocers and other small businessmen and peddlers, joined Albany's Odd Fellow lodges. In each lodge, like its working-class members, men with both large and small business interests can be found holding all the different Odd Fellow degrees.

Another way of analyzing Albany's Odd Fellow membership is to determine its religious and ethnic makeup. Judging from the names on the 1845 list, the city's Odd Fellows were predominantly Protestant, or at least not Irish Catholic. Many Dutch names appear, but German names appear more frequently and in larger proportion than the German population in Albany. Although German names can be found on the lists for all lodges, the greatest number, as would be expected, belonged to German Colonial Lodge No. 16. But this was not an exclusively German lodge.

In 1845, Odd Fellow membership typified the socioeconomic and ethnic mix of at least the Protestant segment of Albany. Primarily a commercial city, Albany's economy depended heavily on the advantages afforded first by the Erie Canal and later by the development of railroads.

The city's small-scale industries still relied on such skilled trades as brewing, stove and ironware molding, boot and shoe making, cigar making, and printing. Looking at Albany's ethnic makeup, the majority of its population in the mid-1840s consisted of early Dutch immigrants, Protestant Yankee emigrants from Connecticut, Massachusetts, and Rhode Island, and more recent German immigrants. Albany also had a large Irish Catholic population at this time, and after the famine migrations of the late 1840s, the Irish Catholics became the majority group. But few Irish had joined the Odd Fellows by 1845.[19]

Later membership lists, for Mountaineer Lodge No. 321 in 1872 and American Lodge No. 32 in 1882, continue to reflect Albany's socioeconomic structure.[20] After 1845 workers still joined the Odd Fellows, if anything in greater numbers, and still achieved all degrees within the lodges. Looking at these two lodges, the growing impact of the railroad on Albany is also clear. Many railroad workers, including engineers, conductors, brakemen, and firemen, now belonged. Machinists, blacksmiths, and carpenters, many of whom probably worked at the shops built by the New York Central Railroad in West Albany, also become members. Molders and other skilled workers continued to join, as did a number of individuals that the city directories identify as foremen.[21] There were still relatively few members specifically cited as laborers.

With the increase in the number of skilled workers among Albany's Odd Fellows came a relative decrease in the number of men following commercial pursuits, either large- or small-scale. Furthermore, almost no attorneys are on the later lists. On the other hand, individuals connected with insurance now appear. As was true for members on the earlier lists, middle-class or professional members of the community can be found in all of the degrees within the lodges.

Albany Odd Fellows continued to be largely Protestant, although Irish names do appear on the later membership lists more often than before.[22] German names remain well represented among the membership. German Colonial Lodge No. 16 continued to exist, as did Albany City Lodge No. 385, which was referred to as a German lodge.

A census of Albany's Odd Fellow elite, constructed from records of the Annual Proceedings of the State Grand Lodge for selected years between 1846 and 1889 and small lists of members of the Albany Patriarch's Lodge No. 1 in 1846 and the Grand Encampment for 1867, confirms that many workers rose to prominent positions within Odd Fellowship. Again, members with other occupations also belonged to the elite, further evidence that all elements of the community participated in Odd Fellowship.

Thus Ross's contention that Odd Fellowship consisted of the "great middle, industrial classes" seems a fair assessment of the membership of Albany's Odd Fellows, particularly in the later nineteenth century. Albany workers, especially skilled workers in the city's dominant trades, did participate in Odd Fellowship. The IOOF in Albany was clearly one community institution where workers met members of other social classes and formed relationships that went beyond those of the work place. The significance of this contact, however, lies within the context of the ideological role of Odd Fellowship.

American fraternal orders developed theories and legends to explain their origins. The Masons traced their ancient mysteries back to the building of King Solomon's Temple, and the Knights of Pythias to the legend of Damon and Pythias. The orders believed that the prestige and stability of their fraternity, as well as the status of individual members were somehow enhanced if it had roots in antiquity.[23]

American Odd Fellowship, in its early years, traced its origins to the Roman legions in Britain and Gaul. But the order soon abandoned this legend and proclaimed that its real genesis lay in the "enlightened civilization" of the "greatest republic," the United States. As one of its leaders declared, "Odd Fellowship, as we know it, is an institution of modern times, grown in *our* midst and fashioned by *our* hands."[24] To adapt Odd Fellowship to American conditions and needs, the order made certain reforms in its practices. Because nineteenth-century Americans tended to move about the country, the IOOF, in one of its earliest changes, provided members with traveling cards. These cards certified that the bearer was an Odd Fellow and recommended that he be afforded the "friendship and protection" of all lodges.[25] In another reform, one aimed at making American Odd Fellowship more respectable than its British counterpart, the order banned all intoxicating beverages and tobacco from its meeting rooms. One official historian of the Odd Fellows praised the "abolition of all social and convivial practices at Lodge meetings" as "among the first improvements to the Order in America required by duty and a decent respect for the opinions of mankind." Since this change, he added, Odd Fellowship has gained "the respect and esteem of the virtuous of all classes" and, consequently, increased its membership greatly.[26]

As it evolved in the United States, Odd Fellowship introduced other reforms to give the American ritual a deeper, more moral, significance. These adaptations reflected a view of the IOOF's essential function, which the fraternity formalized in the 1840s, years of phenomenal growth for the order and a period of significant reform movements in American society. During this decade, the American order withdrew from the Manchester Unity, the supreme English Odd Fellow society, and developed its own distinctive ritual.[27] James D. Ridgely, often called the father of modern, ethical Odd Fellowship, led this movement. At the Sovereign Grand Lodge session of 1844 Ridgely described the prevailing mood as a call for change: "There came . . . a demand, general, earnest, irresistible, for an improved work, a moral more distinctive and didactic, a sentiment more elevated and inspiring, a principle of deeper significance, a purer and truer tone, and the embodiment of all these in a literature worthy of a cause so noble and a work so great."[28]

By breaking with England, American Odd Fellows sought to establish the order as a major moral reform institution. The ritual adopted by the national organization in 1845 remained virtually unchanged to 1880. An official history of the order called this period the "Golden Years" of Odd Fellowship. Odd Fellows identified the order's role in society during these years as encompassing a more exalted moral function.[29] Cornelius Glen, an Albany Odd Fellow who in 1858 rose to be the Most Worshipful Grand Master of New York State, stated: "Our lodges were instituted for higher and holier objects than those of pecuniary gain—we seek to improve and elevate the character of man, and imbue him with proper conceptions of his fellow man."[30]

Odd Fellowship sought to accomplish these higher and more noble objectives by teaching Americans those lessons of morality that formed a "proper education." A leading Odd Fellow in Ohio described how the order went about this task: "In the Lodge-room under the stimulus and magnetism of numbers, exciting the brain to highest activity, these great fundamental principles of our Order, and of society, are evolved and pressed weekly upon the minds of members."[31] The experience of being an Odd Fellow was in itself educational: "Lessons taught by example are more thrilling than those gathered from the history of past events. There is no school so good as that of self-experience."[32] The lessons Odd Fellows needed to learn were imbedded in the structure and regulations of the order and in the form and substance of the degrees. These lessons emphasized the moral obligations of the industrial work ethic and the dominant free labor social views.

The order infused its lectures and charges with moral and religious instruction designed to instill in members a religious spirit, temperance, industriousness, and self-discipline.[33] In order to become members, as noted earlier, all Odd Fellows had to affirm their belief in the Supreme Being. At least one Albany lodge opened each meeting with a prayer. Albany Union Lodge No. 8 asserted that Odd Fellowship protected members from the evils of the world "by the shield of Omnipotence. . . . We are as if all Christians were united in one sect, assisted and assisting—a band of brothers!"[34] In the lecture of initiation, the All-seeing Eye reminded the Odd Fellow that "the omniscience of God pierces into every secret of the heart. . . . Let us, therefore, so regulate our conduct [that] we may not fear the scrutinizing eye of anyone."[35]

Part of Odd Fellowship's religious instruction was the moral dictum of temperance. As already noted, Odd Fellowship adopted regulations banning liquor from the lodge rooms early in its existence in the United States. According to A. B. Grosh in *The Odd Fellow's Improved Manual*, "Our laws teach us respect for ourselves, temperance in our desires, chastity of person, and purity in heart and mind. Drunkenness is a worse than beastly vice."[36] The lectures of the first degree of Odd Fellowship required initiates to pronounce drunkenness "the vilest and-most pernicious of all vices." Subordinate lodges provided for the expulsion or suspension of members found guilty of repeated intoxication.[37]

Odd Fellowship warned members not only to be temperate but also to "keep free from all excess and pollution."[38] One Albany lodge specified that a prospective member "be of good moral character, of industrious habits, and exempt from all infirmaties which may prevent him from gaining a livelihood for himself and family."[39] Lodge regulations governing relief benefits for illness stipulated that they be given only if the prospective recipient's "sickness or disability does not proceed from immoral conduct."[40]

Odd Fellows believed that relief benefits made the order a practical reform, whose advantages "worthy men of all capacities may enjoy, and in which all can assist in practical benevolence." A lodge must give aid to a member in distress with "cheerful alacrity . . . and without taking away from his independence." This was done "as the duty of his brothers."[41] Odd Fellowship desired to enhance, not diminish, a member's self-reliance.

The procedures, lectures, and degrees illustrate the character-forming features of Odd Fellowship. The system of graduated admission reinforced the order's control over a member's behavior. At one point in the rules, initiates were told that "the solemnities may be novel, even startling by their novelty, but they are perfectly chaste, dignified, and serious as the lessons they are designed to teach. . . . Give yourself, then, passively to your guides, to lead you withersoever they will."[42] The attainment of higher degrees was equated with both "receiving the unqualified blessings of society and recognition of the individual's fraternal worthiness."[43] According to Ridgely, the degrees aimed by successive steps "to form a workman, and to put him to appropriate labor. The treatment is pictorial, by example, and didactic."[44]

Each degree had its own series of emblems and symbols revealing the lessons of that degree and of Odd Fellowship in general. Within the different degrees, symbols of united effort, mortality, and religion reinforced the order's moral purpose. Above all, the emblems reiterated the necessity of industriousness and self-discipline. They warned an Odd Fellow not to waste time, to use his time wisely. The Hour Glass, an emblem of the third degree, reminded the Odd Fellow that " 'procrastination is the thief of time' and that constant and persistent labors are bound to result in deserved and merited success." The symbol of the Arrows directed "that we shall pursue our daily tasks and perform our bounden obligations in the straight, direct and narrow path of duty."[45]

In sum, the structure and literature of Odd Fellowship stressed certain moral precepts endorsed by the society at large. Odd Fellowship sought to inculcate in its members a religious spirit, self-discipline, industriousness, and temperance in all things. As written in the introduction to the bylaws of Albany Union Lodge No. 8, "The only and sole object of the Independent Order of Odd Fellows, is to carry into effect social and benevolent purposes, to inculcate principles of faithful intercourse with all men, charity, and useful moral precepts."[46] In promoting what are often called bourgeois habits, Odd Fellowship acted as a moral policing institution within the community.

By emphasizing the moral values accepted by the community at large, fraternal societies became "bulwarks of the *status quo*, conservers of traditional morality, transmitters of existing social values."[47] In mid-nineteenth-century Albany, the free labor ideology best describes this dominant consciousness. Adherents of free labor ideas defined American society in optimistic terms, as progressive and dynamic, as providing the means for workers to advance upward on the social scale. Although they recognized there were differences among individuals and groups, they anticipated that these differences would not become fixed as class relationships. In free labor terms all that was thought necessary for society's well-being was for both capital and labor to acknowledge their shared interests.[48] In its symbols and regulations Odd Fellowship reflected these free labor values.

Committed to a fluid social structure, free labor adherents still emphasized the importance of hierarchy and place as well as of mobility. Based on his standing within the Odd Fellows each member was assigned a particular spot in the lodge room during such ceremonies as initiation. In public processions, every Odd Fellow had a proper place according to his rank in the lodge. All Albany lodges had rules governing the asking of questions during meetings, and assessed penalties for improper language or use of disrespectful expressions towards officers or other members.[49]

Odd Fellowship assigned status to its members in accordance with the degree they had attained. Regulations reinforced these status distinctions among members. The most important work of a lodge took place in the Scarlet Degree, and only members of this degree could hold elective office in the lodge. Procedures to regulate the use of traveling cards also recognized these distinctions. To insure that a brother received the honors to which he was entitled, all traveling cards had to state the member's rank and degree. A lodge could bar a traveling brother if it was holding a meeting in a degree higher than his.[50]

Each degree had appropriate regalia, and Odd Fellow regulations mandated the wearing of these costumes. The bylaws of one Albany lodge forbade a member "to enter the Lodge unless he was clothed in suitable regalia; nor shall he be allowed to speak or vote on any question, unless clothed in the regalia appropriate to his rank or degree."[51] Thus the regalia became a "criterion of social distance not only between members and non-members but among the members themselves."[52]

In their study of working-class culture during the American industrial revolution, Alan Dawley and Paul Faler argue that the new industrial values "were constructed out of older materials. . . . In preindustrial times, individual initiative was fused with deference to social superiors, while in the new setting individualism was alloyed with a belief in equality of opportunity."[53] Equality of opportunity, as will be shown, was a notable theme in the ideology of Odd Fellowship, but this did not preclude deference to those who had made the most of their opportunities.

While recognizing social distinctions, in common with the larger society Odd Fellowship emphasized social mobility and the success ethic. In the United States the success ethic meant, in the dominant middle-class view, freedom of opportunity—an open path upward for men of talent and energy. Yet to free labor adherents equality did not denote a leveling process but rather an equal chance in the race for wealth.[54]

The leaders of the Odd Fellows in the United States dedicated the order to functioning as an open-class society. The central symbol of Odd Fellowship was the Three Link Chain, symbolizing Friendship, Love, and Truth. The order defined "love" as that which bound Odd Fellows together "without reference to those artificial distinctions which exist among mankind, and separate them into a diversity of grades and of classes, each laying peculiar claim to notice."[55] As should be true in the larger society, worthy individuals from varied social backgrounds moved up in the order to achieve the highest degree. An Odd Fellow earned the right to advance by exhibiting the proper habits of good citizenship, truthfulness, temperance, religious feeling, and industriousness, and by learning the ritual of the higher degree. As Ridgely observed, Odd Fellow degrees were not open to the multitude but were earned by the worthy and well qualified.[56]

In order to expand its scope and significance, American Odd Fellowship, in its earliest years, added a higher degree, the Patriarchal, which brought Odd Fellows together into Encampments formed outside the subordinate lodges. Subordinate lodges were thought to unite Odd Fellows into a single family; the mission of the Patriarchs was to unite Odd Fellowship with the world.[57] By joining an Encampment, an Odd Fellow might rise to an even higher station than he could achieve in the subordinate lodge. Believing that American society depended on giving "free scope to ability, perserverance, courage and ambition," Odd Fellowship had instituted "a higher summit" in the Patriarchal Degree.[58] By creating a structure that encouraged mobility, Odd Fellowship exemplified a society that provided upward movement for men of talent and energy.[59]

In promoting the fraternal relations that should exist among "brothers," Odd Fellowship symbolized the free labor principle of an inherent mutuality of interests between labor and capital. In Odd Fellowship the spirit of fraternity was "inspired by our cardinal idea of tolerance, [and] the mutuality of human obligations and sympathies, elaborately embodied as generic truths in our codes."[60] The authors of *The Odd Fellows' Pocket Companion* observed that "the sentiment upon which our institution depends most for support and existence, is the sentiment of *true brotherhood*; that mutual principle which should prompt [us] to lay aside all personal differences and sacrifice all party considerations for the benefit of the general weal."[61] In the term "united effort," Odd Fellowship expressed the concept of mutuality. For example, the emblem known as the Tee Square and Sword reminded the Odd Fellow "that justice and mercy should be administered without reference to the refined and subtle distinctions of men. Let us weigh well our conduct, and do unto others according to the injunction of the Golden Rule."[62]

The beneficial features of the order provided a way for members to express their mutual obligations. In Odd Fellowship "the bonds of fraternity draw us together in our lodges; they induce us to feel and relieve each other's distresses; they lead us to console the afflicted . . . [as] a family of brothers."[63] The order did not consider its benefits to be charity; rather, whatever his "circumstances of life" a fraternal brother was to receive the aid, counsel, and protection of his fellow members, "*not as a favor merely, but as a right.*"[64]

At a time when government provided few social services, when unemployment insurance and workmen's compensation were unknown, the benefits provided by the IOOF and other fraternal societies made a difference. Between 1824 and 1886 the New York State Grand Lodge spent $4,500,000 on relief programs. In Albany County alone the order had disbursed over $150,000 by 1886. Nor was an Odd Fellow barred from receiving these benefits by distance from his lodge. In fact, in 1870 Albany's lodges jointly inaugurated an Odd Fellow Board of Relief and specifically charged it with responsibility for assisting "the distressed traveling members" of the order. In times of particular need, such as the depression of the 1870s, Odd Fellows in New York City and Albany increased substantially the amount they expended on relief.[65]

The concept of mutuality was integral to the ideals of brotherhood expressed by Odd Fellowship. As one Odd Fellow noted,

> The conflicting and discordant elements of society can find repose and safety, only in the conservative spirit of philanthropic institutions . . . whose mission is to teach us that "no one liveth to himself," but that we are created and placed here to labor for our fellow-men, to improve our social condition.[66]

Ridgely wrote that within the degrees of Odd Fellowship lay the remedy for the world's evils: "That remedy is FRATERNITY. It has but one form: *association*; but one principle, *benevolence*; but one doctrine, *toleration*; but one order, *equality*. Thus all the workmen are one, and the work itself is in unity. It follows that the end is to unite all mankind into a vast and loving brotherhood."[67] Viewing society as an organic whole, believers in the free labor ideology assigned to each part duties and responsibilities, the whole being dependent on the contributions that each part made. It is this conception of the social order that Odd Fellowship most exemplified.

The leaders of nineteenth-century American Odd Fellowship assumed that moral and social reform were closely related and that Odd Fellowship, through its moral lessons, would insure social stability and cohesion. Looking back over a period of more than thirty years of the American ritual, Ridgely concluded,

> It is the experience of the world, and the teaching of history supplemented by careful observation, that of all the powers that exert a controlling influence upon society, none exceeds "moral power." It gives to citizenship the highest incentive to character, which forms the basis and bulwark of society, and supplies the general virtue and intelligence upon which the State relies.

He further observed that Odd Fellowship constituted

> an important organization, not only in controlling the general sentiment but in educating the popular feeling. . . . Society is enlightened and trained under a proper education; the people became happy, industrious, thrifty, and liberty, restrained by law, is supremely triumphant.[68]

During the nineteenth century workers formed relationships among themselves in their taverns, unions, and social clubs, and with members of other classes in community social institutions. Odd Fellowship was just one such community institution that helped shape workers' perception of industrialization in nineteenth-century Albany. By participating in noneconomic voluntary societies such as the IOOF, Albany workers met as brothers with individuals from all classes in the community. Further, as Odd Fellows, workers were instructed in conventional habits, including self-discipline, temperance, and industriousness. In so educating its members, Odd Fellowship contributed to the general acceptance of those personal habits felt essential to an industrial work ethic.

Community institutions such as Odd Fellowship transmitted the dominant social values. In Albany during the period of its industrialization, these values included a belief in hierarchy and place, in the success ethic, and, fundamentally, that a mutuality of interests existed among all groups in the community. These values were both symbolized and realized in the regulations, literature, and benefits of Odd Fellowship.

6

The Albany Penitentiary: Model for an Orderly Society

In communities throughout the United States in the antebellum period, middle-class elites sought to maintain an orderly and cohesive society in the face of the unsettling changes generated by economic growth and industrialization. Their free labor world view made them more comfortable with the economic changes, and less with the social changes, brought on by industrialization. While enthusiastic about the opportunity for social mobility made possible by economic growth, they also stressed the need to preserve order and balance in society. Believing that the protection of property safeguarded all other rights, middle-class elites manifested a particular concern over the perceived surge in petty crime in the first half of the nineteenth century.[1]

In the 1840s, Albany's middle-class leaders—its "thoughtful and influential citizens"—began to consider how they might lessen the growing "evils of crime." In May 1843 the Albany County Board of Supervisors, prompted by Samuel Pruyn, a prominent local merchant, appointed a five-member committee to see what could be done to better protect property and to "reform" or reduce, the rising expenses of the county.[2] In February 1844, the committee recommended to the board that Albany County build a penitentiary for the "confinement, employment, and reformation of vagrants and petty criminals," and the supervisors adopted its recommendation.[3] Constructed between 1845 and 1848, the Albany Penitentiary became "the first large county industrial prison for misdemeanants in America."[4]

After traveling through the United States inspecting prisons in the 1830s, Alexis de Tocqueville and Gustave Auguste de Beaumont commented that Americans seemed caught up by the "monomania" of regarding the penitentiary system as a "remedy for all the evils of society."[5] Yet Albany's public officials had no illusions that a correctional institution, "no matter how perfect its administration," could by itself "root out crime." They hoped that the penitentiary might control crime by inspiring wrongdoers with "honest purposes."[6] For this to occur, the criminal had to be separated from society, his old associations and habits broken. Once the criminal was incarcerated, the penitentiary's demands on him—to follow an unwavering routine, to remain silent at all times, to spend long hours at hard labor—would effect his reform.

The civic leaders who established the Albany Penitentiary did envision the institution as accomplishing more than just reclaiming society's errant members. They considered the discipline and order that would be imposed within the prison's walls as indispensible in the larger society as well. Albany's middle-class leaders believed that a successful penal institution would by its example encourage self-restraint throughout the whole community. Apprehensive about the disorder that seemed to follow in the wake of the city's economic growth, they regarded the penitentiary as one community institution capable of restoring social equilibrium.[7]

Albany's middle-class leaders never doubted that their community needed a new prison. Clearly dissatisfied with the county jail, they were likewise disinclined to accept the state prison system as a solution to managing the growing number of petty criminals and disorderly persons in Albany. Proponents of a county penitentiary called confinement in state prisons of those persons "whose habits had not yet hardened" a practice that confounded "mere poverty as such with crime."[8] Yet these community leaders did not want their sympathy for the wrongdoer to be misconstrued: "Our commiseration for the criminal should not cover up the fact that our peace and happiness as members of the social compact are held by the tenure of law; that property and life itself, is secure as crime is punished."[9] Maintenance of a stable community demanded that criminals be punished and that punishment be within sight of the community. The Albany Penitentiary fulfilled this purpose.

In colonial America jails functioned neither as instruments of discipline nor as places for the correction of inmates' personal habits. Colonial jails merely held debtors or persons awaiting trial or sentencing. Punishment itself was usually swift and corporal.[10] However, beginning in the late eighteenth century the concept emerged of a prison as a reformatory, as a place for treating and remaking the offender. In 1789 the Pennsylvania legislature mandated that part of Philadelphia's Walnut Street jail be set aside to confine at hard labor all convicted felons from throughout the state. Seven years later New York City opened its Newgate prison, which was patterned after the Walnut Street jail. In both institutions convicts worked together in workshops. To prison authorities, convict labor served the dual purpose of inculcating in prisoners the habits of industry while at the same time helping to defray the community's cost for incarcerating them.[11] The pattern of linking labor with reform continued throughout the nineteenth century.

By the 1820s prison management followed either the system adopted at the New York State prison at Auburn, New York, built in 1817, or the system at the Eastern State Penitentiary at Cherry Hill, near Philadelphia, opened in 1821. Both prisons sought to reform the criminal by isolating him from society and forcing him to adhere to a rigid routine. In the "Auburn system" a prisoner worked with others in silence ("congregate labor") during the day but resided in solitary confinement at night. As an alternative, the "Pennsylvania system" kept the prisoner totally isolated from his fellow inmates for the entire period of his confinement. Prisoners ate, slept, read their Bibles, and worked alone in separate cells.[12]

By the 1830s the state prison at Auburn had become synonymous with terror. During the tenure of Elam Lynds as warden, visitors accused Auburn of reducing its inmates to "silent and insulated working machines."[13] Frequent use of the cat-o'-nine-tails and other such punishments at Auburn transformed strict discipline into brutality.[14] On the other hand, critics of the Pennsylvania system charged that the "unnatural" condition of complete isolation resulted in general ill health, including a high incidence of insanity and suicide, among prison inmates.[15] The humanitarian reformer Dorothea Dix despaired at the "mind poisoning moral miasma" she found in state prisons and county jails during her investigation of conditions in these facilities in 1840.[16] By midcentury acceptance of its custodial function as the sole purpose of prisons was common.[17]

The widespread disenchantment with the reformatory potential of the existing state prison system had little effect on the proponents of a penitentiary in Albany. As they saw it, the failure of the county jail to contain the cost of crime to the community had to be remedied. Although Albany's population had less than doubled since 1815, the city's crime rate had risen by 400 percent during that time and the resultant costs to the county had nearly tripled.[18] In fact, conditions at the jail made it "a fruitful source" of, rather than a solution to, crime.[19] Under these circumstances, the Pruyn committee recommended to the Board of Supervisors that it apply immediately to the state legislature for a law enabling the county to erect a penitentiary.[20] In April 1844 New York's legislature empowered the board to construct a penitentiary in Albany County and appointed three commissioners, including Samuel Pruyn, to plan for the institution's management. Eight months later the commissioners issued their report, written by Pruyn.[21]

The moral earnestness that informed the penitentiary movement in Albany is evident from the commissioners' review of existing prison systems. Pruyn rejected the Pennsylvania system, declaring total isolation "incompatible with the natural rights of man, and with the laws of God." Because such punishments "degrade humanity, . . . render the better feelings callous, unhinge the reason and sink the human nature to the level of the brute, . . . the system is unquestionably wrong." With an eye on more mundane matters as well, he added that the great expense of the Pennsylvania system made it "impracticable" for Albany County.[22]

The penitentiary commissioners advised the county to adopt the Auburn system for the new Albany Penitentiary, especially in the form that system was practiced in Connecticut's Wethersfield prison. Unlike the Albany jail, Wethersfield had accumulated a large surplus, had averaged few second commitments (only 5 percent), and had had no third commitments. Pruyn found that at Wethersfield "silence, order and industry are *completely* exemplified."[23] Acting immediately on the commissioners' report, the Board of Supervisors selected a site for the new penitentiary and, in order to "forestall" any mistakes "from inexperience," hired Amos Pilsbury, the warden of the Wethersfield prison, to be the superintendent at Albany.[24]

The Pilsbury family played an important role in nineteenth-century prison reform. Amos's father, Moses Pilsbury, supervised New Hampshire's state prison before being appointed warden at Wethersfield in 1827. When Moses retired three years later, Amos, who had been his father's deputy, succeeded him. Similarly, in 1872, Amos's son Louis replaced his father at Albany. In 1877 Louis became the first superintendent of prisons for New York State.[25]

During Wethersfield's twenty years under Pilsbury guidance the penitentiary earned a reputation as the "pattern prison of the Auburn plan."[26] In her *Remarks on Prisons and Prison Discipline in the United States*, Dix cited Wethersfield as "the best example" of the silent system in the nation, a prison with greater potential "for more correct, moral discipline" of its inmates than any other.[27] The Auburn system as practiced at Wethersfield—congregate labor during the day, isolation in the evening, rigid discipline enforcing silence at all times—was the system that Pilsbury introduced in the new Albany Penitentiary.

The board chose Pilsbury because they wanted to establish professional standards for the new prison's management. To Pilsbury the prerequisite for professional prison management was the institution's freedom from outside interference. Successful prison administration, he declared, depended on "the elimination of political control and political appointments." He insisted that the convicts' care be entrusted only "to those who have aptitude and capacity for that peculiar function, independent of their political leanings or opinions."[28] The penitentiary's founders were of the same mind, insisting at the outset that "no political or partisan considerations should enter or influence" prison affairs.[29]

To help guarantee nonpartisan management of the Albany Penitentiary, its founders entrusted responsibility for overseeing conditions to an unpaid three-member board of inspectors, jointly appointed by the county Board of Supervisors and the city of Albany's mayor and recorder. Until 1885, when the New York State legislature revised the procedures governing the pentitentiary, the board of inspectors consisted of Democrats and Republicans, representative of the city and county.[30] By severing penitentiary governance from party politics, the Albany community demonstrated the special place it accorded the institution.

The middle-class founders of the Albany Penitentiary assumed that reforming criminal and disorderly persons fulfilled "purely benevolent and philanthropic" purposes.[31] They characterized the movement behind the penitentiary as one arising not from "selfish motives, but from the higher principle of desiring to arrest the ruinous tendency of the present state of things upon the public morals."[32] From the perspective of the city's middle-class leaders, the Albany Penitentiary was a public-spirited attempt to offset rising crime and disorder. They never doubted that their solution was in the general interest. Certainly this assumption by the penitentiary's founders contains a degree of self-delusion. Nevertheless, the movement for construction of a penitentiary in Albany represents a sincere effort by the local middle-class elite to provide responsible moral leadership.[33]

Proponents of the penitentiary explained the upsurge in crime in Albany as an unfortunate consequence of the city's economic success. As a "centre of a vast and increasing system of internal intercourse," Albany naturally became "the peculiar haunt of vice and crime."[34] The penitentiary supporters did not, however, equate "the growth of petty crime, vagrancy, and pauperism" in Albany with a particular part of the community. They identified criminals solely as individuals with particular habits, not as representatives of an ethnic group or class.[35] The intention of the reformers was to insure that what they believed to be right conduct would become the standard in Albany.

Prison authorities routinely recorded an inmate's age, literacy, marital status, and habits (temperate or intemperate) at the time of his incarceration. Most nineteenth-century American prison reformers cited a criminal's personal habits as proof that certain character defects had led him to crime. For example, in 1841 Alonzo Potter, a founder of the New York State Normal School, attributed a decline in crimes requiring knowledge and foresight to an increase in "ignorance and mental debasement."[36] But the Reverend A. D. Mayo of Albany's First Unitarian Church considered idleness, intemperance, and ignorance to be symptoms, not causes, of crime: "The real cause of crime is a weakening of moral decision, which is the gradual result of a thousand influences."[37] The main sources of this moral weakness, according to Mayo and other prison reformers, could be found in the criminal's early training and home life.

Advocates of a penitentiary in Albany believed crime symptomatic of the failure of traditional institutions, especially the family, to instill proper respect for order and authority in the individual. "The family is the great school," Mayo contended, "where children are fitted for honor or dishonor."[38] The Albany Penitentiary's first chaplain, the Reverend T. R. Dawson, observed that "in nine out of ten cases" the inmates' evil deeds "may be easily traced to the neglect of the needful discipline in their childhood."[39] Deprived of guidance and discipline in their youth, these individuals succumbed to society's many temptations and became criminals.[40]

The failure of the family to perform its designated function, to instill proper habits in its members, made it only prudent that the community fashion an alternative agency that could do so. Pilsbury accepted this as the penitentiary's main challenge, "I have endeavored to make it a school where the young, at least, while suffering confinement for crime should be taught principles and habits of industry and personal morality calculated to govern them in their future lives."[41] According to Mayo, the wrongdoer needs "the fatherly hand of society laid on him for wholesome restraint; needs to be sequestered from his old temptations and crimes . . . needs the whole moral force of society concentrated for his reformation."[42] To these ends the Albany Penitentiary's proponents dedicated the institution.

When completed in 1848, the Albany Penitentiary consisted of a three-story central building with two wings, each of which was flanked by an octagonal tower. Ninety-six cells, four tiers high, each cell a scant seven feet by four feet and seven feet high, made up most of the south wing. These cells (which, according to an inmate, allowed little more than two steps forward and back) and ten larger rooms in the tower constituted the men's cell block. Female prisoners were housed in the forty cells and eight tower rooms of the north wing. The prison superintendent resided in rooms at the front of the main building; the rest of the building included a dispensary, separate hospital rooms for men and women, and a chapel. A fourteen-foot-high brick wall surrounded these buildings. Atop the wall were guardhouses and a sentry walk, and within it was the male convicts' workshop. The design of the buildings not only facilitated surveillance of the prisoners but also permitted optimal ventilation and sunlight.[43]

Like most prison reformers, Amos Pilsbury believed that the facility's design—its arrangement of cells and workshops— contributed to its function as a reformatory. Pilsbury considered "a plain, simple straight plan of building," such as adopted for the Albany Penitentiary, with workshops and cells in separate buildings, to be "the best" for the operation of the silent, congregate system.[44] A penitentiary's location helped it achieve its reform goals. A visitor to the Albany Penitentiary some years after its completion commented that the "undulating grasses" of the institution's twelve-acre site one-half mile west of the Capitol precluded "the hum and bustle of the city" from distracting convicts at labor in the workshops.[45] The internal discipline vital to a penitentiary's success needed an orderly and peaceful environment.

Any description of the discipline inside the Albany Penitentiary lends truth to the saying "the road to Hell is paved with good intentions." Inmates woke at daylight and worked until 7:00 a.m., when a bell rang signalling breakfast. Then, as the rules set out, the prisoners ceased all work, rose, and formed a line: "At the word *right*, each man will turn right; at the word *up*, each man will take his bucket upon his left arm, they will then form into sections in close order."[46] The prisoners marched through the penitentiary in lockstep, left hand on breast and right hand on the right shoulder of the prisoner in front, and always with eyes downcast. One visitor described having seen "200 men march out with one tread" when the command "right up, forward" was given.[47] Such regimentation typified the quasi-military conditions most penitentiary advocates deemed essential to reforming the criminal.[48]

Having rejected the Pennsylvania system as "inhumane," Albany officials insisted that while punishment of an inmate for any infraction of the rules should be "adequate" to his offense, it should also be such as would tend to "effect" the convict's "moral reformation."[49] Prison rules at the Albany Penitentiary forbade use of a whip, or the "cat." But the rules did permit the "shower bath" and solitary confinement. In a shower bath the offending prisoner had buckets of cold water poured over him through a quarter-inch hole twelve inches above his head. The prison's rules also specified that the warden alone had responsibility for carrying out any punishment.[50] By all accounts Pilsbury maintained effective discipline in the penitentiary.[51]

More than their punishment, the inmates' nearly constant labor in the prison's workshops was the key element in the discipline imposed in the Albany Penitentiary. Once marched by lockstep back to the shops after breakfast, prisoners immediately resumed their work, laboring until noon, when they had an hour's dinner, and then again until 6:00 p.m. On the second day of an inmate's incarceration prison authorities determined the amount of labor he could perform "without taxing his powers to such an extent as to produce absolute fatigue."[52] This then became the standard applied until that inmate's release. Some male, and all female, convicts worked at prison maintenance, for example, as groundskeepers or cooks. Most male prisoners, however, worked in the shops. But whatever the task, prison administrators expected all prisoners to "labor diligently" whenever they were not in their cells.[53]

The founders of the Albany Penitentiary expected the labor performed by inmates in the prison's workshops to generate enough income to support the institution. To fulfill this goal Pilsbury entered into contract with private entrepreneurs. For the length of a contract the businessman paid the penitentiary a per diem rate for each prisoner who produced goods for him. The contractor then sold the convict-made products for his own profit.

A number of forces intervened to limit the kind of labor Pilsbury could secure contracts for. From the beginning officials in Albany recognized the "sensitiveness of the public" with regard to the competition of convict-made goods with the products of free labor.[54] The founders mandated that only work that did not interfere with "the lawful association of any citizen" be performed at the penitentiary.[55] The prison population itself probably had most influence in shaping the contract system at the Albany Penitentiary. Inmates were mostly vagrants and disorderly persons. Besides lacking skills, they usually served short terms, which hindered efficient utilization of convict labor. This became an even greater problem after 1855 when a change in New York's temperance laws created a "new class of prisoners" whose presence in great numbers, officials feared, was turning the institution into an "Inebriate Hospital." Individuals charged with public intoxication were now sentenced to the penitentiary for a mere ten days—time only for them to dry out, the *Argus* lamented, and not time enough for them to perform any profitable labor.[56]

These circumstances made the introduction of skilled trades into the prison's workshops improbable. Only labor of the "simplest character" could be carried out in the penitentiary.[57] Basketmaking, caning chairs, and brushmaking were among the simple jobs inmates performed. Even a somewhat more skilled task, shoemaking, was done in the simplest manner. One contractor with the Albany Penitentiary, James R. Busley, an Albany shoe dealer, estimated he could make a prisoner of ordinary intelligence a first-rate worker in only three weeks.[58]

The revenue generated by contract labor was but one advantage of the system touted by its supporters. A convict's labor was the key to transforming a dissolute (and unproductive) criminal into a useful member of society. The penitentiary's original design called for the institution to be built by the convicts themselves.[59] The penitentiary's founders intended not only to save the county money but, equally important, to extract "labor from those who, by crime, had made themselves a public charge."[60] A productively employed criminal quickly learned that his confinement was part of his repayment to society.[61]

Many of those associated with the penitentiary agreed with Pilsbury that "the most prolific parent of crime is idleness, for which the best remedy is a careful training in habits of industry."[62] According to one prison chaplain, the constant labor demanded of inmates gave them "that which few of them had previously, habits of regularity and industry."[63] The Reverend Mayo called the penitentiary's inculcating habits of industry in the convict "the first element" in his reformation.[64] The routine of labor once learned inside the prison would produce hard-working citizens outside.

Reforming the criminal depended not merely on his being kept busy but also on how he was made to go about his tasks. Prison guards saw to it that inmates worked continuously and silently and always with their attention focused on the task at hand. In an early report the inspectors of the penitentiary commended the prisoners' "submissive deportment" while working in "unbroken silence."[65] Visitors to the institution took special note of convict workers' penitent behavior. They know that "you are there," one visitor wrote in *Appleton's Journal* in 1874, "yet not one man raises his head, . . . not one eye turns. It is the rule of the place that none shall."[66] To the penitentiary's supporters such comments confirmed the institution's success.

Few persons in Albany questioned the need for total control over inmate behavior. Only through vigorous discipline could the institution break the criminal's evil habits and instill in him new and productive ones. Yet, in his history of the penitentiary, a former chaplain wondered if prison discipline were not too strict: "In passing through the workshops and viewing the men at their labors, one seems to be looking at machines rather than at human beings. . . . It is too hard, cold, unsympathetic, repressive. It works against rather than with nature.''[67] A former deputy to Pilsbury at both Wethersfield and Albany also acknowledged that ''the stringency of control maintained at Albany was not so much for safety as it was for the sake of serviceable industrial efficiency, the increase of prison earnings.''[68] But the penitentiary's supporters believed that the productivity and revenue that such discipline produced only enhanced the institution's role as a reformatory.

Convict labor was but one component, albeit a critical one, of the process whereby the Albany Penitentiary transformed the criminal. The institution also provided its inmates with moral and religious guidance. A chapel occupied part of the penitentiary's central building, and prison authorities employed a chaplain to encourage the inmates' ''subordination, reformation and spiritual welfare.''[69] The penitentiary's middle-class advocates regarded the moral and religious care prisoners received in the facility to be a ''powerful auxiliary in producing amendment and reformation.''[70] By incarcerating a wrongdoer, society might check ''perverse passions for a time,'' prison chaplain David Dyer stated. But without moral and spiritual care he would again become an ''inveterate slave to his passions and a greater injury to the state'' once ''these appliances'' were removed. Neglect the moral and religious attributes of the inmate, ''the mainspring of thought and action, the director of the whole man,'' Dyer pronounced, and the system is deranged, ''readjustment and reformation . . . impossible.''[71] If less millennial in their expectations than Dyer, the penitentiary's civil supporters agreed that only when its inmates had internalized the prison's system of industry and discipline could the institution be counted a success. This change did indeed require moral training.

Allied to their faith in moral training, penitentiary authorities emphasized that reformation required discipline. They had been critical of the county jail because its inmates were ''herded together in promiscuous intercourse and utter idleness.''[72] To prevent similar corruption in the new penitentiary, its founders promulgated regulations demanding silence at all times. The regulations even stipulated that guards move about the cell blocks ''with socks on, in a silent manner,'' in order to better detect any unnecessary noise.[73] Responding to questions about communication among prisoners in the penitentiary, Pilsbury stated simply: ''Silence is enforced—strictly.''[74] Prisoners not only had to remain silent when outside their cells, as in the workshops, they had always to gaze downward—the rules forbade eye contact.

The injunction that the silent prisoners keep their heads bowed was meant to reinforce their submissiveness. In 1864 Pilsbury told the New York Prison Association that his system, by relying on ''strict, rigid discipline'' of inmates and the ''unceasing attention'' of all officers, achieved unyielding obedience to all the prison's rules and regulations.[75] The reliance on complete submissiveness was less for safety in the prison than to teach the inmate deference to authority. Pilsbury resolutely tried to carry out the mandate of the penitentiary's founders that the institution operate so that the convict ''feel his imprisonment is an iron yoke to be borne.''[76]

The founders of the Albany Penitentiary believed that the rigid routine and discipline imposed within the institution would have a restraining influence on the outside community. The Albany city jail had deterred few persons from committing crimes. In fact, because the jail held no ''terrors,'' it had an ''opposite effect.''[77] Looking back over the penitentiary's first quarter century, its supporters congratulated themselves because the prison was from the very beginning ''a terror to evil-doers . . . more dreaded than State prisons, by habitual criminals.''[78] Public officials had worried that Albany was destined to be a ''rendezvous for criminal and disorderly persons.'' Instead, the penitentiary's ''unrelaxed industry and perfect impartiality of the system'' had been ''potent agencies'' deterring crime in Albany.[79] Pilsbury's ''iron yoke'' inside the penitentiary had ''exerted a great and beneficient influence'' outside the prison's walls.

The public acclaim bestowed on Pilsbury further testifies to the esteem with which the community held the system in force at the Albany Penitentiary. Every three years the joint board governing the institution renewed Pilsbury's contract as a matter of course. Prison inspections became something of an annual celebration (with more than a hint of self-congratulation) of the Pilsbury administration and of the institution. After the first year, penitentiary officials expressed their conviction that the institution would be ''the pioneer of a new system of criminal punishment.''[80] Fifteen years later, in 1863, the joint board unanimously offered ''cordial congratulations'' to Pilsbury. Its resolution stated, ''We hold in the highest estimation the fidelity with which he has managed [the penitentiary's] affairs, and the perfect system of order and discipline which has made it the model penal institution of the United States.''[81] Albany's press echoed the board's praise, pointing out that the Albany Penitentiary was regarded ''as *the* model institution of prison discipline.'' The editor of the *Argus* insisted that the penitentiary ''must be visited. . . . there are many useful lessons to be learned even in an hour's visit.'' Forgetting for the moment that he had been observing unfree workers, the newspaper's editor described the workshops as ''a perfect bee-hive of industry. . . . INDUSTRY and ORDER, if not printed in capitals at each doorway, stare you in the face at every step.''

But perhaps the most "useful lesson," according to the *Argus*, was that each prisoner worked for the common good, "Everyone has a duty to perform, and it is performed."[82] For many of Albany's leading citizens the harmonious and stable order that Pilsbury fostered inside the penitentiary was a model for the community outside.

As spokesmen for a free labor society, Albany's middle-class civic elite praised the ideal of a community composed of self-governing individuals. In developing institutions to encourage self-restraint, they could either call on the coercive power of government or attempt reform through voluntary agencies that emphasized moral suasion. In nineteenth-century America reformers frequently endorsed both strategies.[83] Yet as Tocqueville concluded, "when they propose to inculcate some truth" Americans preferred to use voluntary agencies. Even in creating and sustaining the penitentiary (in reality, of course, an agency of government), its founders saw themselves acting as they might in any voluntary reform endeavor. Like members of any association for moral reform, they thought of the penitentiary in terms of the free labor values commonly accepted in Albany.

In the free labor world view society's well-being depended on getting the diverse interests of the community to work in harmony for the common good.[84] The penitentiary could only function as a reformatory if the institution facilitated that purpose. A thousand forces might cause crime, but, according to the Reverend Mayo, "Every influence that unites the several interests and classes is a preventative of crime." Because the penitentiary had just such a unifying influence, Mayo called it a "symbol of the capital" city, Albany.[85] Supporters of the penitentiary believed that its success as an agency of reform came not only through its impact on those incarcerated but also through the subtle influence of its example in the community.

The founders of the Albany Penitentiary consciously chose a design for the institution's buildings that would enhance their ability to impose order and discipline within. They saw the institution sending a corresponding message to the community. Looking like the armories that would be built across the United States after the nationwide railroad strike in 1877, the penitentiary's imposing building occupied a "beautiful and commanding elevation" in Albany. Its founders had selected a site that would isolate inmates from the community in order to reform them, yet be conspicuous.[86] The prison's monumental structure (it expanded to six times its original size by the 1880s) reinforced the institution's role as a model. Both in location and size the penitentiary stood as a silent yet powerful symbol of order in the community.

Pilsbury attributed the order and discipline maintained within the institution "in a great measure" to the support the penitentiary received "from the authorities and citizens" of Albany. Prisoners entered the institution "feeling and *knowing* that the community approved and had confidence in the discipline and management" of the prison.[87] Its founders had charged the penitentiary with the responsibility for reforming Albany's petty criminals, disorderly persons, and vagrants. The institution would "reclaim" its inmates by inculcating self-discipline, respect for order, industriousness, self-restraint, and a sense of one's rightful place in society. By its physical appearance the institution also reminded those on the outside that they too belonged to a community that was to be orderly, cohesive, and strictly hierarchical.[88]

Public officials in Albany assumed that the penitentiary's ability to be self-sustaining contributed to its reformatory role. Prison authorities brought in revenue not only from contracts for convict labor but also from contracts for confining prisoners from counties throughout New York State. An 1847 amendment to the law establishing the Albany Penitentiary authorized such contracts, and in 1854 the Board of Supervisors for Albany County arranged with officials of Dutchess County to house all its convicted vagrants and disorderly persons at Albany. In 1855 the board worked out a similar agreement with Washington County officials, and other such contracts followed.[89] Pilsbury greatly augmented this source of revenue in 1862 when he arranged with the federal government for all prisoners then kept in Washington, D.C., to be sent instead to the Albany Penitentiary. With their sentences ranging from six months to nineteen years, 131 convicts were immediately transferred to Albany. Over the next nineteen years the national government paid the penitentiary $1.25 per week or $65 per year for each federal prisoner maintained at the Albany facility.[90] More than the fees paid in Albany County for housing federal prisoners, the infusion of inmates with more skills and longer sentences into the shops enabled Pilsbury to make more profitable labor contracts, thereby adding to the penitentiary's ability to sustain itself.[91]

However, a growing inmate population also caused problems. The penitentiary had to be enlarged to accommodate the increased numbers. Three years after the prison opened, officials added 120 cells; ten years later, 36 more cells were constructed, as well as rooms for washing, ironing, drying, and other laundry chores. In 1865, to take advantage of the federal prisoners, the county erected a new two-story building with additional workshops.[92] By 1886 the penitentiary had added another new workshop.[93] Penitentiary officials emphasized that this expansion was paid for out of prison earnings from greater productivity rather than tax revenue.[94]

To some contemporary observers of American penal conditions, the growing size and diversity of Albany's inmate population divested the penitentiary of its special mission as a county institution. By the 1860s clearly it had become a state and national rather than local institution.[95] Albany officials seem to have turned a deaf ear to these charges, and, at least into the middle 1870s, their praise for the penitentiary continued unabated. Certainly no one questioned Pilsbury's ability to control the enlarged inmate population. Nevertheless, Pilsbury had told the New York Prison Association in 1850 that he opposed confinement of more than four hundred prisoners in one prison under one director. Once a prison grows larger, he said, it becomes impossible for the warden to know the "general character and moral feeling of each prisoner," which he must in order to do his job.[96] By the 1870s the Albany Penitentiary held over nine hundred prisoners, more than twice what Pilsbury had characterized as the optimal population, and it is unlikely that such phenomenal growth had no impact on the institution's management.[97] And there is evidence that by the 1870s the community's faith in the penitentiary as a reformatory had slackened.

Pilsbury resigned shortly before his death in 1873, and, as they had once before, the penitentiary's governing authorities chose a Pilsbury, Amos's son Louis, to be warden.[98] Although there was no visible diminution in the public's esteem for the Albany Penitentiary during Louis Pilsbury's four-year tenure, there are hints of political partisanship becoming a factor in prison goverance. At an 1876 Board of Supervisors meeting a discussion on the reappointment of a prison inspector to the joint board included political considerations for the first time.[99] In addition, in 1878, more than a year after Louis Pilsbury resigned to become the superintendent of prisons for New York State, the Albany County Board of Supervisors selected his successor by a straight party vote.[100] Party politics clearly had entered prison affairs.

Nonpartisanship had been the cornerstone of the reform system adopted for the penitentiary's administration by Amos Pilsbury and Albany's public officials. The change in this policy in the 1870s indicates a shift in the special role assigned the penitentiary by community leaders. "The impression is fast fading in the public mind that prisons are to be considered reformatories," the Reverend Charles Reynolds, chaplain at the penitentiary, reported to the Board of Supervisors in 1881. "They are places of punishment for misdeeds committed, and are so regarded by prisoners"—and, most likely, by the community.[101] By the 1880s, although Albany's officials continued to praise the institution, the penitentiary appears to have lost its reformatory purpose and become a purely custodial facility. The institution persisted, but the community no longer looked to the penitentiary system to inspire a general reform of behavior and habits.

Like a number of institutions that date from the Jacksonian era, the Albany Penitentiary was built because of a perception of greater disorder caused by an expanding economy. It had seemed to the Pruyn committee "a wise and prudent policy, to adopt timely measures, if not to check, at least to guard [the] community against" these dangers.[102] Its founders believed that because the prison's success would inspire a general reformation of manners and habits, the penitentiary was just such a "timely" measure. Its supporters were committed to a community order based upon the self-restraint, industriousness, and discipline of its members. They intended the penitentiary to spread these virtues throughout Albany. The penitentiary became one means of preserving order and stability in nineteenth-century Albany.

7

Socialization and Acculturation: Religion, Ethnicity, and Politics in Albany

Nineteenth-century communities depended on a range of voluntary associations to mediate class relations as well as guide behavior. American churches, Tocqueville found, unlike those in Europe, functioned without the authoritative backing of the state. Even so, he observed, religion in the United States managed to direct the affairs of the community through its regulation of "domestic life," by which Tocqueville meant the manners and beliefs of the people.[1] In communities like Albany, religion exerted moral and social influence through organized churches and through an affiliated network of voluntary moral and benevolent associations. Prominent lay people joined church leaders to make these voluntary associations into agencies for promoting common values.

As had the founders of the Albany Penitentiary, middle-class Protestant leaders of Albany sought to sustain a community order that they thought of as the normal one. This assumption stemmed from a deep conviction that they had a moral responsibility to form and guide behavior. In particular, the religious voluntary associations that this middle-class elite sponsored endeavored to win communitywide adherence to a standard of "right conduct," the basis for an enduring moral order.[2] The character traits that Albany's Protestant elite encouraged were those desirable in the new economic order—self-reliance, temperance, and industriousness.

Albany's Catholic population, many of whom were recent immigrants, often found themselves the objects of the moral "reform" aspirations of Protestant-sponsored associations. In order to resist Protestant evangelism, Catholics in Albany, as they did elsewhere, established an alternative system of benevolent associations. While serving as social clubs and societies of mutual support, Catholic voluntary associations also helped preserve Catholic traditions and identity.

The parallel charity and welfare system that Catholics organized in Albany does not mean that they segregated themselves from the larger community. Even while providing Catholics with necessary sanctuary, their voluntary associations paved the way for eventual Catholic participation in the full range of Albany's social and political life. In Europe, parish organization had been a rural concept. In cities like Albany, the Catholic Church transformed the parish through these voluntary associations into an agency for sustaining religious faith and helping immigrant members adjust to their new urban environment. By acting as "brokers," that is, as the representatives of their congregants in dealing with Albany's power structure, the Church hierarchy facilitated the Catholic immigrant's accommodation to the prevailing community order.[3] Ethnic leaders joined Church leaders in this role. Because by 1855 Irish Catholics (first and second generation) constituted almost 40 percent of Albany's population, their adjustment to the city merits special attention.

Albany's Irish Catholic elite was most often drawn from the middle and business classes. The more prosperous Irish secured the esteem of fellow Irish-Americans through their leadership of ethnic voluntary associations that usually combined welfare and Irish nationalist purposes. These "lace-curtain" Irish leaders not only served as models for their ethnic group, they also acted as mediators between it and the larger community.[4] In common with the Catholic hierarchy, the leaders of Albany's Irish community participated in what is best described as a bargaining process between the elites of the city's more recent arrivals and its already entrenched groups.[5] As leaders of their ethnic community in Albany the Irish elite gained political and social recognition for themselves and their ethnic group. In Albany, acculturation of the Irish became an integrative process meant to maintain social harmony.

In emphasizing their respectability, lay and religious leaders of Albany's Irish Catholics subscribed to free labor social values. The cultural identity these leaders encouraged should, therefore, be contrasted with the class identity that was the object of Albany's trade union and labor reform movements. Irish preponderance in Albany's trade union and labor reform movements has led one historian to conclude that this was "the real base of Irish economic power in Albany."[6] Irish workers held office in many local unions and in the city trades assembly. Albany's militant iron molders, who operated two cooperative foundries in the 1860s, were mostly Irish-Americans.[7] Independent of middle-class leadership, working-class members of Albany's Irish community often rejected the accommodation to the free labor order that the city's Irish elite tried to foster. The commonwealth ideals that animated the cooperative and eight-hour movements in Albany reflect social values that diverged from the prevailing free labor ideology.

However, in Albany and elsewhere workers consistently failed to show in their political behavior the class consciousness that marked their economic actions. More often than not in the political sphere issues raised by workers' ethnic and cultural identity mitigated their class consciousness.[8] The alternating claims on workers in Albany of their class and cultural identities are very apparent in the city's 1878 mayoral election. Albany workers exhibited little interest in independent labor politics prior to the 1870s. But the Panic of 1873 and the depression that followed, the national rail strikes in 1877, and especially the long, bitter strike by molders in 1876 and 1877 reawakened Albany workers' interest in an independent political party. In 1878 workers organized the Independent Labor Democratic party and nominated their own candidates for the municipal elections. The Democrats countered by nominating an Irish Catholic businessman for mayor, and the election became a test between the antipodal attractions of class and cultural identity.[9]

Guided by a local elite, voluntary associations promoted adjustment to the social norms that dominated Albany in the midnineteenth century. More consciously than fraternal societies such as the Independent Order of Odd Fellows, religious and ethnic voluntary associations encouraged the city's diverse groups and people to feel themselves to be members of a common community, knit by shared moral and social values. In particular, the participation of Irish workers in politics enhanced their ties to a middle-class ethnic leadership and thereby undermined organization of an independent class-based political party in Albany. For the city's Irish workers, such accommodation meant shedding those values that had made them radical.[10]

The earliest Protestant religious institutions in Albany date from the seventeenth century. One of the oldest churches in the United States, The First Reformed (Dutch) Church, was erected in 1642 near Fort Orange, the original site of the city of Albany. Over the next 125 years, Lutherans, Episcopalians, and Presbyterians all built houses of worship.[11] Although Methodists and Baptists did later establish themselves in the city, Albany throughout its history remained dominated by the more conservative Protestant churches. Little of the liberating spirit of the nineteenth-century Finney revivals in Northern New York's "burned-over district" touched Albany.[12]

Although revivalism in Albany was weak, many of the more conservative reform societies that proliferated in its wake became part of the city's daily life in the course of the nineteenth century.[13] A local branch of the Young Men's Christian Association (YMCA) opened in Albany in 1857 in order to improve "the spiritual, mental and social condition of the young men of the city." The YMCA offered lectures, a library, reading rooms, and religious services to its members, providing an environment where they could "resort at the close of the daily labors" free from "degrading influences."[14] In 1877 a Railroad YMCA opened in West Albany, offering similar opportunities for "mutual improvement" to railroad workers.[15] Poor women in Albany received the attention of the Ladies Protestant Union Aid Society. Founded in 1866, the society furnished employment (generally sewing) and provided temporary relief. The "Christian ladies" who ran the society visited the "worthy poor" in their homes to "incite them to a higher standard of moral character and action."[16] As did similar "uplifting" associations, the Ladies Protestant Union Aid Society concentrated on inculcating proper moral values and improving personal behavior.

The YMCA and the Union Aid Society were only two such associations in what may be characterized as the Protestant benevolent empire in Albany. By 1870, the forty-nine churches of the city's various Protestant denominations ran more than sixty Sunday schools; many sponsored a "Young People's Society" or similar groups for religious education and sociability.[17] Albany's Protestants also united behind the Albany County Bible Society, Albany County Sunday School Union, Women's Christian Temperance Union, and other local associations promoting morality. Moreover, Protestant churches and their wealthy lay members donated money to support numerous welfare institutions, including three hospitals, the Albany Guardian Society and Home for Aged Men, the Open Door Mission, the Children's Friend Society (which ran two industrial schools for vagrant children), the House of Shelter (for "wayward" girls), and the Albany Orphan Asylum.[18] Taken together, these associations and institutions formed a Protestant religious and moral establishment that, much more than local government, ministered to the needs of Albany's poor.[19]

The most ambitious agency of the Protestant establishment in Albany was the nondenominational Albany City Tract and Missionary

Society. Organized as the City Tract Society (CTS) in 1835, the society focused on reaching those individuals and families who did not attend the city's churches.[20] The CTS operated through volunteers who visited nonattenders at home. These volunteers would try to gain the confidence of those they visited by reading portions of the Bible to them if they were illiterate or by praying with them. The society enjoined its visitors to be "prudent, affectionate, and gentle" and to scrupulously refrain from inculcating sectarian views.[21]

The CTS divided Albany into districts of roughly twenty-five to seventy-five families, and assigned one or two visitors to each district. Visiting was the heart of the society's mission. As one Albany minister explained, "The simple scheme of bringing into close contact single minds, somewhat elevated, with other minds, more or less degraded, must have a mighty effect in bringing about the moral regeneration of society."[22] The Reverend William Buell Sprague, pastor of the Second Presbyterian Church and a force behind the society in its early years, stressed the impact societies like the CTS had on preserving moral standards in the community. In his sermon "Religion and Rank," Sprague commended the person of rank who moved "among his inferiors with affability and kindness,—apparently forgetful of his wealth and his honors."[23] Men from higher and lower social stations must be encouraged to meet together so that they might discharge their reciprocal responsibilities. Such intercourse brought those in humble circumstances "consolation and relief" and fostered within them a "spirit of contentment." For men of high rank the exchange "enlarge[d] the circle of their sympathies and their influence" and made them "feel more strongly the value of religion, and the hallowed nature of the tie that binds the Christian brotherhood together."[24] Clearly Albany's Protestant elite believed that moral reform had to come from the top down.[25]

During the 1850s the City Tract Society underwent an ambitious transformation. In 1852 the CTS brought the Reverend David Dyer to Albany from Dorchester, Massachusetts, to superintend the society's operations and act as its minister at large. During his first six months of ministry in Albany, Dyer preached some fifty sermons in churches around the city, held many religious meetings, especially at the society's Bowery Mission, and supervised the distribution among boatmen and immigrants along the city's docks of some 266,000 pages of tracts. "These varied and commendable labors," the society confidently announced, "happily contributed to comfort the destitute, instruct the ignorant, reform the vicious, and convert the unconverted."[26]

In 1855 the City Tract Society became the Albany City Tract and Missionary Society (ACTMS). The change in its name signaled the society's commitment to the more aggressive "missionary" policy it had adopted under Dyer. In particular, Dyer wanted the society to extend "*the benign influence it exerts on our foreign population.*"[27]

In 1853 CTS managers had engaged the Reverend A. Von Puttkammer as its missionary to Albany's German population. The following year he became pastor of a German mission started in the western part of the city, and another minister, the Reverend F. N. Wieskotten, was assigned to the area south of Hudson Street. Despite this missionary effort in Albany, it seemed to Dyer that the CTS must reach still further into the community. Many, "not the poor only, but respectable laborers, mechanics and others," seldom if ever attended church or had any formal connection with religion. "Have we no duty to perform in reference to them?" he asked. "Do they not form a part of the community in which we dwell? . . . Do not their irreligious habits directly tend to the subordination of their moral nature, and thus to the production of ignorance, poverty, crime, and social desolation?"[28] In April 1854, in order to identify the areas of Albany in greatest need of its ministry, the CTS undertook a survey of attendance at all places of public worship in the city. The society found that on what was reported to be one of the pleasantest Sundays of the year not quite 26 percent of the city's residents attended religious services. To the CTS, these statistics confirmed that thousands in Albany were living in spiritual ignorance. The society accepted its obligation to reach these persons, for if it did nothing then the community faced "public evils" that would "certainly and most injuriously affect every interest of the city—commercial, educational, scientific and religious."[29]

In the 1850s the CTS concluded that in order to accomplish its spiritual mission among the unchurched poor, it must help provide some of their "temporal wants."[30] In 1854, at the behest of "several gentlemen," the society became a quasi-official welfare agency in Albany.[31] Since its visitors entered the dwellings of the poor and could ascertain "their real condition," relief could be distributed by the society with more "precision and certainty, and administered with kind, moral and elevating influences."[32] Just six months after Dyer arrived in 1852, the society's treasurer reported that the CTS was spending on relief more than one-third what had been its total operating budget the previous year.[33] Over the next two years, more than two thousand persons received some form of aid through the society. The winter of 1854–55 alone saw the ACTMS distribute coal, wood, shoes, and bedding, and fill 7,769 food orders for 1,454 Albany families.[34]

Despite its increased relief activities, meeting the temporal needs of the poor remained a secondary objective for the ACTMS. The society stood fast to its founding purpose, ministering to the unchurched.[35] Nor did its intensified missionary activities indicate a fundamental shift in its principles. In August 1858, when churches in Albany were traditionally closed for the month, Dyer gave a series of five lectures on personal religion, the first of which was entitled "The Influence of Personal Religion in Leading to Decision and Independence of Character."[36] Dyer assured the "friends of the poor" that the society denied many applicants for aid "because it was ascertained they were either intemperate, vicious, pauperized in spirit, practiced beggars . . . or individuals who gave no hope of improvement, and were likely to be permanently dependent."[37] Clearly the individual was held responsible for his own spiritual and temporal condition. Still, the ACTMS believed that its more extended operations had been "healthful [because] adapted to the wants and interests of the community."[38] In summing up his first decade as superintendent of the society, Dyer observed that the ACTMS had labored "to correct the very springs of society; to make that which is impure, holy; that which is disorderly and baneful, peaceful and beneficient, . . . and to promote on earth the kingdom of heaven."[39] Ministering to the material needs of the poor advanced the ACTMS's spiritual mission of creating a moral order in Albany. By reaching out to bring all members of the community under religious influence, the society helped assure social harmony.[40]

The socially tense 1870s strained the ACTMS's optimism and made the society more conscious of its welfare role. Reflecting on the 1877 railroad strike, the Reverend Charles Reynolds, a subsequent superintendent of the ACTMS, stated, "The fact is we are resting upon slumbering volcanoes of corruption and crime ready to break out at any time in riot and plunder." Reynolds contended that the only way to avoid such danger was through "education and evangelization," processes that were based on "fast removing the discomfort and privations surrounding these people." Relief could no longer be administered as a specific response to a temporary need but had to be part of an ongoing process that made "the masses" aware "of a better social life than they have known before."[41] The ACTMS proposed to facilitate this process through a new mission. In May 1874 the society's managers decided to concentrate its efforts in only one district rather than continue to serve the entire city. The area south of the Capitol, in which many of the city's poorest (and Catholic) citizens lived, seemed to issue the loudest "call," and the ACTMS began construction of its new mission building there.[42]

In December 1877, *Our Work at Home*, the official newspaper of the ACTMS, heralded the opening of "A GRAND CHARITY"—the society's new mission building. The facility had three stories. The basement housed a dining room (soon called the temperance coffee room), clothes washing and drying rooms, and bathing rooms. Above the basement, the "audience room story" comprised a large room with galleries that could seat some eight hundred to nine hundred people. The third story held the mission's educational facilities—its reading room/library and sewing room/workroom, the former apparently intended for men, the latter for women.[43] The building's facade, the ACTMS managers proudly announced, resembled a bank rather than a church, and, as such, it embodied the mission's purpose as "*a business house for God's work in saving men.*"[44]

The key responsibility of the new facility was to teach the poor to abide by middle-class standards of behavior.[45] "The work of the mission," its managers emphasized, was "to educate to better things" the community it served. Each service available in the mission had a morally and socially didactic purpose. The temperance coffee room, one of the most publicized of the mission's enterprises, offered "a workingman's meal"—a bowl of stew, a large cup of coffee, and two slices of bread—for just six cents.[46] But the coffee room was envisioned as more than just a place where workers might get an inexpensive meal. "The coffee room is intended not only to feed so many people," the ACTMS stated, "but to serve as a factor in the culture of those who attend."[47] By "culture" the society's managers meant the mission's inherent uplifting function, its intended salutary influence over personal habits and behavior, over "domestic life" as Tocqueville called it.[48]

Of course, the mission's founders considered temperance to be absolutely essential to reforming domestic life. The society charged so little for the "workingman's meal" in order to place it "within the means of even the poorest" and so induce them to begin each day with good food rather than with just a slice of dry bread and a glass of beer.[49] "Drink and bad expenditures of wages stripped many a home even of its necessities," *Our Work at Home* pointed out.[50] Two years after the "model" coffee room opened, the ACTMS congratulated itself on its achievement as a "practical gospel." The society claimed that workers either ate in the coffee room or ordered their dinners sent out from it. The same ten cents that brought the laborer "two glasses of hard liquor and sent the drinker home to abuse his family" provided him instead with a very "comfortable meal." The coffee room's success proved that workers had learned to calculate which kind of expenditure was the more worthwhile.[51]

The ACTMS intended the services it offered at the mission to strike at the root causes of contemporary social ills. According to Reynolds, the facility would accomplish its reform goal by surrounding the individual and the family with proper moral influences. The society provided the washing and drying rooms and bathing rooms not merely as charity but as means "to help into a better morality and surround with better physical and moral circumstances all who come in contact and whom we can reach."[52] The goal of moral uplift also led the ACTMS to organize the City Mission Social Society in 1879. Readings, singing, essays, debates, and addresses made up the social society's program. Dues were set low, at two cents each week. Bringing together "the families of our mechanics, laborers etc. . . . at least once a week for a literary treat and a pleasant entertainment" cultivated their self-respect and made "a man feel that although he is a workingman, he can at the same time be a gentleman."[53] The ACTMS expected the social society to "wean" the worker from pubs and other low entertainments, thereby insuring that his subsequent life would "be under mental and moral training."[54] As a voluntary agency, the mission endeavored to fulfill its ultimate reform goals by inculcating self-respect and self-control in those it reached rather than by relying on the coercive powers of government.

The lesson of self-help lay behind the nominal fee the society charged for each service the mission offered. The ACTMS wanted to avoid the mission's becoming an almshouse, "It will not be permitted as a lounging place for idlers."[55] The idea of work was the "truest charity" the mission could teach. Alms conferred no "permanent benefit," because without their appreciating the importance of work, "chronic mendicants" could not be reformed.[56] The ACTMS board believed that "so long as people can be supported for nothing, so long pauperism will be encouraged and will increase. . . . [The] best charity to our own people is to give help in such a way that they will be encouraged to help themselves."[57] Only when the poor internalized the lessons that the mission taught could the ACTMS feel sure that its reform goals had been achieved.

From its inception the ACTMS relied on religious and lay leaders in Albany acting as moral stewards. The society reminded the city's men of means that they would be judged "for their stewardship," that is, on what they had done for the poor.[58] The "man of means" who dined at the temperance coffee room would demonstrate that the room was hardly intended to be a "cheap soup house" charity. Of course, the ACTMS also depended on the largesse of wealthy Albanians to fund the mission and the other good works of the society. For those who contributed fifty dollars or more to it, the society created a category of giving called "directors for life." These generous sustainers of the society included Erastus Corning, the city's leading banker, merchant, and political figure; Thomas W. Olcott, president of the Mechanics and Farmers Bank; and Robert H. Wells, a prominent attorney; as well as a large number of persons active in commerce. In the 1870s members of Albany's middle class figured prominently among the society's presidents and managers and subscribers to the new mission. By sustaining the ACTMS from the beginning, the middle-class Protestant establishment in Albany fulfilled its self-defined role as moral steward.[59]

In opening the new mission the ACTMS was putting a new face on what had always been its traditional role, to be a moral guide inspiring each individual to assume responsibility for his personal salvation. The ACTMS reiterated that the main purpose of the mission's services was to make the society better able to improve "the spiritual condition of those who are willing to be benefitted by them. The more of Christ we can teach, and the closer humanity can be induced to follow Him, the greater will be the success of this mission."[60] The ACTMS was just one of the benevolent associations through which the city's Protestant elite endeavored to develop new supports for a community order that they regarded as normal.[61] The same social and moral aspirations that motivated the founders of the penitentiary or the Odd Fellows led the ACTMS to build its new mission.

The poor that the Protestant establishment in Albany wanted to reach were mostly the city's Catholic immigrants. Yet beginning with the opening of St. Mary's Church in 1798, the Catholic Church created numerous institutions and voluntary associations intended to protect religious traditions as well as to meet real needs. These institutions and associations would help to establish a Catholic presence in Albany. But even as the Catholic Church resisted Protestant evangelism, it was adapting to rather than challenging the prevailing community moral and social standards.

Most Catholic migrants to Albany found themselves welcome. Early histories of the city refer to the Jesuit Father Isaac Jogues, who, in 1643, had apparently found refuge in Albany after being forced to flee Mohawk Indians unsympathetic to his missionary endeavors. However, not until the 1790s was Albany's Catholic population large enough to support a permanent church in place of weekly meetings at each others' homes. Leading Catholics in the city organized a board of trustees and incorporated "The Roman Catholic Church in the City of Albany." Constructed on land donated by the city, St. Mary's was completed with the aid of contributions from many prominent local Protestants. Small, only fifty feet square, St. Mary's nevertheless stood as the only Catholic church between New York City and Detroit in the 1790s.[62]

St. Mary's congregation grew slowly over the next twenty years, reaching over three hundred members by 1820.[63] Initially, the church seems to have had problems retaining a priest for more than a year or two at a time. But in the 1820s the canal boom doubled Albany's population, drawing many Catholics to the city. In 1828 St. Mary's began its first Sunday school, staffed by Sisters of Charity from Emmitsburg, Maryland. The following year Albany's prominent Catholic families (including the Cassidys, Caggers, Goughs, and Mahers), many of whom had helped found St. Mary's, oversaw the construction of a larger and more handsome church. Over the next fifteen years the Diocese of New York added two parishes in Albany, St. John's in 1837 and St. Joseph's in 1843, to minister to the city's burgeoning Catholic populaton.[64]

The growth of Catholicism in Albany had taken place under the direction of lay leadership. The influence of lay trustees over church affairs in Albany (and Troy) inevitably led to conflict with the Church hierarchy based in New York City. Rumor had it that St. Mary's lay trustees had used Masonic ritual, a practice completely contrary to Catholic doctrine, during the consecration of the new church building in 1829. In 1844, during one typical dispute involving St. Mary's, Archbishop John Hughes declared that sooner or later "the trustee system as it has existed, will destroy or will be destroyed by the Catholic religion."[65] At Hughes's behest in 1847 Pope Pius IX created two dioceses in upstate New York, Albany and Buffalo. Hughes chose Brooklyn-born Father John McCloskey, his coadjutor in New York, to be the first bishop of the Diocese of Albany. Under Bishop McCloskey the trustee system ended, as he firmly established hierarchical control in his new diocese.[66]

Bishop McCloskey transformed the Roman Catholic Church in Albany into a potent medium for nurturing and promoting its communicants' prestige in the city. At its inception the Diocese of Albany embraced twenty-five churches and thirty-four priests, two orphan asylums (in Albany and Utica), and two free schools (in Utica and East Troy). During Bishop McCloskey's seventeen years as archbishop, the Albany diocese added over one hundred fifty churches, chapels, and missions, and sixty-one priests. By 1864 it served 134,500 communicants.[67] Within the city of Albany the diocese erected two new churches, in 1851 the Church of the Holy Cross, which ministered mainly to French and German Catholics, and in 1858 St. Patrick's Church.[68] But the most important new Catholic building in Albany was the Cathedral of the Immaculate Conception, which McCloskey built as his procathedral. An impressive Gothic structure, the cathedral, completed in 1852, seated 2,500 persons, and, in the words of one historian, towered "over the South End as a symbol of Irish Catholic power."[69]

McCloskey's institutionalization of a Catholic presence in Albany rested less on construction of new houses of worship than on making the

Church the center of an impressive social welfare services network that catered especially to Catholic newcomers and needy. He helped raise funds for Irish immigrants fleeing the Potato Famine in Ireland and, mediating between the immigrants, travel agents, and city authorities, arranged for their arrival and settlement in Albany. The diocese's most substantial relief efforts, however, involved the Society of St. Vincent de Paul, founded in Albany during the winter of 1847–48. Like their counterparts in the Protestant ACTMS, members of the St. Vincent de Paul society's relief committee visited the homes of the worthy Catholic poor in Albany and distributed aid (either provisions or relief tickets redeemable through the city's grocers) to them. Three members of the society's relief committee also taught catechism at the Albany Alms House.[70] Official historians of Albany calculate that by 1886 the Society of St. Vincent de Paul had distributed roughly $100,000 in cash as well as vast quantities of provisions and clothing. Also, visitors for the society had made some twelve thousand five hundred visits to families totaling about forty thousand members.[71] By the 1870s, with the founding both of St. Peter's Hospital and St. Agnes Cemetery (located next to the Protestant Albany Rural Cemetery), Catholic benevolent agencies in Albany could provide the same cradle-to-grave services that the Protestant community offered.[72]

His concern for preserving Catholic traditons and teachings as well as for alleviating actual distress had induced McCloskey to develop a Catholic benevolent empire. Catholic poor often found themselves the focus of efforts by the ACTMS and other Protestant voluntary agencies to build a Christian moral order in Albany. One incident, which occurred at the Albany Alms House in 1855, illustrates how religious conflict stimulated the development in the city of a Catholic alternative to the Protestant social service system.[73]

The "Alms House Affair" involved the education of poor orphans. By 1854 the Irish comprised about 60 percent of the poor cared for at the facility. Most of these Irish probably were Catholic. William Hurst, who had been appointed superintendent of the almshouse in spring 1854, roused Catholic fears when he declared that Catholic orphans were "*not* to be brought up as Catholics."[74] In January 1855 four Catholic lay teachers at the almshouse confiscated 150 nondenominational Sunday School Union picture books that the wife and daughters of Albany's Mayor William Parmelee had distributed the previous day. The city's nativist press condemned the confiscation of "non-sectarian stories and moral tales with pictures" as "inquisitorial."[75] This particular episode seems to have been quietly and informally resolved by Bishop McCloskey in a letter to Mayor Parmelee. Yet its lesson for Albany's Catholic hierarchy, and the lesson of similar incidents, was that the Church would have to rely on Catholic institutions such as St. John's Boys Orphan Asylum and St. Vincent's Female Orphan Asylum to preserve Catholic identity.[76]

Not surprisingly, in Albany as elsewhere, Catholic sensitivity about religious education focused on the public schools. The attempts by Archbishop Hughes during the 1850s to "de-Protestantize" New York State's public schools failed, predictably, over Catholic refusal to accept the nonsectarian Protestant version of the Bible. Consequently, Hughes decided to leave public schools in the state as a semi-Protestant domain and concentrate on building Catholic parochial schools.[77] McCloskey agreed with Hughes's strategy. He asserted that there was great need for Catholic schools because "in the public schools . . . every effort was made to destroy the faith of Catholic children."[78] For McCloskey, like Hughes, the preservation of Catholic identity required development of an alternative institution, namely, the parochial school system.

Although at least one Catholic school had opened in Albany before 1847, McCloskey laid the foundation for the parochial school system in the city. By 1855 Albany's Catholic schools enrolled about six hundred pupils. St. Mary's, St. Joseph's, and St. John's churches all opened parochial schools, followed by the Albany cathedral and the Church of the Holy Cross. McCloskey brought to Albany the Daughters of Charity, the Brothers of the Christian Schools, and members of other Catholic orders to teach in these schools.[79] What began under McCloskey's direction accelerated under his successors; by 1875 more than two thousand students attended the city's twelve parochial schools and two Catholic high schools.[80]

The Church in Albany did not make training in Catholic precepts exclusively the province of the parochial school system. Church-sponsored cultural and social societies also helped preserve a common Catholic heritage. Just as Protestant youth in Albany joined the YMCA, Catholic young men could, by the 1850s, become members of the city's Catholic Young Men's Institute.[81] Young Catholics also joined the Library Association and the Catholic Literary Society, which brought to Albany itinerant lecturers such as Orestes Brownson and James A. McMaster.[82] The Catholic Young Men's Lyceum, started in 1871 to promote social intercourse among Catholics and "their moral and intellectual improvement," maintained a library and reading rooms and sponsored lectures on such topics as "Indifferentism in Religion."[83] In addition, each parish in the Albany diocese had its own sodality, library association, or young men's association. According to the priest at St. Mary's Church church sodalities were a basic part of parish life: "The word of God must be preached in season and out of season, the faith must be instilled especially into the young, . . . and for this the monthly communion is most important."[84] Like their Protestant counterparts, Catholic voluntary associations defined Catholic education and identity.[85]

The effort by Catholics in Albany as elsewhere to preserve their religious identity by creating distinct associations and institutions led nativists to attack Roman Catholicism as alien to the American way of life. To win acceptance for Catholics in the United States, the Church hierarchy sought to prove the opposite. For example, Archbishop Hughes defended parochial education as patriotic. He called on "everyone who has the interest of the country at heart" to recognize that Catholic schools "are among the strongest bulwarks of the country and the best safeguards of the social order."[86] When the Albany cathedral opened its parochial school in 1861, McCloskey summed up his views on the importance of religious education: "Education is not education if it is to be completely divested of its main element, religion. . . . The educated man without religion is more dangerous to society than the uneducated with religion."[87] McCloskey's sentiments easily could have been expressed by a supporter of public education. Like Hughes, McCloskey agreed with his Protestant "adversaries" that the importance of religious education lay in maintaining moral order.[88]

After McCloskey left Albany in 1864, Clarence A. Walworth, the priest at St. Mary's Church from 1866 until his death in 1900, became the leading exponent of the prevailing moral and social concepts for Catholics in Albany. Born in 1820 in Plattsburgh, New York, to a family prominent in New York State affairs, Walworth had been raised as a Presbyterian. His classmates at the Albany Academy included Pruyns, Townsends, and Van Rensselaers, sons of families that were the pillars of Albany's Protestant establishment. After a brief career in law, Walworth turned to religion. He was ordained an Episcopal minister in 1843. Two years later he converted to Catholicism.[89]

Like the Protestant managers of the ACTMS, Walworth and other prominent Albany Catholics linked poverty with intemperance, whose solution lay in teaching self-restraint. Walworth, a founder of the Total Abstinence Guild in Albany, numbered temperance among the "cardinal virtues," along with justice, fortitude, and prudence.[90] He administered the pledge to parishioners and, as did most temperance reformers in Albany, put his faith in individual restraint rather than state-imposed prohibition. It was a mistake to look to civil law to do all the work, Walworth contended, for only by working together could the forces of morality and religion lead the individual to true reform.[91]

Walworth preached the Catholic hierarchy's faith in the prevailing free labor ideology. He fervantly believed that the sanctity of private property underlay all "civilized society." Echoing sentiments expressed almost a quarter century earlier by Abraham Lincoln, Walworth insisted that the "rights of labor" meant the opportunity of a man to acquire property by his labor, to use it freely, and to transmit it to his children. "A man works in the hopes of earning something," Walworth stated, and "that something when earned becomes his property." Since the opportunity to own property made each worker a potential capitalist, the interests of labor and capital were necessarily in harmony: "What is the employer, then, if not the laboring man reaping at last the fruits of his industry, the reward of honest labor?" Walworth labelled the socialist, indeed any person who might try "to limit the honest ambition of industry," the laboring man's "natural mortal enemy."[92] Like Walworth, most Catholic leaders subscribed to the dominant American belief in the free labor system.

The prestige of Catholics in Albany after 1847 was due in no small measure to the direct, if informal, intervention of the local Church hierarchy on behalf of its communicants. In negotiating with Albany's civic leaders, as McCloskey had in the almshouse affair, the Church hierarchy functioned as a broker on behalf of the city's Catholics. While acting to preserve religious traditions and identity, Catholic leadership in Albany also paved the way for Catholics to participate in the larger community.[93] As one index of the development of Catholic respectability in Albany, in 1864 thirty-five prominent Protestants invited McCloskey, as he prepared to leave Albany, to a dinner honoring his episcopal labors, "the reflected light of which we see in the elevated conditon of your people."[94] By the 1870s municipal authorities allowed Catholic priests to regularly visit the Albany Alms House, and a Catholic priest, Father Noethen of the Church of the Holy Cross, became a chaplain at the Albany Penitentiary.[95] In securing these concessions, the Catholic hierarchy was assisted by leaders of the Irish business and middle class in Albany, who, in addition to aiding their Church, served their ethnic community by organizing numerous Irish voluntary benevolent associations. The large Irish Catholic population in Albany found itself guided by both a religious and a business elite committed to the dominant community values.

As already noted, most Catholics in Albany were Irish. The city's lay Catholic elite, which had founded St. Mary's Church and been its trustees prior to Bishop McCloskey's arrival, also helped to organize Albany's many Irish voluntary associations. These ethnic associations functioned like their religious counterparts, aiding immigrants' adjustment to their new community while preserving their Irish identity. The ethnic leadership, like the Catholic hierarchy, acted as mediators within the larger community. Through their control of ethnic voluntary associations an Irish elite encouraged accommodation to the city's social structure.[96]

The lives of two early Irish immigrants to Albany, James Maher and John Cassidy, are archetypical of the role played by the Irish elite during the nineteenth century. Maher and Cassidy were both born in Ireland and emigrated with their families to Albany in the 1790s. Self-made men, Maher made his fortune in the wholesale and retail grocery business, Cassidy as a meat and cattle dealer. Together the two men organized and served as officers of the Republican Green Rifles, an Irish company that fought in the War of 1812. Maher and Cassidy also helped found the Association of Friends of Ireland, an Irish nationalist group, and the St. Patrick's Society, a benevolent association incorporated for the purpose of aiding Irish immigrants. Both men were active in Catholic affairs, and by the 1820s each was a trustee of St. Mary's Church. The pattern of group leadership exemplified by Maher and Cassidy combined economic success with nationalist, benevolent, and religious activities in their ethnic community.[97]

Equally important, Maher and Cassidy had successful careers as politicians in Albany. A hero after his military exploits as captain of the Green Rifles, Maher served as a ward leader for the Albany Regency and then was rewarded with patronage posts as clerk of the market and state librarian. Similarly, Cassidy held appointive jobs under the Democratic-Republican party. In 1820 each man won election as an assistant alderman and the following year as alderman from his ward. In 1829, an election year marked by nativist sentiments throughout New York State and by charges of an increase in "popery in Albany," the Democrats nominated Maher for sheriff of Albany County. Although he lost that election, both he and Cassidy had gained places of influence for themselves and opened the way for other Irish-Americans to enter the inner councils of political power in Albany.[98]

John Cassidy died in 1829. According to the *Argus*, his funeral, attended by New York's governor, Albany city officers, and 300 Masons, as well as by many members of the city's ethnic associations, was the largest in Albany since that held for Governor DeWitt Clinton.[99] But the model provided by Cassidy lived on. In 1833, James Maher and other members of Albany's Irish elite organized a new relief agency, the Hibernian Provident Society (HPS). Although workingmen joined the Hibernian Society, generally businessmen or other middle-class Irish composed its leadership and provided the financial backing for its benevolent activities. In addition to offering temporary aid to sick or incapacitated members, the HPS also looked to enhance Irish prestige within Albany. The society dedicated itself to bringing before the American people the "republican features" of Irish character "and of procuring for themselves, in proper time, the privileges of all American citizens."[100] HPS efforts to bolster the repute of Irish-Americans included sponsoring an annual St. Patrick's Day dinner. Prominent Albanians often attended and would join Hibernians in toasting the "perfect tact and . . . beautiful harmony" that should always exist "amongst the American born and adopted citizens."[101] By celebrating Albany's pluralism in this way, these ethnic leaders indicated their acquiesence to those values dominant in the larger community.

James Maher and John Cassidy exemplify the success achieved by some of Albany's early Irish-American immigrants. These respectable Irish-American leaders gained a foothold in the local community. Cassidy's two sons, William and DeWitt Clinton, capitalized on their advantages and became full-fledged members of Albany's social and political elite. Both Cassidy boys attended the exclusive Albany Academy along with the sons of Albany's Dutch and Yankee aristocracy. After graduation, William went to Union College in nearby Schenectady, where he studied law. He eventually turned to journalism as a profession and in 1843 became editor of the *Atlas*. The *Atlas* spoke for the "Barnburner" and "Free Soil" factions of the Democratic party that, in the 1840s and 1850s, challenged the conservative "Hunker" wing of the party. Ambition more than ideological differences appears to have fueled an ongoing feud between Cassidy's *Atlas* and its rival the *Argus*, which spoke for established Democratic interests. In 1856 New York Democrats faced challenges from both a growing Know-Nothing movement and the newly organized Republican party. As a consequence, New York's Democratic governor, Horatio Seymour, intervened to end the Barnburner–Hunker feud. In Albany, he helped arrange the merger of the *Atlas* and the *Argus* under Cassidy's editorship in 1856, which cemented Democratic unity in the city. Cassidy served as editor of the *Argus* until his death in 1873. Under Cassidy, the *Argus* continued as the voice of the conservative wing of the Democratic party and, in addition, established itself as the journal of respectable Irish Catholic opinion in Albany.[102]

Nativism in Albany during the 1850s also pushed DeWitt Clinton Cassidy, William's brother, into the public spotlight. More than just a partisan political issue, nativism affected all community institutions. In 1855 the editor of a local nativist newspaper ran for president of the Young Men's Association for Mutual Improvement (YMA). The city's Yankee and Dutch elite dominated the YMA, a secular society that maintained a library, ran debates, and held lectures in order to promote moral and intellectual improvement in Albany. A number of Irish were also members of the YMA, including both Cassidy brothers.[103] In what the *Albany Evening Journal* called "a merited rebuke," the nativist candidate lost the election. The YMA then chose DeWitt Clinton Cassidy to be the association's orator at Albany's Fourth of July celebration.[104] In the spirit of pluralism and accommodation endorsed by his forebears in Albany, Cassidy praised New York State's "cosmopolitan character," that tendency not only to be hospitable to differences "of language, of birth, of religion" but also to recognize Americans' "common allegiance."[105] Two years later Cassidy won the YMA's presidency. As one study of the Irish in Albany concludes, his victory was probably as much a victory for Irish political power as for the city's pluralist tradition.[106]

By midcentury the Cassidys and Mahers along with other respectable middle-class Irish-American families in Albany constituted a local ethnic elite. But this entrenched elite would be challenged by more recent enterprising immigrants, most notably Terence Quinn and Michael N. Nolan. Ambitious on their own behalf, these "Young Turks" nevertheless affirmed the social values endorsed by earlier ethnic leaders. Through the 1860s and 1870s, even as the city's working-class and poor Irish joined radical nationalist and labor movements, the middle-class Irish elite in Albany was able to maintain its authority.

The Fenian Brotherhood, a secret society begun in Ireland, first appeared in the United States in 1857. Operating on both sides of the Atlantic, Fenians sought the independence of Ireland through armed force. The Irish-American community in Albany warmly supported the cause of Irish nationalism. Working through agencies such as the Association of Friends of Ireland they sought to improve conditions in their native land. These secular associations often received Church support for their cause. For example, in 1847, just after the formation of the Albany diocese, three of the city's Catholic churches spearheaded a drive that raised over $5,000 for Ireland's aid.[107] However, Albany's entrenched Irish Catholic leadership, although sympathetic to respectable Irish aid societies, rejected Fenian revolutionary republicanism.[108]

Fenianism served as an important social link as well as political force in Albany's Irish community. Fenians formed local lodges known as circles. In Albany during the 1860s and early 1870s Fenian circles frequently held lectures and sponsored balls, picnics, and other social gatherings. The *Argus* reported that some fifteen hundred persons, including many state legislators, attended a Fenian ball in January 1866.[109] A picnic in July 1867, which featured a "sham battle" between Troy and

Albany Fenians, was called the largest meeting of Irish people in the region ever held.[110] The Fenian Brotherhood appears to have been a popular ethnic society in Albany, attracting Irish-Americans from all classes.

The Fenian Brotherhood in the United States is best known for its abortive "invasion" of Canada in an effort to force Great Britain to free Ireland. In June 1866 a division of the Roberts Circle, a Fenian group from New York City, reached Albany en route to Canada. The city's Irish Catholic elite immediately spoke out against the intended invasion. Bishop McCloskey branded it "mischief" that could "incite perhaps the anger and distrust of the American people against us."[111] William Cassidy, in an *Argus* editorial, expressed his dismay at the "warlike" Fenian demonstrations and called it incredible that "a considerable body of men could be induced to engaging on an expedition that will only lead to mischief and the most deplorable results."[112] An older, more conservative Irish elite obviously resisted any movement that might undermine Irish Catholic respectability in Albany.

Ignoring such warnings, Albany's Irish Catholics enthusiastically rallied to the Fenian cause.[113] At a large public meeting held at City Hall on April 17, 1866, reportedly some four hundred men enlisted in the Fenian army, and several persons donated arms and ammunition. On June 7 a company from Albany estimated at one hundred fifty men departed for Canada under Brigadier General James Heffernan and Colonel Terence Quinn.[114] As self-made businessmen, Heffernan and Quinn were indistinguishable from Albany's existing Irish elite. Yet in openly championing the Fenian cause, they proved more responsive to the emotional appeal that the Brotherhood had among Albany's Irish Catholics.[115]

Although Albany's Irish elite remained skeptical, the popularity of Fenianism eventually prodded them to reconsider their opposition. At a mass rally for Fenians organized by Quinn in May 1870, "many of our most prominent citizens," the *Argus* reported, addressed the crowd and donated money to the Irish nationalist cause. Modifying his opposition to Fenianism, Cassidy now referred in the *Argus* to the "strong patriotism and love of fatherland" among those willing to "buckle on the armor and meet death or an English prison."[116] By the 1870s Fenianism had become good politics in Albany.

Albany's Republicans as well as Democrats tried to capitalize on the obvious appeal of Fenian leaders in the Irish-American community. Yet the Democratic party proved to be the party more open to rising young Irish-American figures. Quinn, who was a graduate of the Albany Academy and owner of a large brewery in Albany, watched his political star soar. A Democratic alderman in 1862, Quinn eventually became, in

1876, Albany's first Irish Catholic congressman.[117] Nor was he the sole beneficiary of the Democrats' manipulation of ethnic politics. By the 1870s the Irish political establishment in Albany included the superintendent of the almshouse as well as the chiefs and much of the personnel of the city's police and fire departments.[118]

Whereas the major political parties might have been open to enterprising individuals, working-class Irish found neither party sufficiently sensitive to their social and political aspirations. In the 1860s and 1870s both Democrats and Republicans paid little more than lip service to the reforms that workers were trying to secure through the state legislature. Indeed, both parties had openly opposed an eight-hour law. Thus despite the rewards the Democratic machine in Albany may have bestowed on individual Irish-Americans, by the mid-1870s working-class Irish believed that an independent labor party was required in order to satisfy their basic grievances. John Perry's contract in 1877 to manufacture stoves at Sing Sing prison would make prison contract labor the fundamental issue of Albany workers' political movement. On the evening of March 20, 1878, Irish workers gathered along with Yankee, German, and other Albany workers at Ames Hall to nominate Nelson H. Chase for mayor of Albany and an entire Independent Labor Democratic ticket. As they had in the 1860s, Albany's workers made class a political issue in the 1878 mayoral election.[119]

Confirmation that class lines were being drawn came quickly. On March 21, some two hundred "citizens" who wanted "honest and economical administration" met at the Albany Board of Trade and nominated William A. Young, a lawyer, as their nonpartisan candidate for mayor. The platform of the Citizens' party defined the purpose of municipal government as insuring public safety and the protection of property and fostering the business interests of the city. During the campaign, the *Albany Evening Journal* urged all Republicans to support Citizens' party nominees. With obvious satisfaction, the *Evening Journal* reported that prominent businessmen attended the party's ward meetings determined "to make their influence felt in the selection of candidates."[120] Although the Citizens' party took no public stand on the prison contract labor issue, in choosing Young, who was an inspector of the Albany Penitentiary, the party was nominating a symbol of that system.[121]

The Democratic party seized the opportunity presented by the opposing labor and business nominees and chose Michael N. Nolan as its mayoral candidate. During the campaign Nolan, an Irish Catholic, the son-in-law and partner of Terence Quinn, was hailed by the Democrats as a successful businessman. Not two weeks before his nomination, the

Argus had done a long feature on the Beverwyck brewery owned by Quinn and Nolan, giving a glowing description of its facilities and celebrating the enterprise and prudence of both owners.[122] By nominating Nolan, the Democratic party obviously hoped to attract widespread support in Albany's Irish Catholic community. But Nolan and the Democrats also recognized that class had become an issue in this election. In a note accepting his party's nomination, Nolan termed prison contract labor "vicious and outrageous" and called for its abolition.[123] Although the party as a whole seems not to have adopted a plank against such practices, virtually every Democratic ward passed resolutions condemning the system. The Fifteenth Ward, for example, declared that prison contract labor was "demoralizing in its effect on honest labor" and the cause of the present "distressed condition of the working classes." The ward meeting called on the Democratic party to achieve the necessary reform.[124] By nominating Nolan, an Irish Catholic, and by seizing the political initiative on the prison contract labor issue, Albany's Democratic party consciously appealed to both the cultural and class loyalties of Irish workers.

Results of the 1878 election indicate that the Democrats had been wise to try to neutralize the appeal of the workers' independent movement. Although Nolan won by a wide margin over his two opponents, Chase, the candidate of the workers' Independent Labor Democratic party, received over eight hundred more votes than the businessmen's Citizens' nominee, Young (Nolan 47.3%, Chase 28.5%, Young 24.1%).[125] The *Albany Evening Journal* claimed that the strong third-party vote had cut deep into Republican ranks. Given the workers' showing despite "desperate" Democratic efforts to forestall it, the newspaper wondered if the election did not hold a portent for both parties.[126] Yet Albany's Democrats had already demonstrated that they understood how to respond to the labor party.

One speaker at a victory celebration outside Nolan's home exulted that the election had proven "that among Democrats it matters not what is a man's nationality, religion or occupation."[127] This was, of course, just the lesson Albany Democrats intended the election to have. As a successful businessman with obvious appeal among the city's Irish Catholic voters, Nolan was typical of earlier Irish leaders in Albany. Still, there were special conditions surrounding the 1878 election. The formation of the Independent Labor Democratic party forced Albany's Democrats to respond to the prison contract labor issue. In this context Nolan represents a new kind of authority figure in the ethnic community, a leader meant to hold the line against a powerful labor movement.[128] Irish-Americans could and did support the independent political alternative offered by and for workers. But Nolan's appeal to the same community undercut the workers' bid for independent power. Nolan's election in 1878 was a victory for accommodation over class consciousness.

Electoral politics was but one mechanism that mitigated class conflict in nineteenth-century communities like Albany. An array of moral and welfare associations and institutions also evolved that functioned as transmitters of the dominant free labor culture. Protestant societies, such as the ACTMS, sought to guide behavior by socializing all members of the community to their mutual social and moral responsibilities. And, even though Albany's Irish Catholics resisted this assimilation and retained their ethnic and religious character, under their own Church and middle-class leaders they did in fact adapt to these community norms.

The cultural and community bonds forged in Albany by benevolent, nationalist, and social voluntary associations, as well as through politics, promoted wide accommodation to, rather than alienation from, the existing economic and social order. But Albany's mayoral election in 1878 did not signify an end to class conflict, or, for that matter, a resolution of the prison contract labor dispute. The prison labor issue would continue to dominate local and then state politics for at least another six years. Although workers would be able finally to win an end to prison contract labor in New York State, how they secured this victory demonstrates the continuing dialectic between class and community consciousness.

Part III

8

The Anti–Prison Contract Labor Movement: A Study in Albany Workers' Evolving Consciousness

John S. Perry's 1877 contract to mold stoves at New York's Sing Sing prison aroused workers' long-standing resentment against prison labor. From the beginning of the state's prison system, penal authorities required convicts to labor. They preferred the contract system because it made the prison self-supporting and advanced inmate reformation by inculcating proper work habits. Throughout the nineteenth century, until an amendment to the state constitution in 1894 abolished prison contract labor, workers continually denounced the system as unfair competition and an affront to their dignity as free laborers.[1] The effort by Albany workers and others to abolish prison contract labor after 1877 was therefore merely the final phase of a seventy-five-year-long protest movement.

Of course the abolition of contract labor was neither the only nor the most important reform that Albany workers pursued in the nineteenth century. Still, the convict labor system provided a constant irritant, and the movement to end it flared up repeatedly, albeit in different contexts. In the Jacksonian era, the 1830s and 1840s, workers opposed contract labor as part of a general protest against economic privilege and monopoly concentration. Workers then invoked the cause of "Equal Rights" as they sought numerous reforms, including free public education and an end to imprisonment for debt, designed to keep open the avenues for social mobility. As workers became more convinced that industrialization posed a threat to their position in society, a growing sense of class antagonism animated their activities against contract labor. By the 1860s the contract system seemed to workers to be further evidence of capital's innate antipathy to labor and of the need, therefore, to fundamentally change the existing free labor order. Workers espoused cooperative production and the eight-hour workday in hopes of establishing a cooperative commonwealth. Through the nineteenth century, and especially after 1877, the dynamic character of the anti–prison labor movement aptly expresses workers' evolving world view.

The anti–prison labor movement in Albany intensified after 1877, as the city's workers engaged in what they understood to be "class politics." In 1878 and again in 1882 they forged a labor party to elect officials to local and state government. But these attempts to exert independent political power met with only limited success, in part because one of the existing political parties, the Democrats, appeared to incorporate the workers' objections to contract labor into its own political agenda. Having failed to sustain class politics, labor leaders in Albany responded by shifting gears. They began to define prison contract labor as one of a number of specific grievances that could be resolved through an appeal to the major parties rather than through an independent political movement. A pattern of interest-group politics evolved as the city's labor leaders pursued limited reforms that did not require fundamental changes in the social order. In keeping with their accommodation to the existing system, Albany's labor leaders invoked the free labor idea of a community of interests. Workers' struggle against prison contract labor chronicles the changes in the consciousness of Albany workers during the later nineteenth century.

The opening of the state prison at Auburn in 1817 marked the real beginning of penal reform in New York. Under the "Auburn system," the model for many later prisons, inmates spent their days working together in silence; at night they returned to their cells. The labor that convicts performed largely depended on the contracts that prison authorities negotiated with private entrepreneurs. During the 1820s prisoners at Auburn worked at coopering, tailoring, shoemaking, weaving, toolmaking, and rifle making; Sing Sing prisoners worked mostly at stonecutting. The 1830s saw the introduction of chain and lock making and of the production of silk hats.[2]

In the early years of the prison system in New York public officials consciously avoided direct competition between convict and free labor. At the same time, in order not to overburden the state's taxpayers, they insisted that prisons be self-sustaining. As a result of rising protests among New York workers against prison labor, the legislature, in 1833, appointed a committee to visit Auburn prison. The committee reported that in some cases the mechanics' complaints were well founded. Nevertheless, it recommended that no changes be made that would threaten the financial benefits that contract labor brought to the state.[3] Unable to prod New York officials into action against the system, workers from across the state gathered in Utica in August 1834 for an anti-prison labor convention. The ninety-nine delegates, including eleven from Albany County, voted to establish a permanent central committee (with headquarters in Utica) and local county associations to carry on the campaign against prison labor. The convention resolved that workers mount a petition drive against the system. Led by their newly formed state and county associations, New York workers besieged the legislature with petitions containing some twenty thousand signatures overall.[4]

Responding to the latest worker protest, the legislative session of 1834 created another commission to study prison labor. This commission included a labor representative, Ely Moore, president of both the National Trades' Union and the General Trades' Union of New York City. Yet its conclusions, published in January 1835, did not differ much from those of the earlier committee. Still, the commissioners did recommend limiting the number of convicts working in any one trade, restricting the items produced to those now supplied by imports, and only letting contracts to the highest bidder after due public notice. In May 1835 the legislature incorporated these recommendations into law.[5]

New York workers attacked the 1835 commissioners' report as "weak" and "shuffling." Nevertheless, after the legislature acted, the anti-prison labor movement faded. For the next several years, as the nation suffered from the effects of the Panic of 1837, the labor movement in general fell on hard times. Under these circumstances, workers could not counter the wholesale evasion of even the partial reforms enacted in 1835. But as economic conditions improved in the early 1840s, workers mounted a new assault on the convict labor system. Again New York's legislature responded by forming a committee to investigate prison labor. However, this committee's report focused more on evidence of corruption and lax discipline in the state's prisons than on the grievances of the workers. The legislature, reluctant to endanger profits from convict labor, did little even to halt the corruption that the committee uncovered. After nearly ten years, the anti-prison labor movement had won only minimal legislative concessions.[6]

Jacksonian workers regarded any monopoly as theft, degrading of their labor and robbing them of their just reward. Prison labor qualified as a monopoly in their view because the state was granting contractors an exclusive privilege that gave them an unfair advantage.[7] Reviling the "hordes of state prison contractors" who created a "*hydra of iniquity*," the workers intended to secure their just rights as citizens.[8] The primary objective of all "just government and righteous laws," the delegates to the 1834 Utica convention proclaimed, was to protect "virtuous citizens" in their lawful occupations, and to punish vice. Because New York State's prison system had the opposite effect, convict labor represented nothing less than the "war of the State upon the property and the rights of the honest and industrious mechanics."[9] The convention called on workers "as men, as citizens, and as mechanics, to assert, demand, and maintain your rights." Workers should "arise" by using the ballot box and supporting only those candidates ready to end the convict labor system.[10] In 1843, at a prison labor protest rally in Albany, "mechanics and citizens" affirmed their role as producers to whom society owed "its comforts, conveniences and improvements." Anything that tended to "cast reproach" on or to diminish the "just reward" of honest labor should not be tolerated, let alone "inflicted" on workers by legal enactment.[11] Jacksonian workers saw prison labor as part of a general trend toward greater economic privilege and the concentration of power in the hands of the few.

In 1864, Spuyten Duyvil, just north of New York City, became the center of renewed worker protest against prison contract labor. In an attempt to break the molders' union, I. G. Johnson, the town's leading iron foundry owner, arranged to have his stoves molded at Sing Sing. Johnson's action prompted the president of the Iron Moulders' International Union, William Sylvis, to lead molders in New York in a drive against convict labor. Early in 1865 the molders presented to the legislature six petitions demanding a law prohibiting prisoners from practicing trades in prison that they had not engaged in prior to commitment. Expressing support for the molders, the New York State Workingmen's Assembly, at its annual meeting in Albany, passed a resolution calling for an end, once and for all, to the competition free workers faced from convict labor. The state legislature, ignoring the workers' petitions, failed even to consider a bill introduced on the molders' behalf during the 1865 session.[12]

In fact, the legislation Sylvis and the molders sought would only have enforced the limitations on contract labor enacted thirty years before. When the legislators finally did act on the issue, during the 1866 session, they moved in the opposite direction. In 1866 New York State dropped all restrictions on prison labor and empowered state prison inspectors to employ convicts at whatever labor would be most financially advantageous. Once again the legislators made a self-supporting prison system the highest priority.[13]

The State Workingmen's Assembly, at its February 1867 meeting, condemned the legislators' backsliding on prison labor and demanded that the state instead exclude all mechanical pursuits from the prisons.[14] In March 1868, as part of a statewide protest movement, the Albany printers' and iron molders' unions organized a rally against the prison labor system. Modifying the Workingmen's Assembly's stand against all mechanical labor in the prisons, rally participants adopted resolutions demanding legislation to abolish the contract system and to exclude from the prisons those types of industry that would compete with outside labor.[15]

New York workers redoubled their protests against prison labor in 1868 when they learned of an arrangement between a New York City printing firm and the state's prison inspector, Henry Barnum, to teach about seventy convicts the printing trade. Printers and other workers throughout the state mobilized to have this contract abrogated and to prohibit its renewal. Reportedly, some two hundred thousand mechanics petitioned the legislature either directly or through their unions against this contract. In this instance, their appeals succeeded; the state legislature overruled Barnum and vacated the contract.[16]

New York workers' protest against prison labor in the 1860s echoed the antimonopoly sentiments of their Jacksonian forebears. Workers still spoke of the unjust competition facing honest laborers from a system that served "no interest but the contractors."[17] But in condemning prison contract labor in the 1860s workers began to express a sense of class more forcefully than they had before. According to the workingman's newspaper, *Fincher's Trades Review*, convict labor offered further proof of the inherent defects in the free labor system. Convict labor was just another weapon of "capitalists and employers" in their war on labor, evidence of "the unmeasurable depth of degradation to which capital would reduce labor." Prison contract labor was a "provocation" that must, *Fincher's* asserted, "awaken the deepest feelings of hostility."[18]

To workers in the 1860s more than the demise of the prison contract labor system was needed to restore the dignity of their labor. As an alternative to the bleak future they foresaw, workers turned in the 1860s to securing such reforms as producers' cooperatives and the eight-hour workday, as well as an end to prison contract labor. According to *Fincher's*, the "lesson" of prison labor was "the mercy we might expect should we fail to guard our rights with those potent weapons, cooperation and combination."[19] Labor leaders like Fincher and Sylvis believed that, allied to their efforts to ensure economic justice for themselves through cooperatives and the eight-hour workday reform, workers would have to join together in a labor party to gain their full rights. Political demogogues might speak in flattering terms of the dignity of labor, Sylvis explained, but only "*the men who work*," using their political power, could save labor from the degradation "which reckless legislation has fastened upon it."[20] More than the specific abuses contract labor inflicted on workers, the system symbolized the growing oppression of labor under the contemporary system. To end this oppression, workers had to act politically and economically, and they had to fundamentally reform the social order.

In the 1860s workers did act on Sylvis's mandate to exercise political power, when they lobbied state legislators on behalf of a broad reform program. Between 1869 and 1872 workers in New York, Massachusetts, and elsewhere capped these efforts by organizing independent political parties.[21] During the 1870 legislative session in New York, probably as a result of workers' political pressure, prison contract labor was once more the subject of intense debate. Indeed, the State Assembly even approved a bill that, in effect, would have abolished the system. But the State Senate, reluctant to endorse such drastic change, decided to form yet another commission to study the problem. During six weeks of hearings, the Senate commission heard testimony from 138 witnesses, including labor leaders and workingmen from across the state. Many of the witnesses, including those representing labor, blamed the convict labor system's failings on the contractors and suggested alternatives, including the public account system. The public account system gave control of prison labor to prison wardens rather than to contractors, whose only interest, reformers complained, was their private profit. Especially important to workers was the fact that under the public account system the goods produced could be used only in public institutions and could not be sold on the free market. At the conclusion of the hearings, the commissioners endorsed the public account system; the legislators, however, failed to take any action.[22]

Despite the obvious priority that the legislature gave to protecting convict labor's revenue-producing features, the state prison system was not self-supporting. In the mid-1870s a broad coalition of New Yorkers, including the state's governor, Samuel Tilden, pressed for reform. In 1876 the legislature once again appointed a commission to study ways to improve prison discipline and to better administer the institutions.[23] In February 1877, acting on a commission recommendation, the legislature created the post of state superintendent of prisons and appointed Louis Pilsbury as the first superintendent. Pilsbury was empowered to make whatever changes necessary so that prison labor would be "more remunerative to the state."[24]

Pilsbury quickly demonstrated that the legislature had chosen well. One of his first acts as superintendent was to reach an agreement with John S. Perry to employ Sing Sing convicts at molding stoves. The original five-year contract called for Perry to use 150 convicts, with an increase in that number "as circumstances warrant."[25] Apparently, both Pilsbury and Perry looked confidently to the future, because the foundry that was then constructed at Sing Sing could accommodate 300 molders plus 500 laborers working in subsidiary branches of the trade.[26] In fact, within two years about 80 percent of Sing Sing's 1,253 inmates were working for Perry.[27] Given the size of this contract, it is no wonder that prison contract labor again became a matter of considerable and immediate importance to New York State workers in general and to Albany workers in particular.

As they had so often in past labor struggles, Albany's iron molders spearheaded the movement to end prison contract labor. In 1877 their national union proposed a boycott of all Perry and other prison-made goods: "Shun the Argand and American [Perry stoves] as you would a viper."[28] One molder offered the following as "The Prayer of John S. Perry": "Good Lord deliver me from the meshes of the I.M.U.N.A. and shower your blessings on the Legislature of the State of New York, / And so enlighten them that they may plainly see that it is their duty to assist me in making my Sing Sing contract a success!"[29] In 1878 the city's molders and other workers organized the Independent Labor Democratic party and made contract labor a pivotal issue in that year's municipal elections.[30] Reacting to the challenge of the new party, every Democratic ward committee as well as the Democratic candidate for mayor denounced contract labor. The support Albany's Democrats offered workers on the contract labor issue helped carry their party to victory in 1878.

Despite the uproar Perry's contract at Sing Sing caused, Albany politicians initially focused their attention on convict labor at the Albany County Penitentiary. At a special meeting of the joint board of the prison held during the 1878 election campaign, Patrick Daly, the Democratic supervisor from the Fifteenth Ward, offered a resolution that a committee be selected to investigate the penitentiary's contracts in order to determine their effect on local manufacturing and skilled labor. The committee would also consider the kinds of labor that might be substituted for the contract system. Charles Knowles, the Republican supervisor from the Fourteenth Ward, proposed an amendment that differed only slightly from Daly's, while John Bowe, from the Third Ward, introduced a resolution to simply abolish the system. The supervisors adopted only Daly's proposal, and the mayor appointed an investigative committee.[31]

The investigative committee never met. Louis Pilsbury challenged the committee's authority, arguing successfully that only the inspectors appointed by the joint board had the right to review the penitentiary's affairs.[32] During the next few years the county supervisors considered other resolutions to abolish or reform the penitentiary's labor system, but did not pass any of them.[33] Once again, the political system had proven unresponsive to workers' entreaties.

Perry's contract with Sing Sing is evidence of the general decline experienced by unions in Albany as a result of the depression of the 1870s.[34] But by 1880, as the economy recovered, the city's workers began rebuilding their organizations. From late 1879 through 1880, the *Argus* reported a union resurgence among Albany's cigar makers, coopers, carpenters and joiners, bricklayers, masons, plasterers, and stonemasons. The city's iron molders had also revived their union activities, even going so far as to strike in August 1879 and successfully raise wages cut during the depression.[35] In January 1882, forty delegates from six unions met in Albany to reorganize the city trades assembly as a means "to promote the principle of trade unionism" and to "benefit all working classes."[36]

The local labor movement added a weapon to its arsenal in May 1882 when the *Albany Evening Union* began publication in Albany as a workingman's newspaper. The *Evening Union* declared itself to be an independent voice, and encouraged workers to serve their own interests by uniting behind "those journals whose voices speak to them and for them in tones which have no uncertain or false sound."[37] Within a short time the city's revived trades assembly designated the *Evening Union* its official journal.[38] The newspaper identified the end of convict labor as the first article in labor's platform.[39]

Weak at the time of Perry's contract with Sing Sing in 1877, a rejuvenated labor movement in Albany was able to take on the prison contract labor system in the 1880s. In March 1882, a state legislator from New York City put before the State Assembly the workers' demand that contract labor in the state's prisons be abolished, or, short of that, that it continue only if convicts were paid the same wages as free labor. But the Assembly ignored these demands as well as a Senate-passed bill to study the best way to end competition between the convict labor system and outside industries.[40] Yet again, New York's political leaders had rebuffed workers on the issue.

Having failed to gain redress on prison labor from elected state officials, workers in Albany resorted once more to independent labor politics. In September 1882, Joseph Delehanty, a leader of a recent cottonspinners' strike in neighboring Cohoes, addressed a prison labor rally in Albany. He called on the workers "to give men power from your own ranks by the ballot box and send them to the legislative halls."[41] Soon after this rally, the city's trades assembly met to discuss the formation of a labor party. These discussions led to the convening of a citizens' labor convention in Albany in October 1882. Besides trades assembly delegates, representatives from the Knights of Labor, individual trade unions, and such local reform groups as the greenbackers, antimonopolists, and Citizens' Association attended. The delegates adopted a platform corresponding to the broad reform interests of the groups represented at the convention—the government to control communication and transportation; public lands to be held in reserve for settlement (not one acre for railroads); introduction of factory inspectors and an end to the labor of children younger than fourteen; the government to issue legal tender directly to the people, independent of banks; and, heading the list, the abolition of prison contract labor. The Citizens' Labor party, which evolved from this convention, nominated candidates for local and statewide offices.[42]

Although Albany workers participated in organizing the Citizens' Labor party, it is difficult to know what they thought of the party's platform. The city's workers had given little support to the greenback movement's legal-tender objectives nor, up to the convention, to most of the other reform planks. The labor party platform represented a very different reform agenda from the cooperative and eight-hour workday struggles of the Albany workers a decade earlier, an agenda geared more closely to contemporary national movements than to matters of local labor interest. What makes participation by workers in the Citizens' Labor party coalition significant has less to do with the party's program than with their helping at all to organize an independent party.

The Citizens' Labor party, like the *Evening Union*, wanted to wean workers from their devotion to the two major political parties. Workers needed to replace "old party leaders" with "new men" whose experience, capacity, and integrity were not "tainted by personal ambition." Such leaders could come only from the ranks of labor.[43] The chairman of a large rally in Albany endorsing Citizens' Labor party candidates stated, "We must rise in our might and control our [political] machines which rule us."[44] The labor party considered it axiomatic that the success of the workers' reform platform required them to gain some control over political institutions.

Despite the new party's high hopes, the Citizens' Labor party saw all but one of its candidates defeated in the November 1882 elections. Joseph Delehanty, who ran with Democratic endorsement in the Fourth Assembly District, was the exception. In the aftermath of the election, the *Evening Union* observed that "the important question they had hoped to decide yesterday was whether honest, respectable men, who owe their livelihood to their own patient toil and industry, should have a voice in the affairs of government or whether their wants and honest requests were to be ignored."That workers had as yet no such voice meant only that their struggle for changes in the prison contract labor system and other reforms would continue. The newspaper predicted that labor would win the struggle if it were effectively organized: "The remedy, and the only remedy, is in organization. There must be a meeting of the people who want real, genuine reform called without delay."[45] The *Evening Union* even raised the possibility of workers taking control of the Albany Penitentiary by electing labor candidates to the County Board of Supervisors in the spring elections.

In January 1883 the *Evening Union* exuded confidence in workers' chances of securing their reform program. The statewide elections in November had brought some positive results. The Democrats, who had deemed it prudent to endorse (at least in the party's platform) labor's position on convict labor, had won resoundingly and now controlled both houses of the state legislature. And, besides Delehanty, two other labor representatives (from Buffalo and Rochester) won election to the State Assembly. Under such favorable circumstances, which also included a "sympathetic Governor," the *Evening Union* predicted that workers in New York were at last in a position to overturn the "bad legislation" responsible for labor's worsening conditions.[46] Presumably, the labor paper based its optimism on workers continuing to apply political pressure through the Citizens' Labor party.

But just one month later, in February 1883, the *Evening Union* abandoned the independent labor party movement. Although it reaffirmed its faith in political action, the newspaper announced that "the time is not yet ripe for the workingman to form a separate political party." The newspaper had concluded that labor's brief experiment with independent political organization and the Citizens' Labor party, far from eliciting public sympathy, provoked "popular dislike and distrust." According to the *Evening Union*, this experience demonstrated to labor's "thoughtful leaders" that workers should avoid appearing to organize "class combinations." A labor party raised fears in the community that workers would try to gain by "intimidation" that which "the people would grant spontaneously" if they could be made properly aware of the workers' grievances. The newspaper suggested that instead of organizing a formal labor party, workers organize to support and vote for candidates, regardless of party affiliation, whose records indicated sympathy with the "Councils of Labor."[47] The *Evening Union* was certain that the democratic process would enable workers to secure a fair hearing and relief for their grievances.

It is likely that no single event precipitated the fundamental shift in workers' attitudes as expressed by the *Albany Evening Union.* But the degree to which labor in Albany turned away from a broad reform program and independent labor politics is striking. Having only recently encouraged workers to organize for the spring 1883 elections, the newspaper and the city trades assembly now declared themselves to be nonpartisan, calling on workers to support any candidate who opposed prison contract labor.[48]

Yet there is good reason to be skeptical of the labor leaders' claim to nonpartisanship. The evidence suggests that as workers moved away from independent politics they moved toward closer ties with the Democratic party, a process probably begun during the 1878 mayoral election. The class and cultural differences revealed in the 1878 election continued to be typical of Albany politics at least into the early 1890s. In 1878, instead of running their own candidate for mayor, the Republican party had endorsed William A. Young, the nominee of the newly organized Citizens' party. The *Albany Evening Journal* called support for Young the "Duty of the Hour" for Republicans if they wanted good government.[49] Two years later the good government forces in Albany led in the formation of the Committee of Thirteen of the Citizens' Association. Leading businessmen dominated the affairs of the committee, whose central concern was that government be run in an efficient, businesslike manner free from political corruption. The committee did not take a formal stand on the current prison contract labor controversy. But its members' stand on increasing prison revenues makes it unlikely that they would support workers' attempts to abolish contract labor.[50]

Workers in Albany could expect little help from Republicans in seeking redress on the prison labor issue. In contrast to the Committee of Thirteen, the *Albany Evening Journal* adamantly opposed workers on this issue. The *Evening Journal* deemed the debate over prison labor to be just one of several "purely economic questions" that had become mixed with politics (a critical reference, no doubt, to the actions of the Democrats) "to a degree that many find it impossible or personally inexpedient to investigate the matter on its own merits." The newspaper held firm in its conviction that if workingmen dispassionately weighed the evidence they would agree that although the present convict labor system was not perfect, "self-sustaining prisons are for the advantage of all."[51]

Albany's Democrats, as already noted, were more willing to accommodate workers on the prison labor issue. In 1878 and again in 1882 city Democrats had declared their opposition to contract labor. Nor was the prison labor issue the only example of a growing labor–Democratic party alliance in Albany. In January 1883, a month before its change of heart, the *Albany Evening Union* reported that Weed and Parsons, printers for the Republican *Evening Journal*, now held the contract for state printing. The labor paper contrasted Weed and Parsons, who employed nonunion labor and paid low wages, with the Argus Company, printers of the Democratic *Argus*, which during its tenure as state printer had employed only union labor and paid good wages.[52]

In its February editorial abandoning independent labor politics, the *Evening Union* reiterated its belief in the importance of the "ballot box" and insisted that "questions of interest" to the workingmen should not be kept out of politics.[53] Less than a month later the newspaper called for workers to organize for the upcoming spring elections. "The independent voter" had to take "matters into his own hands" against "machine rule."[54] The labor paper recommended that the Albany trades assembly resolve "as a body" to endorse for the county Board of Supervisors those nominees from "different party tickets" who openly favored abolition of the contract system at the Albany Penitentiary.[55] Given the respective positions of the Democratic and Republican parties on this critical issue, there could be little doubt that labor would support the Democrats. Despite the declaration of nonpartisanship, then, in rejecting independent politics Albany's labor movement was becoming an interest group within the Democratic party.

The shift by Albany's labor movement away from class-defined independence, as seen in the *Albany Evening Union*'s repudiation of a labor party, is also apparent in the evolution of workers' understanding of the prison contract labor issue. By 1883, spokesmen for the city's labor community no longer (as they had in the 1860s) invoked contract labor as a tool of the capitalist against the worker. Indeed, workers in Albany now claimed that they shared with their employers a need to overturn the contract system. At a "monster meeting" in March 1883, a broad cross-section of the community marched under banners reading "LABOR AND CAPITAL UNITE TO ABOLISH PRISON CONTRACTS." The *Evening Union* reported that nothing in the past twenty years had aroused so much antipathy as prison labor: "Merchants, mechanics, tradesmen and manufacturers, all joined in the monster turnout." The meeting paid homage to labor as the "foundation of all wealth, of individual happiness and national prosperity," and adopted resolutions calling for an end to the contract system. One state senator told the participants that "capital and labor . . . were here assembled on a common basis, their interest in this question were identical." Other speakers, including some professional men—members of a "class"reputedly "unsympathetic" to workingmen—similarly expressed the conviction that workers and employers must join together to eliminate the prison contract labor system.[56]

Rather than the "wages system" labor's *bête noire*, the real enemy of both workers and employers became simply the individual prison contractor. Perry's contract with Sing Sing, which enabled him to produce and sell stoves far more cheaply than other Albany founders, injured the other employers as well as their employees. The testimony in March 1883 of Franklin M. Danaher, a lawyer representing Albany's trade unions before a State Senate committee on New York prisons, shows the shift in workers' arguments against contract labor. Workers do not oppose prison labor per se, Danaher claimed. If the state directly supervised the convicts' labor and did not farm it out to a private contractor "who uses it against them, the workingmen would not object to the amount or character of any work" imposed on prisoners. What hurt workers was that the goods produced by inmates ended up competing with the goods that they produced, the goods sold by the men who hired and paid them. By paying low wages for convict labor, contractors gained an unfair advantage over other employers, which resulted in reduced wages for all workingmen.[57] Workers still had a vital stake in abolishing prison contract labor, but now they judged their interests to coincide with those of the general community.

Albany workers' greater identification with the Democratic party (and their public rejection of class politics) parallels their acceptance of the prevailing free labor ethos (and their rejection of class consciousness). Like the city's middle-class Irish Catholic elite, Albany's labor leaders seemed intent on proving the working man's respectability by shedding all vestiges of class antagonism. Workers in Albany, especially during the 1860s and early 1870s, had looked to reform permanently the free labor order. By the 1880s, however, the city's workers had significantly moderated their views. The prison contract labor issue enabled the more respectable leaders, those who favored accommodation over class conflict, to take charge of the labor movement in Albany.

Accommodation did not mean passivity. Albany's "monster" rally in March demanded that during the current (1882–83) legislative session the Democratic party redeem its platform pledge to end contract labor competition. Workers became impatient when the Democrats appeared to be "floundering," too concerned about how to employ convicts once the contracts were abolished. The *Albany Evening Union* felt, "it matters not what system may be adopted hereafter, it can scarcely be worse than the present one which cannot and will not be longer tolerated."[58] Albany workers united behind a bill, introduced by Assemblyman Butts of Monroe County, that would simply not have renewed existing contracts for convict labor. But the State Senate passed instead a bill submitting the issue to a nonbinding popular referendum. Over workers' objections, the Butts bill died, and the "submission bill" became law.[59]

In assessing the 1883 session, the *Evening Union* expressed satisfaction that at least some labor legislation had passed. Still, the legislature had failed on the main issue, to end contract labor. The newspaper blamed this failure on a coalition in the state legislature of Republicans and dissident Democrats hostile to labor.[60] Workers now faced the question of what to do in the fall election. Both the *Evening Union* and the state Workingmen's Assembly interpreted the Democrats' endorsement of the submission bill rather than of the Butts bill as a cynical move calculated to help the party in the coming election. The only recourse, according to Workingmen's Assembly President Walter Thayer, was for workers to elect their own representatives to the state legislature; where workers could not field a candidate, they should continue to endorse Democratic and Republican candidates friendly to them.[61] In the 1883 fall elections, Albany labor leaders proved to be more sympathetic to the second part of Thayer's suggestion than to the first.

In July 1883, John Parr, a former compositor with the *Argus* and a long-time member of the printers' union, became the editor of the *Albany Evening Union*. His editorial views attest to the moderate direction Albany workers' world view was taking, as well as to the workers' greater attachment to interest-group rather than class ideology. Parr considered strikes a last resort, one that unions should avoid. The "main object" of unions, Parr maintained, was "to meet capital on a reasonable basis, to study into the relative value of labor and capital, to ascertain what is fair and just to both, and to arbitrate in a spirit of friendly feeling and justice the right to both—to bring the employers into harmony with the employees, and to develop the fact that their interests are identical and inseparable."[62] Strikes at best were "heroic remedies," a means of demonstrating workers' willingness to fight. But "arbitration should take the place of mere physical weapons of attack and defense in industrial conflicts."[63] Parr believed that more could be gained by peaceful competition than warlike confrontation.

Parr was equally conciliatory on labor politics. Labor could satisfy its legitimate claims through the existing political system. The failure of "remonstrance and petition" compelled workers to seek relief through "the recognized and legal coercion of the ballot box." Like other labor leaders, Parr spoke of labor's political role as nonpartisan; only by supporting those "who support us" could workers secure advantageous laws, such as one ending prison contract labor.[64] Parr declared the worst enemy of the "labor party" to be the "disgruntled political crank." In what seems an obvious indictment of the Citizens' Labor party, he warned workers to avoid the "disappointed office seeker," who having been rejected by other political parties forms his own, calling it "Reform," "Citizens'," "Greenback," or "Temperance." Labor had to turn its back on all such "political heresies. It is time for this thing to stop, and for the Labor Party pure, simple and unadulterated."[65] By "labor party," Parr meant workers continually pressing labor's interests "until our grievances are considered, our wrongs righted, and prison contract labor a thing—a dream of the past."[66] Workers' politics in the future, according to Parr, would be pressure group politics on behalf of their particular interests.

At an 1883 meeting of the New York State Workingmen's Assembly, the *Albany Evening Union* submitted a plan for workers' political action. The newspaper asserted that a worker had a responsibility to belong to a political association as well as to a trade union.[67] The labor paper proposed that workers establish Workingmen's Republican and Workingmen's Democratic clubs. Club members would attend their respective party's caucus and help elect delegates to the party's nominating convention who, in turn, would choose candidates for the legislature sympathetic to labor. In the fall elections, Albany workers acted on the *Evening Union*'s proposal.

The litmus test for labor support was a "yes" vote on the submission bill. Although the *Evening Union* would have preferred the referendum be binding on the legislature, the newspaper was willing to accept it as a symbol: "We will show them that the people are with us, and they will not dare to refuse us justice."[68] The labor paper cautioned workers to watch out for the "visionary element" in their ranks, those who promoted an independent labor party. A small minority of those attending a recent city trades assembly meeting had proposed nominating a full slate of labor candidates for the upcoming fall elections. But the majority of members present, the newspaper reported with relief, voted to seek the nomination of major party candidates pledged to support labor's bills.[69]

Just before the fall 1883 elections, delegations of workers from Albany attended the county conventions of both the Republican and Democratic parties. At each convention the workers solicited the support of party officials on the contract labor issue. In response, county Democrats unanimously voted to denounce contract labor and agreed to distribute ballots for its abolition at the polls.[70] The Republicans were less receptive to the workers' overtures.[71] The *Albany Evening Union* concluded that workers had to support the Democrats: "The Democratic party, after all, is the only hope of the workingmen, and we advise them to vote the ticket straight."[72]

As it had five years earlier, the Democratic party in 1883 appeared willing to accommodate workers' opposition to the prison contract labor system. Despite some equivocating by the state party, local Democrats endorsed the workers' demand for abolition. The *Argus* repeated the workers' claims that prison labor competition undermined free industry: "The loss to the honest workingmen of the State by convict labor, at competitive employments, has been tenfold greater than the gain to the revenue of the State by such employments."[73] The Republican *Albany Evening Journal*, in contrast, branded abolition of contract labor a "Labor Bugbear" and insisted that "the proposition to do away with the contract system in our prisons is not supported by an healthy public sentiment."[74] By 1883 so strong had the bond become between the Democrats and Albany's labor leadership that even the party's failure to renominate Delehanty in the Fourth Assembly District did not break it.[75]

Election day November 1883 brought gratifying results for labor. The referendum vote throughout the state for abolition of prison contract labor was 405,882 in favor, 266,966 against, a three-to-two majority. In Albany County the abolition majority was almost four to one, and in the city proper the difference in votes reached almost ten to one.[76] The *Albany Evening Union* applauded the election results as evidence of the effectiveness of workers when properly organized. Clearly, workers could exert pressure on the political process through judicious use of the ballot. Their role in politics, the labor paper maintained, was not to vie as a class for the power to remake the system but to work within the system for limited, albeit necessary, reforms.[77]

The New York legislature convened in 1884 knowing that the majority of the state's voters supported an end to prison contract labor. Nevertheless, the legislators continued to equivocate. They voiced concern over the burden a prison system that could not pay for itself might place on taxpayers, and asked for time to consider alternative systems. But the momentum of the anti-contract labor forces at last proved irresistible, and the legislators voted that no contract for convict labor be negotiated, renewed, or extended. However, even this legislative action did not end the system outright, and debate over contract labor lingered. Not until 1894, with an amendment to the state constitution, was prison contract labor finally laid to rest as an issue for New York's—and Albany's—workers.[78]

In 1884 Albany workers stood poised with one foot in the future and one in the past. While articulating the emerging interest-group ideas of Samuel Gompers and the American Federation of Labor, they nevertheless reasserted basic nineteenth-century free labor concepts.[79] In the future they would remain organized, politically and in trade unions, but as a pressure group to win limited reforms. Moreover, according to the *Albany Evening Union* workers recognized that they shared common interests with the larger community. Thus by the mid-1880s workers had adopted the values of the prevailing community consciousness.

The middle-class world that free labor adherents in the 1850s had spoken of preserving—the self-sufficient world of the individual entrepreneur, independent farmer, and free worker—had changed fundamentally by the 1880s. Large-scale industry and corporate concentration, no longer forces to be imagined, were pressing facts of economic life. The early 1870s, as David Montgomery notes, marked the end of American industry's "take-off period."[80]

America's transformation in the 1870s and 1880s was not merely a matter of economic change. All institutions and associations characteristic of the 1840s and 1850s were also changing. In the mid-1880s the Independent Order of Odd Fellows, which had revised its ritual in 1844 to suit American conditions, began to minimize its larger social reformist role, emphasizing instead such benefits as its life insurance program. The Albany Penitentiary, founded in the 1840s by a middle-class elite looking to keep the peace and to guide behavior, had also been shorn of its larger reformatory role by the 1880s. Created after 1847 in large measure to preserve Catholic autonomy, Catholic institutions and associations had lost their immediacy. By the 1880s Albany's Irish Catholics were full participants in the political and social life of the Albany community.

Through most of the nineteenth century voluntary associations in Albany tended to have an interclass membership. Affiliation with such associations was part of a social process intended to stimulate formation of community rather than class loyalties. The Committee of Thirteen is one example of how an aristocratic social elite began to express itself in Albany by 1880. The Fort Orange Club is another. In 1880, 200 of Albany's leading citizens, instead of joining one of the city's interclass voluntary associations as they would have in the 1840s, formed the Fort Orange Club—a social club for the "best men in Albany." According to its official historian, Grange Sard, "Albany needed a club composed of gentlemen who represented that which was best in Albany, the men of distinction, of culture, . . . the men who were born on the top, as well as those who possessed the qualities which make good men and had risen to the top.''[81] Leading Irish Catholics in Albany joined the Yankee-Dutch ''men at the top'' in the Fort Orange Club. The club provided a congenial atmosphere for class and cultural accommodation among the city's elite.[82]

The world described by the free labor ideology may have been fundamentally transformed by the 1880s, but it had not disappeared. The struggle against prison contract labor was waged on behalf of the mutuality of interests of employers and employees. Yet by the 1880s Albany workers still combined a nascent interest-group consciousness with the free labor tradition. The organized labor movement in Albany emphasized peaceful competition for limited benefits within the prevailing system.

A dialectic between identification with class and with free labor characterized the world view of Albany workers from the 1850s on. The 1860s in particular had been a decade of intense militancy by workers as they sought fundamental changes in the social order. Although by the 1880s Albany's labor movement had mostly turned its back on its more radical past, a ''visionary element,'' to use John Parr's phrase, remained. In the 1880s those workers who rejected the prevailing pure and simple trade unionism joined the Knights of Labor.[83] If Albany workers had not realized their ideal of a cooperative commonwealth, many still sought an alternative to capitalist industrialization.

Notes

Introduction

1. Alan Dawley, *Class and Community: The Industrial Revolution in Lynn* (Cambridge, Mass.: Harvard University Press, 1976), pp. 31-32; Herbert G. Gutman, "Work, Culture, and Society in Industrializing America, 1815-1919," *American Historical Review* 78 (June 1973), pp. 531-88; David Montgomery, *Beyond Equality: Labor and the Radical Republicans, 1862-1872* (New York: Knopf, 1967), pp. 25-26. For Montgomery the change from independent mechanic to wage earner marked the emergence of the industrial worker.

2. Bruce Laurie distinguishes class as a structural category from class consciousness as a social and cultural formulation. See *Working People of Philadelphia, 1800-1850* (Philadelphia: Temple University Press, 1980), pp. xi-xii. Like other new labor historians, Laurie follows the work of E. P. Thompson, *The Making of the English Working Class* (New York: Vintage Books, 1963), pp. 9-10, 193-95.

3. On free labor ideology, see Eric Foner, *Free Soil, Free Labor, Free Men: The Ideology of the Republican Party before the Civil War* (New York: Oxford University Press, 1970); Montgomery, *Beyond Equality*, pp. 30-31. Foner focuses on the free labor outlook inherent in the Republican party's emergence in the 1850s. But the free labor ideology characterized middle-class thinking more generally as well, at least through the 1870s. See also Paul Boyer, *Urban Masses and Moral Order in America, 1820-1920* (Cambridge, Mass.: Harvard University Press, 1978), pp. 54-64.

4. Herbert G. Gutman, "The Workers' Search for Power," in *The Gilded Age*, ed. H. Wayne Morgan (Syracuse, N.Y.: Syracuse University Press, 1970). See also Gutman's collected essays, *Work, Culture, and Society in Industrializing America: Essays in American Working-Class and Social History* (New York: Vintage Books, 1977).

5. *Argus*, May 27, 1867.

6. Ibid., June 18, 1872; *Albany Evening Journal*, June 18, 1872.

7. *Argus*, April 15, 1867; *Albany Evening Journal*, May 3, 1867.

8. Walter Licht, "Labor and Capital and the American Community," *Journal of Urban History* 7 (February 1981), pp. 219–20; Dawley, *Class and Community*; Paul G. Faler, *Mechanics and Manufacturers in the Early Industrial Revolution: Lynn, Massachusetts, 1780–1860* (Albany: State University of New York Press, 1981); John T. Cumbler, *Working-Class Community in Industrial America: Work, Leisure, and Struggle in Two Industrial Cities, 1880–1930* (Westport, Conn.: Greenwood Press, 1979); Howard Rock, *Artisans of the New Republic: The Tradesmen of New York City in the Age of Jefferson* (New York: New York University Press, 1979); Daniel J. Walkowitz, *Worker City, Company Town: Iron and Cotton Worker Protest in Troy and Cohoes, New York, 1855–1884* (Urbana: University of Illinois Press, 1978); Laurie, *Working People of Philadelphia*; Susan E. Hirsch, *Roots of the American Working Class: The Industrialization of Crafts in Newark, 1800–1860* (Philadelphia: University of Pennsylvania Press, 1978). For "worker culture" I have adapted Robert Baker's definition. See "Labor History, Social Science, and the Concept of the Working Class," *Labor History* 14 (Winter 1973), pp. 100–1.

9. David Montgomery, "To Study the People: The American Working Class," *Labor History* 21 (Fall 1980), p. 503, and "Gutman's Nineteenth-Century America," *Labor History* 19 (Summer 1978), pp. 416–29.

10. Gutman, "Work, Culture, and Society," p. 536.

11. Daniel T. Rodgers, "Tradition, Modernity, and the American Industrial Worker: Reflections and Critique," *Journal of Interdisciplinary History* 7 (Spring 1977), pp. 656–60; Montgomery, "Gutman's Nineteenth-Century America," pp. 425–26.

12. Alan Dawley and Paul G. Faler, "Working-Class Culture and Politics in the Industrial Revolution: Sources of Loyalism and Rebellion," *Journal of Social History* 9 (Summer 1976), pp. 468–71; Laurie, *Working People of Philadelphia*, pp. 33–52.

13. Thomas Bender offers a similar critique of community studies that tend to contrast *Gemeinschaft* (traditional community) with *Gesellschaft* (modern society) in *Community and Social Change in America* (New Brunswick, N.J.: Rutgers University Press, 1978), pp. 15–43. See also Rodgers, "Tradition, Modernity, and the Worker," p. 680; G. David Garson, "Radical Issues in the History of the American Working Class," *Politics and Society* 3 (Fall 1972), pp. 25–30.

14. Gutman, "Work, Culture, and Society," p. 567; David Montgomery, "The Shuttle and the Cross: Weavers and Artisans in the Kensington Riots of 1844," *Journal of Social History* 5 (Summer 1972), pp. 411–46; Stanley Aronowitz, *False Promises: The Shaping of American Working-Class Consciousness* (New York: McGraw-Hill, 1972).

15. Foner refers to Weber's use of "worldly asceticism" in *Free Soil, Free Labor, Free Men*, pp. 12–13.

16. Gwyn A. Williams, "The Concept of 'Egemonia' in the Thought of Antonio Gramsci: Some Notes on Interpretation," *Journal of the History of Ideas* 21 (October–December 1960), p. 587.

17. Ibid., p. 591; Raymond Williams, "Base and Superstructure in Marxist Cultural Theory," *New Left Review* no. 82 (November–December 1973), pp. 8–10; Eugene Genovese, "On Antonio Gramsci," in *In Red and Black: Marxian Explorations in Southern and Afro-American History* (New York: Random House, 1971); Eric J. Hobsbawm, "The Great Gramsci," *New York Review of Books* (April 4, 1974); *Selections from the Prison Notebooks of Antonio Gramsci*, ed. and trans. Quentin Hoare and Geoffrey Nowell Smith (New York: International Publishers, 1971), pp. 3-23, 180–82, 242–76. Robert Q. Gray applies Gramsci's concept of hegemony to nineteenth-century Scotland in *The Labour Aristocracy in Victorian Edinburgh* (Oxford: Clarendon Press, 1976).

18. R. Williams, "Base and Superstructure," pp. 8–10. In a review of Gutman's *The Black Family in Slavery and Freedom, 1750–1925*, David Brion Davis criticizes him for reifying culture to the point of denying the realities of power. See *American Historical Review* 82 (June 1977), p. 745.

Chapter One

1. Allan R. Pred, *The Spatial Dynamics of U.S. Urban-Industrial Growth, 1800–1914: Interpretive and Theoretical Essays* (Cambridge, Mass.: M.I.T. Press, 1966), pp. 16–24. See also David Ward, *Cities and Immigrants: A Geography of Change in Nineteenth-Century America* (New York: Oxford University Press, 1971), pp. 32–49; George Rogers Taylor, *The Transportation Revolution, 1815–1860* (New York: Rinehart, 1951), pp. 243–49.

2. Pred, *Spatial Dynamics*, pp. 63–71. The same pattern of change occurred in brewing and iron and steel manufacture.

	Average Number Employed		
	1860	*1880*	*1910*
Brewing	5.1	12.0	38.6
Iron & Steel	53.8	140.3	425.8

3. Dawley, *Class and Community*. See also Faler, *Mechanics and Manufacturers*, pp. 8–27.

4. Laurie, *Working People of Philadelphia*, pp. 3–30; Hirsch, *Roots of the American Working Class*, pp. 15–36; Licht, "Labor and Capital and the American Community," pp. 223–26.

5. Montgomery, *Beyond Equality*, pp. 3–44; Gutman, *Work, Culture, and Society in Industrializing America*, p. 33; Robert Higgs, *The Transformation of the American Economy, 1865–1914; An Essay in Interpretation* (New York: Wiley, 1971), p. 47.

6. Montgomery, *Beyond Equality*, pp. 29–31, 448–52; Daniel T. Rodgers, *The Work Ethic in Industrial America, 1850–1920* (Chicago: University of Chicago Press, 1974), pp. 37, 250–51. In calculating the number of wage earners in Pennsylvania and Massachusetts, Rodgers modifies Montgomery's procedure. Like Rodgers, I use the number of "hands employed" in the census of manufactures and find that about three-fourths of all employed persons in Albany in 1870 were wage earners. See U.S. Census Office, *Ninth Census of the United States: Population and Social Statistics* (Washington, D.C., 1872), p. 775. In *The Incorporation of America: Culture and Society in the Gilded Age* (New York: Hill and Wang, 1982), Alan Trachtenberg asserts that given the "free labor" consensus before the Civil War, the Gilded Age became a battleground for the meaning of America, that is, for "the political and cultural authority to define the term and thus to say what reality was and ought to be" (p. 73). In many ways that struggle is what the present study is all about.

7. Unless otherwise noted, the description of the sequential and regional patterns of American industrialization comes from Ward, *Cities and Immigrants*, pp. 18–49.

8. Richard L. Ehrlich, "The Development of Manufacturing in Selected Counties in the Erie Canal Corridor, 1815–1860" (Ph.D. diss., State University of New York at Buffalo, 1972), pp. 35–40.

9. Ehrlich, "Manufacturing in the Erie Canal Corridor," pp. 40–41; George R. Howell and Jonathan Tenney, *Bi-Centennial History of Albany: History of the County of Albany, New York, from 1609 to 1886* (New York: W. W. Munsell, 1886), p. 610; David M. Ellis, "Albany and Troy—Commercial Rivals," *New York History* 24 (October 1943), pp. 507–9; William E. Rowley, "Albany: A Tale of Two Cities, 1820–1880" (Ph.D. diss., Harvard University, 1967), pp. 53–57 (copy in author's possession).

10. Joel Munsell, ed., *Collections on the History of Albany, from Its Discovery to the Present Time*, 4 vols. (Albany: J. Munsell, 1865–71), vol. 3, pp. 313–14; Rowley, "Albany," pp. 54–59.

11. Rowley, "Albany," pp. 176–78.

12. Howell and Tenney, *Bi-Centennial History of Albany*, p. 643; Munsell, *Collections on the History of Albany*, vol. 2, pp. 391–93; Rowley, "Albany," pp. 31–32.

13. Howell and Tenney, *Bi-Centennial History of Albany*, pp. 566–73; Rowley, "Albany," p. 60; Ehrlich, "Manufacturing in the Erie Canal Corridor," pp. 49–51; John Leander Bishop, *A History of American Manufactures from 1608 to 1860*, 2 vols. (Philadelphia: Edward Young, 1864), vol. 2, pp. 623–25;

Tammis Kane Groft, *Cast with Style: Nineteenth Century Cast-Iron Stoves from the Albany Area* (Albany: Albany Institute of History and Art, 1981), pp. 11–12.

14. Ehrlich, "Manufacturing in the Erie Canal Corridor," pp. 73–74; Bishop, *History of American Manufactures*, vol. 2, pp. 626–30; Rowley, "Albany," pp. 58–59.

15. *Argus*, September 28, 1861.

16. Munsell, *Collections on the History of Albany*, vol. 2, pp. 393–95; *Argus*, September 28, 1861.

17. Ehrlich, "Manufacturing in the Erie Canal Corridor," pp. 88–89; U.S. Census Office, *Seventh Census, 1850. Abstract of the Statistics of Manufactures* (Washington, D.C., 1858), p. 143. In 1850 the national averages for all manufactories were 7.8 workers and $8,284 in value of goods produced annually. Unless otherwise noted, all data concerning Albany industry in 1850 is based upon the 1850 manuscript census. See U.S. Census Office, *Census of the United States, Census of Industry*, Albany County, 1850 (microfilm, MSS, New York State Library, Albany, N.Y.).

18. The average value of production per establishment in Albany's boot and shoe industry was $7,500 a year, and each averaged 10 employees. Not all industries fit the pattern. For example, 10 brickmakers produced an average $5,030 worth of goods each year and employed an average of 12.8 persons. Taking the four largest brickmaking establishments, the average per brickyard was $5,425's worth of production annually and 19 persons employed.

19. Howell and Tenney, *Bi-Centennial History of Albany*, p. 608. Ehrlich calculates that the average for Albany excluding these 20 firms was 9.58 workers per establishment ("Manufacturing in the Erie Canal Corridor," pp. 88–90). The national average was 9.34. It is likely that the invention of the sewing machine in 1854 had boosted Albany's boot and shoe production.

20. Unfortunately, the manuscript census for 1880 contains almost no industrial returns for Albany. Instead, for 1880, I have used Table VI, "Manufactures of 100 Principal Cities by Specified Industries: 1880, City of Albany, N.Y.," U.S. Census Office, *Tenth Census of the United States, 1880. Report on the Manufactures* (Washington, D.C., 1883), p. 381. In 1880 iron stove casting was listed under foundry and machine-shop products. Inclusion of machine shops, which were generally not as large as stove foundries, makes the average size per establishment appear, if anything, smaller than it actually was. The average number of persons employed per establishment in 1880 was 10.8 for the United States, 14.7 for Albany.

21. Howell and Tenney, *Bi-Centennial History of Albany*, pp. 566–72; Bishop, *History of American Manufactures*, vol. 2, pp. 623–26; *Albany Illustrated* (Albany: Argus, 1892), p. 74; *Argus*, May 2 and 18, June 8, 1878.

22. *The Albany Hand-Book. A Strangers' Guide and Residents Manual*, comp. Henry P. Phelps (Albany: Brandon and Barton, 1884), p. 81.

23. *Albany Hand-Book*, p. 8; Howell and Tenney, *Bi-Centennial History of Albany*, pp. 605–6; *Argus*, May 18, 1867, October 24, 1879.

24. In 1900 the census used three variables to rank each city's manufacturing: the value of products, the number of establishments, and the average number of wage earners. In 1880 Albany ranked 29th in the value of products and 20th in the number of manufacturing establishments. Twenty years later Albany had fallen to 55th in the value of products; it ranked 24th in the number of establishments. Clearly, industry remained important in Albany, but relatively small-scale. A comparison of Albany's iron foundries with Pittsburgh's iron and steel mills makes the same point—that large-scale production did not develop in Albany. In 1880 Albany had 28 foundries and machine shops, producing $2.6 million worth of goods (average, just under $95,000) and employing 2,215 persons (average, just under 80). Pittsburgh's 39 iron and steel mills in 1880 produced over $35 million worth of goods (average, under $900,000) and employed 15,500 persons (average, over 400). By 1900 Albany's 21 iron foundries and machine shops employed only 777 persons (average, 37), while Pittsburgh's 36 iron and steel mills employed 24,418 wage earners (average 678.3). In addition, in 1900, of the 1,566 manufacturing establishments of all sorts in Albany, 916 or 58.5 percent were still hand trades, while for the United States, it was 48.7 percent, and for Pittsburgh, 42.2 percent. See Pred, *Spatial Dynamics*, pp. 66–71; U.S. Census, *Tenth Census. Manufactures*, p. 381, and *Twelfth Census. Manufactures* (Washington, D.C., 1902), part 1, pp. ccxlii-ccxliii, and part 2, p. 1060.

25. On slaughtering and meat packing in Chicago, see Pred, *Spatial Dynamics*, pp. 54–55; Rowley, "Albany," pp. 381–82, 382 n. 41; *Argus*, October 4 and 16, 1882; Howell and Tenney, *Bi-Centennial History of Albany*, p. 643. As the figures on employment in iron foundries and machine shops in 1900 show, stove molding in Albany was also rapidly declining (see note 24).

26. R. Williams, "Base and Superstructure," pp. 8–9.

27. Many works of the new labor history focus on the Jacksonian period. See Laurie, *Working People of Philadelphia*; Faler, *Mechanics and Manufacturers*; Dawley, *Class and Community*; Hirsch, *Roots of the American Working Class*. Older but still very useful works are Edward Pessen, *Most Uncommon Jacksonians: The Radical Leaders of the Early Labor Movement* (Albany: State University of New York Press, 1970); Douglas T. Miller, *Jacksonian Aristocracy: Class and Democracy in New York, 1830–1860* (New York: Oxford University Press, 1967); Walter Hugins, *Jacksonian Democracy and the Working Class: A Study of the New York Working Men's Movement, 1829–1837* (Stanford, Calif.: Stanford University Press, 1960). The term "rapacious tyrants" is from a lecture by Sean Wilentz on Jacksonian labor given at Princeton University, October 1979 (copy in author's possession).

28. Rowley, "Albany," pp. 112–28; Hugins, *Jacksonian Democracy and the Working Class*, pp. 11–23.

29. Rowley, "Albany," p. 116.

30. As quoted in Rowley, "Albany," pp. 104–12. The Lancaster School was based on the English monitorial system, in which one teacher taught 390 pupils.

31. As quoted in Rowley, "Albany," p. 115, 115 n. 132; Joseph G. Rayback, *A History of American Labor* (New York: Macmillan, 1959), p. 65. Most of those imprisoned for debt owed under $20.

32. Rowley, "Albany," pp. 124–26.

33. As quoted in Rowley, "Albany," pp. 116–28; Charles E. Gotsch, "The Albany Workingmen's Party and the Rise of Popular Politics" (Ph.D. diss., State University of New York at Albany, 1976).

34. As quoted in Rowley, "Albany," p. 117; Wilentz lecture.

Chapter Two

1. David Glassberg, "Public Ritual and Cultural Change: Philadelphia's Civic Celebrations at the Turn of the Twentieth Century" (paper delivered at the Mid-Atlantic Regional Meeting of the American Studies Association, Philadelphia, November 1982), p. 1.

2. *Argus*, March 1, 1850.

3. Unless otherwise noted, all quotes are from the *Argus* report of the dinner, June 6 and 7, 1850.

4. Foner, *Free Soil, Free Labor, Free Men*, pp. 16–17.

5. *Argus*, March 1, 1850.

6. Foner, *Free Soil, Free Labor, Free Men*, pp. 38–39.

7. *Argus*, August 30, 1858. The celebration proved premature as faulty insulation led to a breakdown of cable communication. After the Civil War a successful Atlantic Cable was completed

8. The other transparencies honored the cable as a joint American-European effort; one depicted Queen Victoria holding a telegraph message from President Buchanan.

9. Unless otherwise noted, all quotes are from the *Argus* report of the cable celebration, September 3, 1858.

10. *Argus*, May 8, 1858.

11. *Albany Evening Journal*, May 27, 1858.

12. *Argus*, January 28, 1857.

13. *Albany Evening Journal*, October 24, 1855.

14. On nativism and the free labor ideology, see Foner, *Free Soil, Free Labor, Free Men*, pp. 226–60.

15. *Argus*, November 26, 1850. The outing prizewinners' affiliations with other volunteer corps (e.g., the Worth Guards and the Emmett Guards) appeared after their names. Members of these units were Irish; apparently they belonged to more than one volunteer corps. On other company-sponsored volunteer corps, see *Argus*, October 25, November 8, 1852, September 23, 1853 (reference to "Mechanics Guards" organized by tin- and coppersmiths), October 22, November 2, 9, and 12, 1855. To my knowledge there are no historical studies of these associations. For one of the best accounts of this kind of employer-sponsored activity, see the English novel, *The Ragged-Trousered Philanthropists* by Robert Tressel (London: Richards Press and *Daily Herald*, 1927), pp. 190–212.

16. *Argus*, November 26, December 17, 1850.

17. Ibid., October 22, 1855. The "company prizes" included a silver watch, six silver tea- and three silver tablespoons, and a clock. The account of this excursion lists the judges, who, with one exception, were from the middle class. The exception was Captain Michael Cassidy, a molder active in numerous Irish organizations. The Rathbone Guards had 126 members. Their names are not given, but it is likely that most if not all were workers.

18. Ibid., November 12, 1855. Among 23 prizes were gold and silver watches, a gold chain, and a silver cake basket.

19. Ibid., November 28, 1856.

20. Such associations flourished and faded over the next thirty years. There is no clear explanation for this pattern. The newpapers record elaborate excursions by the Perry Guards and the Rathbone Guards in 1880; see ibid., September 3, 4, 10, 17, and 23, 1880.

21. Ibid., August 9, 1856.

22. Ibid., December 19, 1855, January 3, 4, and 11, 1856.

23. Ibid., June 23, 1851. Emphasis in original.

24. Ibid. Other speakers included two lawyers, Charles W. Mink and James Brice.

25. The *Albany Directory* for 1850 lists two Patrick Gradys, one a laborer, the other a cartman, Edward Grimes as a teamster, and Isaac Neville as a grocer. Although it does not list David Mahoney, a majority of the committee definitely were not waterworks laborers. It is likely that some of the middle-class committee members participated from a desire to boost their political careers. Yet James Kilbourn was also active in party politics. His career conforms to the pattern that

Montgomery points to, in which politics was seized on as an opportunity to move out of the working class. See *Beyond Equality*, pp. 208–15.

26. *Argus*, June 25, 1851.

27. William D. Guernsey, "A Brief History of Albany Typographical Union No. 4," in *Commemorating the 90th Anniversary of Albany Typographical Union No. 4* (Albany: J. B. Lyon, 1940), p. 26. Reproduced from the original minutes.

28. *Argus*, June 1, 1850.

29. Unless otherwise noted, all quotes are from the *Albany Evening Journal*, which reprinted the committee's report, September 14, 1850. The report noted that in the 14 printing offices there were 192 printers—110 journeymen, 57 boys, and 18 girls. This was further broken down into 15 foremen, 87 compositors, 15 pressmen, 49 boys at case, 8 boys at press, and 18 girls at press. These figures are estimates only.

30. Norman Ware points out that by 1850 the Napier press and the use of steam power in printing had superseded the hand press in all but job work and extra fine book work. He states that boys with one or two years' experience as typesetters became "two-thirders" who were paid "18¾ to 20 cents per 1000 ems." See *The Industrial Worker, 1840–1860: The Reaction of American Industrial Society to the Advance of the Industrial Revolution* (Chicago: Quadrangle Books, 1964), p. 55.

31. Emphasis in original.

32. Ware, *Industrial Worker*, p. 58. Ware cites the National Typographical Society's address to printers across the nation in 1850 as an example of "a new spirit of denial of the accepted doctrine of a community interest between employer and employed" among American workers. Note the difference between the printers' committee report in Albany and the part of the address that Ware quotes: "It is useless for us to disguise from ourselves the fact that, under the present arrangement of things, there is a perpetual antagonism between Labor and Capital, . . . one striving to sell their labor for as much, and the other striving to buy it for as little, as they can."

33. Jonathan Grossman, *William Sylvis, Pioneer of American Labor: A Study of the Labor Movement during the Era of the Civil War* (New York: Columbia University Press, 1945), p. 24.

34. *Iron Moulders' International Journal*, August 1872. The union claimed that the system being introduced at Eagle Furnace was common prior to 1861.

35. *Albany Evening Journal*, April 10, 1852.

36. Ibid.

37. *Argus*, April 10, 1852.

38. Grossman, *William Sylvis*, pp. 24–25. "Berkshire," or "bucks," was the name given to paid helpers, and refers to a system used in England. Payment in "truck" means that at least part of a worker's remuneration could take the form of orders at company-owned or -operated stores. *Iron Moulders' International Journal*, October 1917, pp. 721–29.

39. On the molders' union constitution, see D. G. Littlefield's and accompanying letters from molders in the *Albany Evening Union*, August 26, 1882, concerning the 1859 strike. See also a letter from a number of Albany founders to the *Argus*, June 25, 1859; *Illustrated History of the Central Federation of Labor Representing the Various Trades Unions of Albany and Vicinity* (Albany: Central Federation of Labor, 1898), pp. 92–93.

40. Littlefield referred to a "leading" Albany firm. On April 30, 1859, the *Argus* reported a strike at Treadwell, Perry, and Norton.

41. *Albany Evening Union*, August 26, 1882. The Troy iron founders also formed an association but immediately gave in to the workers' demands.

42. National Convention of Iron Moulders, *Annual Proceedings and Records*, First Annual Session, Philadelphia, July 5–7, 1859, pp. 5–6.

43. Iron Moulders' International Union No. 2, of Troy, New York, "Minutes," April 28, 1858–March 29, 1866, pp. 56, 58.

44. *Argus*, June 4, 1859.

45. Ibid., June 25, 1859. Emphasis in original.

46. Reprinted in ibid., July 11, 1859.

47. *Albany Evening Union*, August 26, 1882.

48. Albany, New York, Common Council, *Proceedings*, 1859, pp. 439–40.

49. The *Argus* of September 7, 1859, reported rumors that many policemen belonged to the molders' union.

50. Ibid., September 13, 1859; Albany Common Council, *Proceedings*, 1859, p. 516. The mayor had offered two $250 rewards for information on the shootings.

51. John Foster cites workers' resistance to becoming employers of other laborers as an example of their class consciousness. See *Class Struggle and the Industrial Revolution: Early Industrial Capitalism in Three English Towns* (New York: St. Martin's Press, 1974), pp. 224–25. On Albany molders' attitudes towards "berkshires," see Chapter 3.

52. *Argus*, May 27, 1850.

53. *Albany Evening Journal*, May 30, 1850.

54. Ibid., September 5, 1859.

55. *Argus*, September 8, 1859.

56. *Albany Evening Journal*, September 6, 1859.

57. Ibid. Emphasis in original.

58. *Argus*, September 8, 1859.

59. *Albany Evening Union*, August 26, 1882.

60. *Argus*, September 8, 1859.

Chapter Three

1. *Fincher's Trades Review*, May 14, 1864.

2. Howell and Tenney, *Bi-Centennial History of Albany*, p. 723. A correspondent from Albany wrote to *Fincher's Trades Review* listing 20 "bona fide" trade organizations in the city, 15 of them reportedly belonging to the Trades' Assembly of the City of Albany and Vicinity (October 8, 1864).

3. "Commonwealth" ideology seems appropriate as a way to describe workers' diverse views in these years. On workers' ideology in the nineteenth century, see Dawley, *Class and Community;* Dawley and Faler, "Working-Class Culture and Politics in the Industrial Revolution," pp. 466–80; Eric Foner, *Tom Paine and Revolutionary America* (New York: Oxford University Press, 1976); Gutman, *Work, Culture, and Society in Industrializing America*; Laurie, *Working People of Philadelphia.*

4. On external factors in determining this outcome, particularly the role of the dominant culture, see Chapters 5 through 8.

5. On the free labor ideology, see especially Foner, *Free Soil, Free Labor, Free Men*, pp. 11–39; Montgomery, *Beyond Equality*, pp. 30–31. A key contradiction involved the goal of economic independence as defined by self-employment, which was fundamental to the free labor ideology. Montgomery correctly points out that free labor exponents failed to come to terms with the fact that because industrialization resulted in far more employees than it did employers, it necessarily limited social mobility.

6. Gutman, "The Workers' Search for Power," p. 50.

7. *Argus*, June 19, 1863; Munsell, *Collections on the History of Albany*, vol. 2, p. 162; Howell and Tenney, *Bi-Centennial History of Albany*, p. 724.

8. *Argus*, June 18, 1863.

9. Ibid. The laborers' demands were reported variously as 9 shillings to 12 shillings, or a 25 cent raise from $1.25 to $1.50 per day. Munsell gives the 37½ cent figure. Just which outside military forces were involved and how they were

brought to bear is unclear. Howell and Tenney speak of a group of citizens inducing the governor to use the National Guard, while the newspapers report that the sheriff called on the Twenty-fifth Regiment. There is a letter in the Erastus Corning Papers at the Albany Historical Society dated June 18, 1863, in which the sheriff tells Corning that the Twenty-fifth Regiment was in the arsenal and adds, "*If you* think it safe to do so I will dismiss (?) them." (Erastus Corning Papers, Albany Historical Society, AP 166. Emphasis in original.)

10. *Argus*, July 3, 1863. But on the same page in another column there is a report of a vast increase in freight business.

11. Ibid., December 21, 1863.

12. *Iron Moulders' International Journal*, March 1874. Albany molders had lost a strike in 1860. In 1860 Albany's printers, who had disbanded their first union six years before, reorganized, forming Albany Typographical Union No. 4. See George A. Tracy, *History of the Typographical Union* (Indianapolis: International Typographical Union, 1913), p. 187.

13. *Fincher's Trades Review*, August 27, October 8, 1864.

14. Ibid., February 18, 1865.

15. Ibid., October 8, 1864; *Argus*, February 11, 1864.

16. *Fincher's Trades Review*, August 27, 1864. Emphasis in original.

17. Ibid., October 8, 1864.

18. Ibid., December 17, 1864.

19. Montgomery, *Beyond Equality*, p. 99; *Argus*, April 22, 1864; *Albany Evening Journal*, April 21, 1864.

20. *Fincher's Trades Review*, March 4, 1865. A number of unions and labor reformers organized the National Labor Union in 1866; it lasted until 1875. See Montgomery, *Beyond Equality*, pp. 176–96.

21. *Argus*, March 17, 1866. Delegates included representatives from all the leading shops in Albany as well as founders from elsewhere in the state and from Pennsylvania, Ohio, and Canada.

22. Ibid.

23. Ibid., March 24, 1866.

24. National Convention of Iron Moulders, *Annual Proceedings and Records*, Eighth Annual Session, Boston, January 2, 1867, pp. 5–7. On Sylvis, see Grossman, *William Sylvis*, pp. 166–70. Grossman's account of the "Great Lockout" differs from the Sylvis account used here. Upon becoming its president in 1863, Sylvis had built up the union to where by 1866, almost unique among national unions, it had firm control over the craft and was able to enforce a closed shop.

25. *Albany Evening Journal*, March 22, 1866.

26. *National Trades Review*, April 14, 1866 (formerly *Fincher's Trades Review*).

27. *Argus*, March 24, 1866.

28. Ibid., March 27, 1866. "Honest Labor" used "Albanian" to refer to people living in Albany.

29. *Troy Daily Press*, April 16, 1866; *National Trades Review*, May 12, 1866.

30. Iron Moulders, *Proceedings*, Eighth Session, p. 6.

31. *Argus*, February 28, 1870.

32. Ibid., March 2, 1870.

33. Ibid., February 28, 1870.

34. Ibid., March 2, 1870. In ibid., February 28, 1870, the Boss Builders' Board of Trade advertised for 100 masons, bricklayers, and plasterers to work at $3.50 per day. On March 1, Cormac McWilliams, president of the BMPU, accused the builders of trying to flood Albany with men from outside the city so as to force local workers to accept the builders' conditions. See ibid., March 1, 1870.

35. Ibid., September 16, 1869, March 9, 1870.

36. *Workingman's Advocate*, June 4, 1870.

37. After 1870 the *Albany Directory* does not list the organization, nor does the *Argus* mention it after the strike.

38. *Argus*, August 31, 1870.

39. *Illustrated History of the Central Federation of Labor*, p. 91.

40. See Introduction.

41. *Argus*, April 11, 1864.

42. *Albany Evening Journal*, February 10, 1866.

43. *Argus*, July 9, 1864.

44. *Fincher's Trades Review*, August 6 and 27, 1864, March 2, 1865.

45. *Argus*, August 25, 1864.

46. Ibid., April 11, 1864.

47. Ibid., March 19, 1866.

48. *Albany Evening Journal*, February 28, 1870.

49. *Iron Moulders' International Journal*, May 1868, p. 244.

50. The reform movement also attacked the system of prison labor and condemned the "forced" immigration of Chinese laborers. The entire crusade against prison labor is the subject of Chapter 8.

51. *Fincher's Trades Review*, September 17, 1864. The Albany trades assembly sent a copy of the cooperative's constitution to *Fincher's*. They thanked the labor newspaper for reprinting the constitutions of other cooperatives, which they had used as models for their own. Many of the themes, phrases, and regulations used in the assembly's constitution are repeated by the Albany molders' union in the constitution for their own cooperative store organized in 1865. See *Argus*, May 31, 1865; Albany Iron Moulders' Cooperative Association, *Constitution and By-Laws* (Albany: Van Benthuysen's, 1865).

52. *Argus*, December 13, 1864.

53. Supporters of cooperation in Albany knew about the British cooperative movement. The constitution of the trade assembly cooperative refers to the "success abroad" of cooperatives. On the British cooperatives, see J. F. C. Harrison, *Quest for the New Moral World: Robert Owen and the Owenites in Britain and America* (New York: Scribner's, 1969), pp. 74–79. On the notion of a moral economy, see E. P. Thompson, "The Moral Economy of the English Crowd in the Eighteenth Century," *Past and Present* no. 50 (February 1971), pp. 76–136.

54. *Fincher's Trades Review*, September 17, 1864.

55. Harrison, *Quest for the New Moral World*, p. 77.

56. There are no records left from the cooperative. The *Argus*, June 10, 1869, listed the association's officers and noted that it had declared a 4 percent semiannual dividend to stockholders on the amount of goods purchased. However, the cooperative also paid a 4 percent premium on the amount of money invested, which indicates that in order to attract capital, the original guidelines had been revised.

57. Ibid., March 31, 1870.

58. *New York Daily Tribune*, May 27, 1867. The newspaper published a letter from an Albany printer to William Jessup, president of the New York State Workingmen's Assembly, which discusses the prospect of a union-organized printers' cooperative.

59. James C. Sylvis, ed., *The Life, Speeches, Labors, and Essays of William H. Sylvis* (New York: Augustus M. Kelley, 1968 [1872]), p. 275.

60. *National Trades Review*, March 31, 1866. The Troy molders completed their cooperative foundry first, opening it in July 1866. By August it was producing seventy-five stoves a day, and in its first six months, as business increased, the foundry expanded. Of fifty employees, thirty to thirty-five were molders, and of these, all but two owned stock. During the next year profits nearly trebled, and

the labor force doubled as the foundry contracted $100,000 worth of business. See *Troy Daily Whig*, August 17, 1866; *Troy Daily Press*, July 23, 1866; Jonathan Grossman, "Co-operative Foundries," *New York History* 24 (April 1943), pp. 202–5.

61. *Argus*, December 7, 1866. At least the leading officers of the UFA belonged to the Albany Iron Moulders' Union.

62. Ibid., January 2, 1867.

63. *Iron Moulders' International Journal*, February 1867.

64. *Argus*, January 21, 1868.

65. New York, Albany County, City of Albany, vol. 4, p. 10, and vol. 10, p. 190, R. G. Dun and Co. Collection, Baker Library, Harvard University Graduate School of Business Administration.

66. Albany County Clerk, MSS. Certificates of Incorporation, vol. 2. The Capital Co-operative Foundry Company filed for incorporation on August 31, 1868. Ninety-four shareholders were listed. See also *Argus*, June 2, 1868.

67. N.Y., Albany, vol. 10, p. 190, R. G. Dun and Co. Collection.

68. *Argus*, June 26, 1872. The Capital Co-operative made "Germania" wood-burning stoves on contract for a number of leading Albany iron founders.

69. *Iron Moulders' International Journal*, May 1867.

70. Because neither of the Albany cooperatives left records, the information here is a composite drawn from Certificates of Incorporation and the Dun and Company reports. It is likely that the Albany cooperative limited voting. The International Iron Moulders' Union adopted such limits for its Pittsburgh cooperative as did the Albany Iron Moulders [consumer] Cooperative Association. See Sylvis, *William H. Sylvis*, pp. 271–72; Milton Derber, *The American Idea of Industrial Democracy, 1865–1965* (Urbana: University of Illinois Press, 1970), pp. 36–39.

71. Sylvis, *William H. Sylvis*, p. 271.

72. On Sylvis and cooperation, see Grossman, *William Sylvis*, pp. 189–219. In his letter to the *Iron Moulders' International Journal*, May 1868, "Co-operation" concluded, "The only solution of the problem of capital and labor is Co-operation."

73. Montgomery, *Beyond Equality*, p. 234.

74. *Argus*, September 27, 1865.

75. Ibid., October 20, 1865. Whether the league actually organized eight-hour committees in each city ward or solicited the Common Council for the eight-hour workday is not clear from existing records.

76. Ibid., November 7, 1865.

77. Ibid., October 20, 1865.

78. *Fincher's Trades Review*, September 16, 1865.

79. *Argus*, October 20, 1865.

80. Montgomery, *Beyond Equality*, pp. 302–3. William Jessup of the New York State Workingmen's Assembly called a special convention in June 1867. The convention asked Congress and President Andrew Johnson to institute the eight-hour workday in government workshops, and urged the National Labor Union to organize a labor party at its next session. See *Argus*, June 26, 27, 28, and 29, 1867.

81. Workers in the railroad shops included carpenters, truckmen, tinsmiths, blacksmiths, painters, wood-machine hands, and machinists. It is unclear from the records if carpenters in the NYCRR shops belonged to the carpenters' union. By 1868 Corning had lost control of the NYCRR to Vanderbilt. While marching through Albany, the shop workers passed by Corning's residence and cheered him. Evidently one aspect of this strike was the workers' resentment of outside control of the shops. On the causes of the strike, see *Argus*, March 16, 1868.

82. Ibid., March 19, 20, and 23, 1868.

83. Ibid., March 23, 1868.

84. Ibid., March 20, 1868. There is little evidence to explain why greater support did not materialize. An Albany "Mechanic" had written the *Workingman's Advocate* in December 1867 that there was a strong potential for eight-hour strikes if business were good. But 1868 was not a good year. In February the *Argus* reported the "Disorganization of Business and the Destitution of Labor." The article mentioned great "apathy" in trade, stoppage of manufacturing, and significant unemployment, nationally and in Albany. Apparently, the shop workers' strike came at a time when other Albany workers could ill afford to give any assistance. See *Workingman's Advocate*, December 7, 1867; *Argus*, February 8, 1868.

85. *Argus*, March 23, 1868. Resolution of the wage dispute did not come for another two weeks. Not all workers received pay increases; of those who did, the increases varied from 12½ cents to 38 cents per day. The workers did not protest these variations, and even passed resolutions thanking Torrence for his cooperation and acknowledging the company's disposition to deal justly with its employees. See ibid., April 8, 1868.

86. Ibid., September 9, 1868. The three community members, Cornelius Halloran, James McNeil, and Lyman Weaver, were secretaries of the meeting.

87. On worker politics, see Chapters 7 and 8.

88. Montgomery, *Beyond Equality*, pp. 323–34.

89. *Albany Evening Journal*, June 17, 1872.

90. *Argus*, June 18 and 20, 1872.

91. Ibid., June 17, 1872; *Albany Evening Journal*, June 17, 1872. This was a new organization and not a continuation of the earlier league.

92. *Argus*, June 17, 1872.

93. Ibid., June 19, 1872.

94. Ibid., June 18 and 19, 1872.

95. Ibid., June 21, 1872.

96. Ibid., June 19, 1872.

97. Ibid. The *Argus* identified a "Mr. Farenbach" as president of the Machinists' and Blacksmiths' International Union.

98. Ibid.

99. Ibid., June 20, 1872.

100. Ibid. These comments were made by two local strike leaders, Thomas Smith and William H. Barnard.

101. Ibid.

102. Ibid.

103. Ibid., June 17, 1872.

104. *Albany Evening Journal*, June 15, 1872.

105. As quoted in Grossman, *William Sylvis*, pp. 204, 210.

106. The *Evening Journal* wondered whether capital, which controlled the supply of raw materials and the market, might combine against workers' cooperatives; see *Albany Evening Journal*, March 19, 1866.

107. *Argus*, March 23, 1866.

108. Ibid., January 29, 1868.

109. *Albany Evening Journal*, April 16, 1866.

110. Foner, *Free Soil, Free Labor, Free Men*, pp. 11–23.

111. *Argus*, June 26, 1869.

112. *Albany Evening Journal*, May 5, 1867.

113. Irwin Yellowitz, *The Position of the Worker in American Society, 1865–1896* (Englewood Cliffs, N.J.: Prentice-Hall, 1969), p. 1.

114. Montgomery, *Beyond Equality*, pp. 30–31.

115. *Albany Evening Journal*, March 14, 1868; *Argus*, March 16, 1868.

116. *Albany Evening Journal*, March 16, 1868.

117. Ibid., March 17, 1868.

118. Ibid., June 18, 1872.

119. *Argus*, June 18, 1872.

120. Ibid., June 24, 1872.

121. *Albany Evening Journal*, June 15, 1872.

122. *Argus*, May 7, 1867.

123. Foner makes this point about adherents of the free labor ideology in *Free Soil, Free Labor, Free Men*, p. 15.

124. *Argus*, June 24, 1872.

125. *Albany Evening Journal*, June 24, 1872.

126. Ibid., May 3, 1867.

127. *Argus*, April 15, 1867.

128. Max Weber, "Class, Status, Party," in *Class, Status, and Power: A Reader in Social Stratification*, ed. Reinhard Bendix and Seymour Martin Lipset (Glencoe, Ill.: Free Press, 1953), p. 64.

129. Laurie, *Working People of Philadelphia*, pp. 75–79.

130. N.Y., Albany, vol. 10, p. 190, R.G. Dun and Co. Collection.

131. *Argus*, September 9, 1874, January 18, 1875.

132. N.Y., Albany, vol. 4, p. 10, R.G. Dun and Co. Collection.

133. Lawrence Goodwyn, *Democratic Promise: The Populist Movement in America* (New York: Oxford University Press, 1976); Harry Boyte, "Lesson from the Populists," *In These Times*, February 15–21, 1978, p. 19. Leon Fink contrasts the use of politics by the Knights of Labor and the populists in "The Uses of Political Power: Toward a Theory of the Labor Movement in the Era of the Knights of Labor," in *Working-Class America: Essays on Labor, Community and American Society*, ed. Michael H. Frisch and Daniel J. Walkowitz (Urbana: University of Illinois Press, 1983), pp. 117–18. But as with the cooperatives, little real change results from labor politics in these years. Here again the workers' localism was a determining factor. For a different perspective, see Charles Stephenson, "A Gathering of Strangers? Mobility, Social Structure, and Political Participation in the Formation of Nineteenth-Century American Workingclass Culture," in *American Workingclass Culture: Explorations in American Labor and Social History*, ed. Milton Cantor (Westport, Conn.: Greenwood Press, 1979), pp. 31–60.

134. Claire Dahlberg Horner, "Producers' Cooperatives in the United States, 1865–1890" (Ph.D. diss., University of Pittsburgh, 1978), pp. 181–84. See also Grossman, *William Sylvis*, pp. 189–219; Frank T. Stockton, "Productive Coöperation in the Molders' Union," *American Economic Review* 21 (June 1931), pp. 263–66.

135. Robert Wiebe, *Search for Order, 1877–1920* (New York: Hill and Wang, 1967), p. xiii.

136. Grossman, *William Sylvis*, pp. 88–91; Warren Van Tine, *The Making of the Labor Bureaucrat: Union Leadership in the United States, 1870–1920* (Amherst: University of Massachusetts Press, 1973), pp. 1–18.

137. Montgomery, *Beyond Equality*, p. 305.

Chapter Four

1. *Argus*, September 20, 1873. On the Panic of 1873, see O. V. Wells, "The Depression of 1873–79," *Agricultural History* 11 (July 1937), pp. 237–49; Samuel Bernstein, "American Labor and the Long Depression, 1873–1878," *Science and Society* 20 (Winter 1956), pp. 59–83; Samuel Rezneck, "Distress, Relief, and Discontent in the United States during the Depression of 1873–78," *Journal of Political Economy* 58 (December 1950), pp. 494–512.

2. Sylvis, *William H. Sylvis*, p. 365.

3. *Albany Evening Journal*, September 22, 1873.

4. *Albany Daily Evening Times*, September 25, 1873.

5. Commissioner of Labor, *The First Annual Report of the Commissioner of Labor. Industrial Depressions* (Washington, D.C., 1886), pp. 60–61.

6. Ibid.; Leah Hannah Feder, *Unemployment Relief in Periods of Depression: A Study of Measures Adopted in Certain American Cities, 1857 through 1922* (New York: Russell Sage Foundation, 1936), pp. 38–39.

7. *Argus*, February 13, 1877, July 26, 1875. The figure for adult males employed is taken from U.S. Census, *Tenth Census. Manufactures*, p. 381.

8. Herbert Gutman found that among workers nationwide only the iron molders attributed the panic to the "evil machinations" of "Money Power." See "Social and Economic Structure and Depression: American Labor in 1873 and 1874" (Ph.D. diss., University of Wisconsin, 1959), p. 22.

9. *Argus*, June 29, 1875, August 7, 1877; *Illustrated History of the Central Federation of Labor*, p. 88.

10. David M. Schneider and Albert Deutsch, *The History of Public Welfare in New York State, 1867–1940* (Chicago: University of Chicago Press, 1941), p.

41. The *Argus*, February 19, 1872, reported that business was "dull." The newspaper also complained that construction of the new Capitol had attracted many laborers who routinely looked to the city for support when work stopped during the winter months.

11. *Argus*, December 4, 1873.

12. Ibid., October 6, 7, and 28, November 8, 1873.

13. *Albany Evening Journal*, December 27, 1873.

14. *Argus*, December 30, 1873, January 14 and 16, February 23 and 25, 1874; *Albany Evening Journal*, December 30, 1873; Thomas R. Lithgow, "Albany's Finest" (paper written for Dr. Goodman, State University of New York at Albany, Fall 1970; copy in the Albany Institute of History and Art).

15. *Albany Evening Times*, December 18, 1873; *Argus*, February 25, March 10, 1874.

16. *Argus*, December 2, 1873. The *Argus* reported that members of the St. Andrew's Society had an average annual income of nearly $1,000.

17. Ibid., October 3, 1873, February 17, 1877.

18. Theodore A. Ross, *Odd Fellowship: Its History and Manual* (New York: Hazen, 1888), pp. 614–15.

19. Ossian Lang, *History of Freemasonry in the State of New York* (New York: Grand Lodge of New York Free and Accepted Masons, 1922), p. 210; *Argus*, August 14, 1876.

20. *Argus*, December 15, 1873.

21. Ibid., February 10, 1874.

22. Ibid., February 26, 1877; *Albany Hand-Book*, p. 18.

23. *Argus*, January 11, 1876; *Our Work at Home*, December 1875, p. 27.

24. Boyer, *Urban Masses and Moral Order in America*, pp. 148–52.

25. *Argus*, February 10, 1874.

26. Ibid., February 26, 1877.

27. Albany City Tract Society, *Sixteenth Annual Report of the City Tract Society* (1851), p. 3. (Hereafter CTS, *Sixteenth Annual Report*, etc.) Reprints the constitution.

28. *Argus*, August 1, 1874; *Albany Evening Journal*, August 5, 1874.

29. *Our Work at Home*, December 1877, p. 26.

30. Ibid., April 1876, p. 59.

31. Ibid., December 1877, p. 26. The area was heavily Roman Catholic, according to the religious census. However, the mission's purpose was less to convert Catholics than to reach the "nominally Protestant population" who did not attend church.

32. Ibid., pp. 25–28. For more on the ACTMS and the mission, see Chapter 7.

33. Ibid., p. 25.

34. William E. Rowley, "The Irish Aristocracy of Albany, 1798–1878," *New York History* 52 (July 1971), pp. 297–98.

35. *Argus*, February 11, 1875.

36. Ibid., January 31, 1874. During a hard winter (1869–70), Hoxie, an Albany grocer, had helped set up a soup kitchen. Apparently, in 1870, following the election of a new mayor, Hoxie was appointed overseer of the poor. Ibid., January 1, May 28, 1870.

37. Ibid., April 8, 1874.

38. Ibid., January 11, 1876.

39. Ibid., January 21, 25, 27, and 31, 1874, February 2 and 7, March 3, 1876.

40. *Albany Evening Journal*, January 17, 1876; *Argus*, January 25, 1876.

41. *Argus*, February 14, 1876. About $3,000 was spent.

42. Ibid., March 22, 1876; Rowley, "Albany," pp. 99, 220. Although the total spent on relief programs did increase during the 1870s, the actual amount was not great. The city's almhouse received the most support, a constant $25,000 during the depression. At no point in the 1870s did the city spend more than 10 percent of its budget on poor relief.

43. *Our Work at Home*, January 1876, p. 34.

44. Schneider and Deutsch, *Public Welfare in New York State*, p. 42.

45. Ibid.

46. Rezneck, "Distress, Relief, and Discontent," p. 500; Gutman, "Social and Economic Structure and Depression," p. 356.

47. *Argus*, January 5 and 18, March 6 and 14, July 7, 1876, January 22, February 13, 1877. Just after such a meeting in January 1876, Mayor Judson issued a special appeal that led to the formation of the Citizens Relief Committee.

48. More than 40 names are listed, but not all can be checked for occupation in the *Albany Directory*. Some names are not listed in the directory, some are too common, and some have no reference to their job.

49. *Argus*, January 8, 1876.

50. Ibid., July 1, 7, 10, 11, and 13, 1876. In a letter to the *Argus*, ''Workingman'' stated that the laborers wanted $1.50 per day, as ''a just demand.'' The contractors offered $1.00. The compromise provided $1.25 per day.

51. Gareth Stedman Jones, *Outcast London: A Study in the Relationship between Classes in Victorian Society* (Baltimore: Penguin Books, 1976), p. 252.

52. *Argus*, August 1, 1874.

53. Ibid., January 20, 1876.

54. Ibid., February 22, 1876.

55. *Our Work at Home*, January 1876, p. 34.

56. Boyer, *Urban Masses and Moral Order*, p. 151; Jones, *Outcast London*, p. 252.

57. *Argus*, September 21, 1875.

58. Ibid., February 13, 1877.

59. Ibid., May 9, 1977.

60. Ibid., January 20, 1876.

61. Ibid., November 18, 1873, November 4, 1875.

62. Ibid., November 11, 1874.

63. *Iron Moulders' International Journal*, August 1875, pp. 442–43.

64. *Argus*, May 12, 1875. Full capacity for each shop was about 1,300 men.

65. On the rise of foundries in western cities, see Chapter 1.

66. *Argus*, February 28, 1876; *Iron Moulders' International Journal*, February 1876, p. 631.

67. *Argus*, February 3 and 29, March 16, October 21, 1876.

68. Ibid., March 28, 1877. Rathbone told an *Argus* reporter that the iron founders had tried to create sufficient stock in 1876 to carry them through 1877.

69. Ibid., December 5 and 19, 1876.

70. Evidently one ''lesson'' that iron founders in Albany and Troy had learned since 1866 was to avoid the appearance of being themselves organized when they condemned the union of interfering with the free labor market. Although Albany and Troy iron founders belonged to the National Society of Stove Manufacturers (organized in 1872), this organization does not seem to have been involved in the local 1876–77 lockout.

71. *Albany Daily Evening Times*, March 26, 1877.

72. Ibid. The molders' unions in the West were not as strong as those in the East.

73. *Argus*, March 28, 1877.

74. Ibid., April 6, 1877.

75. Ibid., February 1, 2, 3, 6, 8, and 20, 1877.

76. Ibid., March 26, 1877; *Iron Moulders' International Journal*, May 1876, p. 364; *Albany Daily Evening Times*, March 26, 1877.

77. *Argus*, May 30 and 31, 1877, April 10, 1878. In February 1881, Perry agreed to pay the state 56 cents per day, an increase of 6 cents, for the labor of each prisoner.

78. Ibid., August 12, 13, 14, 16, 20, and 25, September 25, 1879; *Iron Moulders' International Journal*, July and August 1877. The struggle against prison contract labor will be covered in detail in Chapter 8.

79. Rezneck, "Distress, Relief, and Discontent," p. 509. On the 1877 rail strike, see Robert V. Bruce, *1877: Year of Violence* (Chicago: Quadrangle Books, 1970); Jeremy Brecher, *Strike!* (San Francisco: Straight Arrow Books, 1972), pp. 1–24.

80. *Argus*, July 23, 1877; *Albany Evening Journal*, July 23, 1877.

81. *Argus*, July 24, 1877.

82. James D. McCabe, *The History of the Great Riots* (Philadelphia: McCurdy, 1877), pp. 263–64.

83. *Argus*, July 27, 1877.

84. Ibid., September 1, 1877; McCabe, *History of the Great Riots*, pp. 278–79. In October 1877 Vanderbilt announced that one-half of the July pay cut would be restored.

85. Brecher, *Strike!*, pp. 23–24.

86. *Argus*, July 24, 1877.

87. Ibid., January 9, 1882.

88. Christopher Lasch, *The New Radicalism in America, 1889–1963: The Intellectual as a Social Type* (New York: Vintage Books 1965), p. xi.

89. Eric J. Hobsbawm, "From Social History to the History of Society," in *Historical Studies Today*, ed. Felix Gilbert and Stephen R. Graubard (New York: Norton, 1972), p. 18.

Chapter Five

1. Alexis de Tocqueville, *Democracy in America*, 2 vols. (New York: Vintage Books, 1945), vol. 2, p. 114.

2. Ibid., p. 115.

3. Noel P. Gist, "Secret Societies: A Cultural Study of Fraternalism in the United States," *University of Missouri Studies* 15 (October 1940), pp. 31–32; Fergus MacDonald, *The Catholic Church and the Secret Societies in the United States*, United States Catholic Historical Society Monograph Series, No. 22 (New York: Catholic Historical Society, 1946), p. 100. Many of the six milion names were probably duplicates. As is apparent in Albany, membership in one fraternity did not preclude joining another.

4. Theodore A. Ross, *Odd Fellowship: Its History and Manual* (New York: M. W. Hazen, 1888), pp. 9–10; MacDonald, *The Catholic Church and Secret Societies*, p. 6; Henry L. Stillson, ed., *The Official History and Literature of Odd Fellowship, The Three-Link Fraternity* (Boston: Fraternity Publishing, 1897), p. 754.

5. Ross, *Odd Fellowship*, pp. 12–27, 32–37.

6. Rev. A. B. Grosh, *The Odd-Fellow's Improved Manual: Containing the History, Defence, Principles and Government of the Order . . .* (New York: Clark and Maynard, 1873), p. 72. The national body was originally called the Supreme Grand Lodge.

7. The "unwritten" work refers to the secret rituals and ceremonies, whereas the "written" work, including the names and lessons of the degrees, the benefits, and the regalia, can be found in the histories and manuals of Odd Fellowship.

8. Ross, *Odd Fellowship*, p. 251.

9. As cited in ibid., pp. 251, 573. The discussion here of the symbols and rituals of the order assumes that the practices described in the manuals were those of the Albany lodges.

10. The order aided the families of deceased Odd Fellows (including providing money for orphans' education) and financial assistance for brothers in distress because of sickness or unemployment.

11. Stillson, *Official History and Literature of Odd Fellowship*, p. 746. Once he had been a member for at least four weeks, an Odd Fellow could apply for a higher degree, pay the fees, and go through the appropriate ritual testing his knowledge of the lessons of that degree. In addition to the four degrees in the subordinate lodge, Odd Fellowship had a Patriarchal Degree, started in 1829, open to Scarlet Degree Odd Fellows. In 1851 the Rebekah Degree was established

for women, and in the 1880s a military degree, the Patriarchs Militant, was introduced.

12. James L. Ridgely, *History of American Odd Fellowship: The First Decade* (Baltimore: By the author, 1878), p. 492. The Masons had similar restrictions but also barred eunuchs from membership.

13. Ross, *Odd Fellowship*, p. 538.

14. Ibid., p. 2.

15. Stillson, *Official History and Literature of Odd Fellowship*, pp. 234, 257.

16. In 1911 the Odd Fellows temple in Albany burned, and most of the records were destroyed. The lists I used are available in the New York State Library. The disparity between the 1845 list and the later occasional records prevents meaningful statistical comparison. Nevertheless, all the names of members on the available records have been checked for occupation in the appropriate Albany city directories.

There is one other methodological problem: In Albany's city directories many Odd Fellows are either not listed, not given a job citation, or have the same name as others in the directories, so that more than one occupational reference is possible. For example, of the 78 members of Hope Lodge No. 3 in 1845, 33 (42 percent) fall into one of these categories; similar gaps in information exist for all of the city's lodges.

17. Using the specific occupations listed, I assume that someone cited in the directories as a carpenter or molder was a skilled worker, and that laborers were listed as such. For a discussion of the problem of occupational classification, see Clyde Griffen, "Occupational Mobility in Nineteenth-Century America: Problems and Possibilities," *Journal of Social History* 5 (Spring 1972), pp. 310–30. Former chief officers, or Noble Grands, of the subordinate lodges were referred to as "Past Grands."

18. The membership of Hope Lodge No. 3 included Robert Pruyn, Cornelius TenBroeck, Abraham Van Vechtan, and other notable attorneys; C. W. Bender, the city chamberlain; Joel Munsell, a book and job printer as well as local archivist and antiquarian; and Rufus King, assistant editor of the *Albany Evening Journal*, the city's leading Republican newspaper. The *Albany Evening Union*, April 25, 1883, noted that 13 past presidents of the Young Men's Association, the city's leading cultural association, were members of Hope Lodge.

19. Rowley, "Albany," pp. 168–75, Appendix, Tables 1–5.

20. A list of members for American Lodge No. 32 in 1850 is similar to the 1845 list.

21. Coming at a time when control over labor was largely informal and left

to the foreman, the evidence of their membership in the IOOF is interesting, but, for Albany, only suggestive, as they are limited to American Lodge No. 32.

22. Irish Catholics may not have joined the Odd Fellows in great numbers because they had their own distinct ethnic, social, and benevolent organizations, like the Hibernian Provident Society. See Chapter 7. See also Rowley, "The Irish Aristocracy of Albany," pp. 275–304.

23. Gist, "Secret Societies," p. 70.

24. Ridgely, *History of American Odd Fellowship*, pp. 2, 10; Ross, *Odd Fellowship*, p. 600.

25. Odd Fellowship is one example of an institutional network that developed to give a volatile people a sense of community. The activities and philosophy of fraternal societies—the provision of traveling cards and practical benefits, the universality of their symbolic secret work, the emphasis on brotherhood, and their perception of themselves as a family—illustrate the portability of nineteenth-century American voluntary institutions. See Brian Greenberg, "Migration and the Working Class" (workshop session at the American Historical Association Convention, Washington, D.C., December 1976). See also Don H. Doyle, "The Social Functions of Voluntary Associations in a Nineteenth-Century American Town," *Social Science History* 1 (Spring 1977), pp. 333–56.

26. Ross, *Odd Fellowship*, p. 44.

27. Stillson, *Official History and Literature of Odd Fellowship*, p. 101.

28. Ridgely, *History of American Odd Fellowship*, p. 319. MacDonald (*The Catholic Church and Secret Societies*) claims the break with the Manchester Unity stemmed from the chartering of a black Odd Fellow lodge in the United States. The official literature of American Odd Fellowship does not mention this; moreover, the literature accounts for the break as a reform. Ridgely was national Grand Secretary for over thirty years.

29. Ridgely, *History of American Odd Fellowship*, pp. 264, 319–20.

30. Independent Order of Odd Fellows, *Journal of Proceedings of the Right Worthy Grand Lodge of the Independent Order of Odd Fellows of Northern New York State for 1858, held in the City of Syracuse* (Syracuse: Curtiss and White, 1858), p. 36.

31. As quoted in Stillson, *Official History and Literature of Odd Fellowship*, p. 817.

32. James L. Ridgely and Paschal Donaldson, *The Odd Fellows' Pocket Companion: A Correct Guide in All Matters Relating to Odd-Fellowship* (Cincinnati: W. Carroll, 1867), p. 321.

33. Grosh, *Odd-Fellow's Improved Manual*, p. 34.

34. Union Lodge No. 8, *Constitution and By-Laws of Union Lodge No. 8 of the Independent Order of Odd Fellows* (Albany, 1845), p. 4; American Lodge No. 32, *Constitution, By-Laws, and Rules of Order of American Lodge No. 32, of the Independent Order of Odd Fellows of the City of Albany* (Albany: J. Munsell, 1850), p. 16.

35. The emblems' "lessons" appear throughout Odd Fellow literature. For examples, see Stillson, *Official History and Literature of Odd Fellowship*, pp. 874–77; Ross, *Odd Fellowship*, pp. 575–78; Grosh, *Odd-Fellow's Improved Manual*, pp. 86–172.

36. Grosh, *Odd-Fellow's Improved Manual*, p. 109.

37. Ezra Cook, *Five Standard Rituals: Odd-Fellowship Illustrated, Knights of Pythias Illustrated, Good Templars Illustrated, Exposition of the Grange, Ritual of the Grand Army of the Republic, and the Machinists' and Blacksmiths' Union* (Chicago: Ezra Cook, 1880), p. 29. Cook opposed secret societies, and in this collection of five pamphlets he revealed their "secret" rituals. According to Gist ("Secret Societies," p. 12), Cook's information was substantially correct. On the expulsion or suspension of members for drunkenness, see, for example, American Lodge No. 32, *Constitution, By-Laws, and Rules of Order*, p. 37. Other reasons for suspension or expulsion included neglect of family, abuse of benevolence, gambling, and conduct unbecoming an Odd Fellow. See Independent Order of Odd Fellows, *Journal of Proceedings of the Annual Communication of the Right Worthy Grand Lodge of Northern New York, held at the City of Auburn, August 1852* (Utica: Curtiss and White, 1852), pp. 193–95.

38. Grosh, *Odd-Fellow's Improved Manual*, p. 52.

39. American Lodge No. 32, *Constitution, By-Laws, and Rules of Order*, pp. 10–11.

40. Union Lodge No. 8, *Constitution and By-Laws*, p. 26.

41. Ibid., p. 3.

42. Grosh, *Odd-Fellow's Improved Manual*, pp. 88–89.

43. Gist, "Secret Societies," p. 66.

44. Ridgely, *History of American Odd Fellowship*, p. 495.

45. Stillson, *Official History and Literature of Odd Fellowship*, pp. 874–77; Ross, *Odd Fellowship*, pp. 575–78; Grosh, *Odd-Fellow's Improved Manual*, pp. 86–172.

46. Union Lodge No. 8, *Constitution and By-Laws*, p. 3.

47. Gist, "Secret Societies," p. 142.

48. On the free labor ideology as the basis for a "community consciousness" in Albany, see Introduction. The critical question of how participation in com-

munity associations like the Odd Fellows modified employer behavior merits its own study.

49. See American Lodge No. 32, *Constitution, By-Laws, and Rules of Order*, p. 13.

50. Ross, *Odd-Fellowship*, p. 569.

51. *Mountaineer Lodge No. 321*, p. 20.

52. Gist, "Secret Societies," p. 120.

53. Dawley and Faler, "Working-Class Culture and Politics in the Industrial Revolution," p. 2.

54. See Yellowitz, *Position of the Worker in American Society*, p. 1; Miller, *Jacksonian Aristocracy*, p. 23. I merely present here the tenets of the success ethic without making any claims for high vertical social mobility in American society in these years. Moreover, as demonstrated by their efforts on behalf of producers' cooperatives and the eight-hour working day, Albany workers did, at times, think of equality as a leveling process.

55. *The Covenant* (May 1845), pp. 227–28.

56. Ridgely, *History of American Odd Fellowship*, pp. 492–93.

57. Ibid., p. 497.

58. Stillson, *Official History and Literature of Odd Fellowship*, p. 545.

59. Gist, "Secret Societies," p. 67.

60. Ross, *Odd Fellowship*, p. 207.

61. Ridgely and Donaldson, *Odd Fellows' Pocket Companion*, p. 304. Emphasis in original.

62. Stillson, *Official History and Literature of Odd Fellowship*, pp. 874–77; Ross, *Odd Fellowship*, pp. 575–78; Grosh, *Odd-Fellow's Improved Manual*, pp. 86–172.

63. Grosh, *Odd-Fellow's Improved Manual*, p. 108.

64. Ridgely and Donaldson, *Odd Fellows' Pocket Companion*, p. 13. Emphasis in original.

65. The statewide order spent more than $50,000 on relief in New York in 1870 and almost $150,000 in 1875. For Albany alone the amounts were over $1,600 in 1870 and almost $7,000 in 1875. The Albany figures represent relief to members only, not to widows for funerals or for the education of orphans. The figures for New York State represent the total amount spent on relief. See Ross, *Odd Fellowship*, pp. 614–15; Howell and Tenney, *Bi-Centennial History of Albany*, p. 720.

66. Ross, *Odd Fellowship*, p. 135.

67. Ridgely, *History of American Odd Fellowship*, p. 495.

68. Quoted in Ross, *Odd Fellowship*, pp. 256–57.

Chapter Six

1. Daniel Walker Howe, *The Political Culture of the American Whigs* (Chicago: University of Chicago Press, 1979), pp. 210–37.

2. David Dyer, *History of the Albany Penitentiary* (Albany: J. Munsell, 1867), p. 7. According to Philip Klein, during the next decade other New York counties followed Albany's lead and built penitentiaries, copying Albany's rules and regulations as well. See *Prison Methods in New York State: A Contribution to the Study of the Theory and Practices of Correctional Institutions in New York State*, Columbia University Studies in History, Economics and Public Law (New York, 1920), p. 222. On changes in penology in New York State in the 1840s, see also M. J. Heale, "The Formative Years of the New York Prison Association, 1844–1862: A Case Study in Antebellum Reform," *New York Historical Society Quarterly* 59 (October 1975), pp. 320–47.

3. *Albany Evening Journal*, February 14, 1844. The newspaper reprinted the committee's report. *Brief Account of the Albany County Penitentiary* (Albany: J. Munsell, 1848), p. 5. This publication is probably the first annual report of the Albany County Penitentiary Board of Inspectors.

4. Zebulon Reed Brockway, *Fifty Years of Prison Service: An Autobiography* (New York: Charities Publications Committee, 1912), p. 27.

5. As quoted in David J. Rothman, *The Discovery of the Asylum: Social Order and Disorder in the New Republic* (Boston: Little, Brown, 1971), p. 84.

6. Albany County, *Third Annual Report of the Inspectors of the Albany County Penitentiary, . . . December, 1851* (Albany: J. Munsell, 1852), pp. 10–11, 15.

7. Rothman, *Discovery of the Asylum*, pp. xii–xx, 79–108; Boyer, *Urban Masses and Moral Order*, p. 58. The work of Rothman and Boyer helped form my understanding of the Albany Penitentiary's social significance.

8. Albany County, *Third Annual Report of the Inspectors of the Penitentiary, 1851*, p. 17.

9. Ibid., p. 19.

10. Rothman, *Discovery of the Asylum*, pp. 43–56.

11. W. David Lewis, *From Newgate to Dannemora: The Rise of the*

Penitentiary in New York, 1796–1848 (Ithaca, N.Y.: Cornell University Press, 1965), pp. 21–23, 29–33. Religious leaders, especially John Howard in England and Thomas Eddy in America, spearheaded the reformatory movement.

12. Rothman, *Discovery of the Asylum*, pp. 82–88.

13. As quoted in W. Lewis, *From Newgate to Dannemora*, p. 88. The penitentiary continued as a place for reform; but the means by which this was accomplished, the prison's internal discipline, had become more severe.

14. Heale, "The Formative Years of the New York Prison Association," p. 325.

15. Rothman, *Discovery of the Asylum*, p. 87.

16. As quoted in Heale, "The Formative Years of the New York Prison Association," p. 326.

17. Rothman, *Discovery of the Asylum*, p. 240.

18. *Brief Account of the Albany County Penitentiary*, p. 5; Dyer, *History of the Albany Penitentiary*, p. 8. The county's expenses for its jail increased from $8,000 per year in 1830 to $22,000 per year by 1843. "Expense" seems to have included jail maintenance and the "attendant costs" of trials, courts, and juries.

19. *Albany Evening Journal*, February 14, 1844.

20. Ibid. The committee of the board which issued the report examined "the subject of Reform in the County expenses" connected with the administration of criminal justice and the distribution of public charity.

21. *Statutes Relating to the Albany County Penitentiary*, comp. Nathaniel C. Moak (Albany: J. Munsell, 1872), pp. 3–6. The legislature placed the penitentiary under the authority of the Board of Supervisors and Albany's mayor and recorder. Once the facility was constructed, this "joint board" appointed the commissioners as its inspectors.

22. Dyer, *History of the Albany Penitentiary*, pp. 15–16.

23. Ibid., p. 16.

24. Ibid., pp. 16–21.

25. *Argus*, February 17 and 21, July 15, 1873, February 20, 1877, May 16, 1878.

26. Orlando F. Lewis, *The Development of American Prisons and Prison Customs, 1776–1845, with Special Reference to Early Institutions in the State of New York* (Montclair, N.J.: Patterson-Smith, 1967 [1922]), p. 175.

27. Dorothea Dix, *Remarks on Prisons and Prison Discipline in the United States* (Philadelphia: Kites, 1845), p. 51.

28. Albany County, *Journal of the Board of Supervisors for 1870*, pp. 175–76. The board had reprinted Pilsbury's testimony to the New York State Committee on Prison Labor.

29. *Brief Account of the Albany County Penitentiary*, p. 6.

30. The Prison Association of New York (hereafter PANY), *Twenty-second Annual Report* (Albany: Van Benthuysen, 1867), p. 456. According to Pilsbury, two inspectors had to be from the city and one from the county. He found the board to be evenly divided politically through the years. Dyer notes that whenever one inspector left the board, his replacement would be from a different party than the remaining two members. Prior to 1854, of course, it would have been Whigs and Democrats. See *History of the Albany Penitentiary*, pp. 154–77.

31. *Brief Account of the Albany County Penitentiary*, p. 6.

32. *Albany Evening Journal*, February 14, 1844.

33. Boyer emphasizes the complex motivations that lay behind nineteenth-century reform. Although he is specifically concerned about those efforts of reform that lay outside the law, I believe he has captured the spirit of the Albany Penitentiary movement as well. See especially *Urban Masses and Moral Order*, pp. vii–ix, 54–63; William Muraskin, "The Social Control Theory in American History: A Critique," *Journal of Social History* 9 (June 1976), pp. 559–69.

34. *Albany Evening Journal*, February 14, 1844.

35. Edward Ayers in his review of *A Just Measure of Pain: The Penitentiary in the Industrial Revolution, 1750–1850*, by Michael Ignatieff, rightly rejects the effort to view the penitentiary movement as a class-conscious attempt to create a disciplined working class. See *Winterthur Portfolio* 15 (Spring 1980), pp. 82–85.

36. "Education and Crime," *The Northern Light*, pp. 49–50. The inspectors of the Albany Penitentiary cited such statistics for that facility as evidence of a close association between intemperance and crime. See Albany County, *Third Annual Report of the Inspectors of the Penitentiary, 1851*, pp. 12–13.

37. A. D. Mayo, *Symbols of the Capital; or Civilization in New York* (New York: Thatcher and Hutchinson, 1859), p. 263.

38. Ibid., p. 261.

39. Albany County, *Third Annual Report of the Inspectors of the Penitentiary, 1851*, p. 41.

40. Rothman, *Discovery of the Asylum*, p. 66.

41. Dyer, *History of the Albany Penitentiary*, p. 70.

42. Mayo, *Symbols of the Capital*, p. 257.

43. For descriptions of the penitentiary buildings, see Dyer, *History of the Albany Penitentiary*, pp. 27–30; Joel Munsell, ed., *The Annals of Albany*, 10 vols. (Albany: J. Munsell, 1850–59), vol. 1, pp. 149–50.

44. PANY, *Sixth Annual Report* (Albany: Van Benthuysen, 1851), p. 76.

45. Dyer, *History of the Albany Penitentiary*, pp. 112–13.

46. PANY, *Tenth Annual Report* (Albany: Van Benthuysen, 1855) includes the prison's rules and bylaws and its "Routine of Duties." See pp. 159–74.

47. Ibid., p. 156.

48. Rothman, *Discovery of the Asylum*, pp. 105–7.

49. *Albany Evening Journal*, February 14, 1844; Dyer, *History of the Albany Penitentiary*, p. 10.

50. PANY, *Nineteenth Annual Report* (Albany: Comstock and Cassidy, 1864), p. 196; PANY, *Tenth Report*, pp. 159, 166.

51. After visiting the penitentiary in 1850, the editor of the *Troy Post* wrote that the prisoners appeared to feel that submission to Pilsbury's authority was "with them a matter of destiny." As quoted in *Argus*, December 28, 1850.

52. PANY, *Tenth Report*, pp. 156, 173–74.

53. Ibid., p. 162.

54. Albany County, *Third Annual Report of the Inspectors of the Penitentiary, 1851*, p. 5.

55. Dyer, *History of the Albany Penitentiary*, p. 10.

56. *Argus*, July 18, November 23, 1855. See also Dyer, *History of the Albany Penitentiary*, pp. 143–47. Of the 1,150 prisoners the Albany Penitentiary received in 1858, more than one-third had sentences of ten days. Not only did short sentences limit the productivity of inmates they also seriously undermined the reformatory function of convict labor. Pilsbury had little hope that during a short confinement the penitentiary could "wean" prisoners "from their vicious and destructive habits" or restore them "to such a bodily condition as would fit them for useful labor." The penitentiary's inspectors concurred, declaring that short sentences rendered "the moral treatment" of inmates less effective than it might be. On short sentences, see Albany County, *Journal of the Board of Supervisors for 1869*, p. 98, and *Second Annual Report of the Inspectors of the Albany County Penitentiary . . . December, 1850* (Albany: Weed, Parsons, 1851), p. 9.

57. Albany County, *Second Annual Report of the Inspectors of the Penitentiary, 1850*, p. 8

58. Glen A. Gildemeister, "Prison Labor and Convict Competition with Free Workers in Industrializing America, 1840–1890" (Ph.D. diss., Northern Il-

linois University, 1977), p. 48. Albany did have a boot and shoe industry, but Pilsbury claimed that prison workshops did not compete with those outside because convict laborers made shoes only of the "coarse kind," which were made nowhere else in the East and sold primarily in the South. PANY, *Fifth Annual Report* (Albany: Weed, Parsons, 1850), p. 291. Yet on another occasion Pilsbury took pains to show how prison labor, because of the division of labor and the use of machinery, did give inmates those skills required by outside industry. According to Pilsbury, in teaching such skills prison labor contributed to the inmates' reform. On the long struggle by New York's workers against the prison contract labor system, see Chapter 8. For Pilsbury on the shoe industry, see Albany County, *Journal of the Board of Supervisors for 1870*, p. 173.

59. *Albany Evening Journal*, February 14, 1844.

60. Dyer, *History of the Albany Penitentiary*, p. 21.

61. On Pilsbury and convict labor, see Gildemeister, "Prison Labor and Convict Competition," pp. 56–59.

62. Albany County, *Journal of the Board of Supervisors for 1870*, p. 154.

63. Albany County, *Journal of the Board of Supervisors for 1874*, p. 193.

64. Mayo, *Symbols of the Capital*, p. 267.

65. Albany County, *Third Annual Report of the Inspectors of the Penitentiary, 1851*, p. 7.

66. As quoted in *Argus*, February 13, 1874.

67. Dyer, *History of the Albany Penitentiary*, pp. 354–55.

68. Brockway, *Fifty Years of Prison Service*, p. 46.

69. PANY, *Tenth Report*, p. 163.

70. Dyer, *History of the Albany Penitentiary*, p. 10.

71. Ibid., pp. 182–83; PANY, *Twenty-fourth Annual Report* (Albany: Argus, 1869), pp. 345–57.

72. *Albany Evening Journal*, February 14, 1844.

73. PANY, *Tenth Report*, p. 172.

74. Ibid., p. 180.

75. PANY, *Nineteenth Report*, p. 194.

76. Albany County, *Third Annual Report of the Inspectors of the Penitentiary, 1851*, p. 15.

77. *Brief Account of the Albany Penitentiary*, p. 5.

78. PANY, *Twenty-eighth Annual Report* (Albany: Argus, 1873), p. 71.

79. Ibid., pp. 71–72.

80. *Brief Account of the Albany County Penitentiary*, p. 6.

81. Albany County, *Journal of the Board of Supervisors for 1863*, p. 35.

82. *Argus*, September 28, 1853. In 1862 a representative from the U.S. Department of the Interior inspected the penitentiary after the transfer of federal prisoners to it. Like the editor of the *Argus*, he found that in the workshops "the impression is produced that they are neat manufacturing establishments, filled with industrious artisans, who are working for wages instead of from compulsion and as punishment." See Dyer, *History of the Albany Penitentiary*, pp. 111–17.

83. Boyer, *Urban Masses and Moral Order*, p. 12. Once again Boyer refers only to moral reforms that did not involve government. In his study of the Second Great Awakening in Rochester, New York, Paul E. Johnson contrasts reform through moral suasion to rcform by the coercive powers of government. See *A Shopkeeper's Millennium: Society and Revivals in Rochester, New York, 1815–1837* (New York: Hill and Wang, 1978), pp. 79–94, 116–35.

84. In her critique of the social control interpretation of religious benevolence in the antebellum period, Lois Banner emphasizes the role voluntary associations played in promoting the social harmony inherent in a "Christian republic." See "Religious Benevolence as Social Control: A Critique of an Interpretation," *Journal of American History* 60 (June 1973), pp. 39–41. See also Chapters 4 and 7 on religious voluntary associations in Albany.

85. Mayo, *Symbols of the Capital*, p. 264. The Reverend Mayo was an outspoken advocate of the free labor system, which he called "the test of national superiority" (p. 74).

86. Munsell, *Annals of Albany*, vol. 1, p. 149; Howell and Tenney, *Bi-Centennial History of Albany*, p. 352.

87. Dyer, *History of the Albany Penitentiary*, p. 70.

88. Boyer, *Urban Masses and Moral Order*, figure following p. 36, caption.

89. PANY, *Thirty-fifth Annual Report* (Albany: Van Benthuysen, 1880), pp. 104–9. This report included New York State's prison laws. Among the other contracts, Rensselaer County officials agreed in 1864 to send to the Albany Penitentiary all of Rensselaer's convicted criminals with sentences of sixty days or more. See *Argus*, December 15, 1864.

90. Dyer, *History of the Albany Penitentiary*, pp. 110–12. Dyer claims that Pilsbury went to Washington after learning of a plan to build a new federal prison. In September 1862 Pilsbury arranged with the secretary of the interior to instead send federal convicts to Albany. Yet on January 30, 1862, the *Argus* had

reported on Pilsbury's contract with the federal government to imprison at Albany all persons convicted in the U.S. Court for the Northern District of New York, the penitentiary receiving ten shillings per week for each convict's board.

91. Dyer, *History of the Albany Penitentiary*, pp. 110–12. In 1856 when the Albany Penitentiary was authorized to receive felony offenders aged sixteen to twenty-one, these younger, long-term prisoners were referred to as a "valuable class" of laborers. See PANY, *Twenty-eighth Report*, pp. 66–67.

92. Dyer, *History of the Albany Penitentiary*, pp. 119–32.

93. Howell and Tenney, *Bi-Centennial History of Albany*, p. 352.

94. For example, see Albany County, *Journal of the Board of Supervisors for 1870*, p. 170.

95. PANY, *Twenty-second Report*, pp. 235–36; PANY, *Thirty-fifth Report*, pp. 8–9.

96. New York State Assembly, *Document No. 120*, December 4, 1850, p. 77.

97. Most statistics on the inmate population at Albany refer to admissions, but the *Argus*, September 20, 1875, did mention that more than 900 prisoners were then confined in the penitentiary.

98. *Argus*, February 17 and 21, July 15, 1873. In 1855 Amos Pilsbury had accepted the position of superintendent at Ward's Island in New York City, overseeing the processing of immigrants into the United States. The joint board chose Louis to replace him as superintendent of the Albany Penitentiary. Three years later Louis resigned to become superintendent of the Illinois state prison at Joliet, and Amos returned to his post at the Albany Penitentiary. Amos left Albany briefly one other time, in 1859, to become superintendent of New York City's Metropolitan Police, but he was not replaced and soon returned to Albany.

99. Albany County, *Journal of the Board of Supervisors for 1876*, pp. 168–71.

100. Albany County, *Journal of the Board of Supervisors for 1878*, pp. 9–10; *Argus*, February 20, 1877, May 16, 1878. The time taken to appoint a new warden is probably a sign of how politicized the penitentiary's management had become. The *Albany Evening Journal*, May 15, 1878, called the final selection the political choice of the Democratic majority.

101. Albany County, *Journal of the Board of Supervisors for 1881*, p. 196. There is no evidence that inmates' daily routine was affected by the changes in prison administration.

102. *Albany Evening Journal*, February 14, 1844.

Chapter Seven

1. Tocqueville, *Democracy in America*, vol. 1, pp. 314–15.

2. Boyer, *Urban Masses and Moral Order*, p. ix.

3. On Catholic acculturation, see Victor Greene, " 'Becoming American': The Role of Ethnic Leaders—Swedes, Poles, Italians, Jews," in *The Ethnic Frontier: Essays in the History of Group Survival in Chicago and the Midwest*, ed. Melvin G. Holli and Peter d'A. Jones (Grand Rapids, Mich.: Eerdmans, 1977), pp. 145–50, 172–75; Eric L. McKitrick and Stanley Elkins, "Institutions in Motion," *American Quarterly* 12 (Summer 1960), pp. 190–91; Philip Gleason, "The Crisis of Americanization," in *Catholicism in America*, ed. Philip Gleason (New York: Harper and Row, 1970), pp. 134–38.

4. Stephan Thernstrom, *Poverty and Progress: Social Mobility in a Nineteenth-Century City* (New York: Atheneum, 1971), p. 177.

5. Matthew Holden, Jr., "Ethnic Accommodation in a Historical Case," *Comparative Studies in Society and History* 8 (January 1966), p. 168. In his study of nineteenth-century ethnic conflict in Cleveland, Ohio, Holden differentiates between what he calls a bargaining process, which seeks accommodation, and a struggling process, which seeks to dictate values.

6. Rowley, "The Irish Aristocracy of Albany," pp. 296–97.

7. Officers for the iron molders' and other Albany unions are listed in the *Albany Directory, Fincher's Trades Review*, and the *Argus.*

8. David Montgomery, "The Shuttle and the Cross," pp. 411–42; Laurie, *Working People of Philadelphia*, pp. 108–33, 199–202.

9. See Chapter 8 on the full significance of the prison contract labor issue in the 1878 election.

10. Paul Buhle, "Debsian Socialism and the 'New Immigrant' Worker," in *Insights and Parallels: Problems and Issues of American Social History*, ed. William L. O'Neill (Minneapolis: Burgess, 1973), p. 276. For a useful discussion of cultural and class consciousness, see Stephenson, "A Gathering of Strangers?," pp. 36–40.

11. Howell and Tenney, *Bi-Centennial History of Albany*, p. 768; *Our Work at Home*, November 1878, p. 114.

12. Rowley, "Albany," pp. 92–99.

13. John L. Thomas, "Romantic Reform in America, 1815–1865," in *Ante-Bellum Reform*, ed. David Brion Davis (New York: Harper and Row, 1967), pp. 154–59.

14. *Argus*, March 28, 1867; Howell and Tenney, *Bi-Centennial History of Albany*, p. 728.

15. *Argus*, November 13, 1877, April 24, May 18, 1878. The *Argus* referred to six Railroad YMCAs along the NYCRR lines, including one in East Albany and one in West Albany. The Albany branches were said to offer rail workers a convenient place to meet, converse, play innocent games, and find good reading matter. The buildings had been fitted by the company. At ceremonies opening the East Albany Railroad YMCA, George Weaver, president of the local chapter, explained that because "the mind of man, when directed in good and virtuous thought, is capable of producing happiness infinitely greater than any indulgence of the passions and appetite," he wished to "dedicate" the organization to moving rail workers in this direction. See *Argus*, June 4 and 5, 1880.

16. Ibid., May 31, 1866.

17. The *Albany Directory* for 1870 lists Albany's churches and Sunday schools. On church social clubs, see, for example, the Young People's Society of the State Street Presbyterian Church, *Constitution* (Albany: J. Munsell, 1871).

18. Rowley, "Albany," pp. 416–17; Howell and Tenney, *Bi-Centennial History of Albany*, pp. 431–32, 727–35.

19. The city spent no more than 4 percent of its budget on relief for any one year during the 1870s. Later in this chapter Catholic relief agencies will be discussed. On relief services during the depression of the 1870s, see Chapter 4.

20. Of the seven ministers on the board of managers during the CTS's first year, three were Presbyterian, two Dutch Reformed, and two Baptist. See also Rowley, "Albany," pp. 224–25.

21. CTS, *Sixteenth Annual Report*, pp. 5–6 (beginning in 1855, ACTMS [Albany City Tract and Missionary Society], *Twentieth Annual Report*, etc.).

22. CTS, *Sixteenth Annual Report*, pp. 8–9.

23. William Buell Sprague, *Religion and Rank: A Sermon Addressed to the Second Presbyterian Congregation in Albany, February 3, 1839, the Sabbath Immediately Succeeding the Funeral of the Honorable Stephen Van Rensselaer* (Albany: Van Benthuysen, 1839), pp. 24–25.

24. William Buell Sprague, *Hints Designed to Regulate the Intercourse of Christians* (New York: Appleton, 1835), pp. 123–28.

25. Johnson, *Shopkeeper's Millennium*, pp. 79–80.

26. CTS, *Seventeenth Annual Report* (1852), pp. 9–11.

27. Emphasis in original. *Albany Evening Journal*, June 18, 1855.

28. ACTMS, *Twentieth Annual Report* (1855), p. 26. It is interesting to note that the transformation of the CTS occurred just a few years after the formation of the Albany Catholic diocese in 1847 and McCloskey's ambitious expansion of Catholic welfare services. Catholic conversion certainly represented an important part of the ACTMS's missionary work.

29. CTS, *Nineteenth Annual Report* (1854), pp. 8–9, 22–23. The survey found that 14,628 persons attended churches in every denomination that day, of whom 5,551 attended "unevangelical" services. The total number represented not quite 26 percent of Albany's population. The report cited an estimate by the "late Dr. Chalmers" that religious attendance in Albany should have been about 62½ percent, but I do not know on what evidence this figure was based.

30. Many of the changes in Albany in the 1850s parallel those in New York City under the influence of the New York City Tract and Missionary Society. See Carroll Smith-Rosenberg, *Religion and the Rise of the American City: The New York City Mission Movement, 1812–1870* (Ithaca, N.Y.: Cornell University Press, 1971), pp. 5–6.

31. These "gentlemen" were not identified. See ACTMS, *Twentieth Annual Report*, p. 15. See Chapter 4 on the belief in Albany that temporary relief was best distributed as alms by voluntary associations. See also CTS, *Seventeenth Annual Report*, pp. 12–13.

32. CTS, *Nineteenth Annual Report*, p. 15.

33. The total CTS budget in 1851 was $600. In 1852, of a total budget of $1,345.74, the society expended $227.75 for relief. The expansion of the CTS's welfare interests does not reflect a change in which churches supported it. Contributions to the society still came mostly from the Presbyterian and Dutch Reform churches in Albany.

34. *Albany Evening Journal*, June 18, 1855.

35. ACTMS, *Twenty-seventh Annual Report* (1862), p. 7.

36. Ibid., *Twenty-third Annual Report* (1858), p. 12.

37. Ibid., p. 15.

38. Ibid., *Twenty-fourth Annual Report* (1859), pp. 14–15.

39. Ibid., *Twenty-seventh Annual Report*, pp. 6–7.

40. Smith-Rosenberg, *Religion and the Rise of the American City*, p. 8.

41. *Our Work at Home*, August 1877, p. 92, October 1879, p. 74.

42. Ibid., December 1877, p. 33. In 1846 the CTS had opened the Rensselaer Street Mission, which served primarily as a Sabbath school. Although the Rensselaer Street facility remained open through the 1870s, the new mission was clearly meant to replace it. Also, by the 1870s the ACTMS seems to have stopped

sending visitors out into the community. Dyer died in 1870, and his successor left after one year. The position was vacant for two years before the society hired Reynolds. On the mission's role as a provider of relief during the depression of the 1870s, see Chapter 4.

43. Ibid., pp. 26–29. Apparently instead of building a boys' gymnasium at the new mission, the ACTMS added one to the Rensselaer Street facility, which also provided lodging for newsboys and for "homeless ones." The society abandoned its intention to house migrants at the new mission because the managers decided it would be impossible to keep the residents' rooms free from vermin. Such an unsanitary situation might "jeopardize the entire work" of the new mission by undermining its educational goals.

44. Ibid., p. 25. Emphasis in original. The city's business leaders were well represented among the new mission's subscribers.

45. Thernstrom discusses the social control aspects of charitable relief assistance in *Poverty and Progress*, pp. 48–49.

46. *Our Work at Home*, October 1879, p. 75.

47. *Albany Evening Journal*, December 21, 1878.

48. In naming its official journal as *Our Work at Home*, the ACTMS distinguished the society's activities in Albany from its support for missions abroad. But the title also points up the society's interest in reforming the domestic life of its client population.

49. *Our Work at Home*, October 1879, p. 76.

50. Ibid., December 1877, p. 27.

51. Ibid., January 1879, p. 4.

52. Ibid., August 1877, p. 92.

53. Ibid., December 1879, p. 92, February 1880, pp. 16–17.

54. Ibid., December 1877, p. 28.

55. *Argus*, March 30, 1877.

56. *Our Work at Home*, January 1876, p. 34.

57. Ibid., December 1877, pp. 27–28.

58. Ibid., January 1876, p. 34.

59. The ACTMS's officers and board of managers are listed in the *Albany Directory*, where their occupations can also be found. Subscriptions to the mission ranged from $2,500, to many between $100 and $1,000, to even more of $1 and less.

60. *Our Work at Home*, December 1877, p. 35.

61. Boyer, *Urban Masses and Moral Order*, p. 58.

62. "Diamond Jubilee Number of the Diocese of Albany, 1847–1922," *The Evangelist*, December 22, 1922, p. 20: Rowley, "The Irish Aristocracy of Albany," pp. 278–79; Robert F. McNamara, *Historic St. Mary's Church, Albany, New York* (Albany: Published by the parish, 1973), p. 5.

63. This figure was equivalent to one-twentieth of Albany's population in 1820.

64. Rowley, "The Irish Aristocracy of Albany," pp. 280–81.

65. John Cardinal Farley, *The Life of John Cardinal McCloskey, First Prince of the Church in America, 1810–1885* (New York: Longmans, Green, 1918), p. 166.

66. Ibid., pp. 160–66; McNamara, *Historic St. Mary's*, p. 21; Rowley, "Albany," pp. 287–88. The Albany diocese covered over thirty thousand square miles and included all or part of twenty-three counties, or two-thirds of the state.

67. Martin Joseph Becker, *A History of Catholic Life in the Diocese of Albany, 1609–1864*, United States Catholic Historical Society Monograph Series, No. 31 (New York: Catholic Historical Society, 1975).

68. *Argus*, August 14, 1851; M. J. Louden, ed., *Catholic Albany: An Illustrated History of the Catholic Churches and Catholic Religious Benevolent and Educational Institutions of the City of Albany* (Albany: Peter Donnelly, 1895), p. 179.

69. Rowley, "The Irish Aristocracy of Albany," pp. 290–91.

70. Ibid. In the 1880s Cardinal McCloskey continued his efforts on behalf of Irish Catholic immigrants by helping to organize the Irish-Catholic Colonization Association. See Aaron I. Abell, *American Catholicism and Social Action: A Search for Social Justice, 1865–1950* (Garden City, N.Y.: Doubleday, 1960), p. 51.

71. Howell and Tenney, *Bi-Centennial History of Albany*, p. 729.

72. Rowley, "The Irish Aristocracy of Albany," pp. 297–98. The Albany city hospital had opened in 1849.

73. Nor was this an isolated incident. See Rowley, "Albany," pp. 356–57.

74. Hurst's appointment followed Whig success in the spring municipal elections. He is quoted in Rowley, "Albany," p. 360. The Catholic lay teachers were permitted to visit on Sundays.

75. Rowley cites the comments of the *Albany Daily State Register* and of the *Albany Morning Express*. See "Albany," p. 359.

76. Ibid., pp. 360–62. On this incident, see also *Argus*, January 4, 13, 15,

and 20, 1855. St. John's Boys Orphan Asylum was built in 1855; St. Vincent's Female Orphan Asylum had opened in 1829, but a new building was finished in 1849.

77. Vincent P. Lannie, "Catholics, Protestants, and Public Education," in *Catholicism in America*, ed. Philip Gleason (New York: Harper and Row, 1970), pp. 52–57.

78. "Diamond Jubilee Number," p. 22.

79. Sister Mary Ancilla Leary, *The History of Catholic Education in the Diocese of Albany* (Washington, D.C.: Catholic University of America Press, 1957), pp. xxx–xxxi.

80. Rowley, "The Irish Aristocracy of Albany," pp. 297–98. In "Albany" (p. 15) Rowley notes the continued growth of parochial education; by 1967 the city's Catholic schools educated almost the same number of students as did its public schools.

81. *Argus*, June 27, 1855.

82. Rowley, "The Irish Aristocracy of Albany," p. 293.

83. *Argus*, May 3 and 17, 1871, February 5, 1872.

84. Ellen H. Walworth, *Life Sketches of Father Walworth with Notes and Letters* (Albany: J. B. Lyon, 1907), p. 207.

85. Of course, a critical difference was that Protestant moral reformers considered themselves to be speaking for the whole community while Catholic leaders focused on the members of their own church.

86. *Metropolitan Record: Official Organ of the Most Rev. Archbishop of New York*, February 4, 1860. Hughes stated that one would find no supporters of disunion or secession among Catholic teachers, who were all faithful to the Constitution and the obligations of citizenship.

87. *Argus*, May 6, 1861.

88. Howard Weisz, "Irish-American Attitudes and the Americanization of the English-Language Parochial School," *New York History* 53 (April 1972), pp. 158–68; Dennis Clark, *The Irish in Philadelphia: Ten Generations of Urban Experience* (Philadelphia: Temple University Press, 1973), pp. 89–99.

89. Walworth, *Life of Father Walworth*, pp. 1–72.

90. Ibid., pp. 260–62.

91. Ibid., pp. 275–76. The penitentiary's founders expressed similar reluctance to using the government's policing powers to achieve reform. See Chapter 6.

92. Walworth, *Life of Father Walworth*, pp. 227–33.

93. Greene, " 'Becoming American,' " pp. 145–46.

94. Rowley, "Albany," p. 392. Among the dinner's organizers were Erastus Corning, Gideon Hawley, Amasa J. Parker, John V. L. Pruyn, Thurlow Weed, Thomas W. Olcott, Ira Harris, Franklin Townsend, and Charles Van Benthuysen. Characteristically, McCloskey declined to participate in such a public display.

95. Rowley, "Albany," p. 393.

96. Rowley, "The Irish Aristocracy of Albany," p. 278. On the special role played by ethnic group leaders, see Greene, " 'Becoming American,' " pp. 144–50; Thernstrom, *Poverty and Progress*, pp. 166–80.

97. Rowley, "The Irish Aristocracy of Albany," pp. 282–83; Richard J. Purcell, "Irish Residents in Albany, 1783-1865," *The Recorder* (February 1950), pp. 11–14.

98. Rowley, "The Irish Aristocracy of Albany," pp. 282–83.

99. Ibid., p. 283.

100. Munsell, *Annals of Albany*, vol. 1, p. 242; Rowley, "Albany," p. 295.

101. *Argus*, March 27, 1855. For a good description of a typical St. Patrick's Day celebration in Albany, see also ibid., March 23, 1850.

102. Rowley, "The Irish Aristocracy of Albany," p. 294, and "Albany," pp. 303–5; Howell and Tenney, *Bi-Centennial History of Albany*, p. 358; *Argus*, February 18, 1856.

103. The YMA in Albany dated from 1833 and attracted the city's commercial and business elite. Erastus Corning had contributed $10,000, which sustained its activities. See Rowley, "Albany," pp. 209–10.

104. *Albany Evening Journal*, February 10, 1855.

105. Rowley, "The Irish Aristocracy of Albany," p. 295.

106. Ibid., p. 296.

107. Cuyler Reynolds, comp., *Albany Chronicles: A History of the City Arranged Chronologically from the Earliest Settlement to the Present Time* (Albany: J. B. Lyon, 1906), p. 573.

108. On Fenianism, see Montgomery, *Beyond Equality*, pp. 127–32; MacDonald, *The Catholic Church and the Secret Societies*, pp. 32–46; Eric Foner, "Class, Ethnicity, and Radicalism in the Gilded Age: The Land League and Irish-America," *Marxist Perspectives* 1 (Summer 1978), pp. 9–11.

109. *Argus*, January 19, 1866.

110. Ibid., July 24, 1867.

111. As quoted in Rowley, "Albany," p. 376 n. 19. By this time McCloskey was archbishop of the Diocese of New York.

112. *Argus*, June 2, 1866.

113. From what we know about the Fenian Brotherhood, it is safe to assume that many who participated in these events in Albany were workers. But no records of the city's Fenian circles survive. Montgomery and Foner stress the working-class nature of Fenianism, yet the fact that in Albany middle-class Irish led the Fenian movement suggests that Fenianism may have been somewhat less radical than these two historians claim it to be. See Montgomery, *Beyond Equality*, pp. 127–32; Foner, "Class, Ethnicity, and Radicalism in the Gilded Age," pp. 9–11.

114. *Argus*, April 18, June 8, 1866.

115. Quinn and Heffernan had won military rank in the Civil War. The Fenian adventure into Canada ended quickly. Both men were arrested, but they returned to Albany in time to lead a non-Fenian Irish nationalist parade on July 4, 1866. See Rowley, "Albany," pp. 377–78.

116. *Argus*, May 26 and 28, 1870. In 1870 Quinn opened a recruiting office in preparation for a second assault on Canada, which, however, never came off. The *Argus* remained firmly opposed to such Fenian escapades.

117. Rowley, "Albany," p. 378. Montgomery contends that Republican party sympathy for the Fenians and Irish nationalism attracted some Fenian leaders to its ranks. Heffernan supported Republican Governor Reuben E. Fenton in 1870. However, little is known of Heffernan's subsequent career.

118. Fifty-eight policemen and 28 firemen in Albany were Irish, according to Rowley. See "Albany," pp. 400–1. Albany Common Council proceedings for 1864 include reports from all city fire departments, listing members and their occupations. See Albany Common Council, *Proceedings*, February 29, 1864, pp. 46–71.

119. Rowley, "Albany," p. 401; *Argus*, September 14, 1877; *Albany Evening Journal*, March 21, 1878.

120. *Albany Evening Journal*, March 23, 1878.

121. Ibid., March 20, 1878; Rowley, "Albany," p. 402.

122. Rowley, "Albany," pp. 404–5; *Argus*, March 28, 1878.

123. *Argus*, March 30, 1878.

124. Ibid., March 26, 1878.

125. Election totals were Nolan 8,916 votes, Chase 5,358 votes, and Young 4,450 votes. Rowley, "Albany," p. 406.

126. *Albany Evening Journal*, April 10, 1878.

127. Rowley, "Albany," p. 406.

128. Rowley, "The Irish Aristocracy of Albany," p. 303.

Chapter Eight

1. W. Lewis, *From Newgate to Dannemora*, p. 44. On New York prisons, see Rothman, *Discovery of the Asylum*, Chapters 3, 4, 10; O. Lewis, *Development of American Prisons and Prison Customs*; Gildemeister, "Prison Labor and Convict Competition," p. 130; John R. Commons et al., *History of Labour in the United States*, 4 vols. (New York: Macmillan, 1918–35), vol. 1, p. 155.

2. W. Lewis, *From Newgate to Dannemora*, pp. 180–83.

3. Charles Z. Lincoln, *The Constitutional History of New York from the Beginning of the Colonial Period to the Year 1905, Showing the Origin, Development, and Judicial Construction of the Constitution*, 5 vols. (Rochester: The Lawyers Cooperative Publishing Co., 1894–1906), vol. 3, pp. 254–58.

4. Ibid., pp. 259–60; W. Lewis, *From Newgate to Dannemora*, pp. 192–200; Commons, *History of Labour*, vol. 1, pp. 369–70; Hugins, *Jacksonian Democracy and the Working Class*, pp. 151–61; O. Lewis, *Development of American Prisons and Prison Customs*, pp. 136–38, 143–45.

5. Lincoln, *Constitutional History of New York*, vol. 3, pp. 264–67; W. Lewis, *From Newgate to Dannemora*, p. 192. On Ely Moore, see Hugins, *Jacksonian Democracy and the Working Class*, pp. 63–67. In 1835, some workers sought, unsuccessfully, Moore's removal from his trade union posts. Even so Moore had little to do with trade unionism after 1835. The legislation passed in 1835 led to experiments with silk production in the state prisons.

6. W. Lewis, *From Newgate to Dannemora*, pp. 197–200; O. Lewis, *Development of American Prisons and Prison Customs*, pp. 143–45. In the 1840s iron production was introduced to Clinton prison in upstate New York.

7. Hugins, *Jacksonian Democracy and the Working Class*, pp. 148–49, 155–56.

8. *Proceedings of the State Convention of Mechanics, Held at Utica, August 21st and 22d, 1834, for the Purpose of Taking into Consideration the Effect Produced on the Various Mechanical Trades by the Present System of State Prison Discipline* (Utica, N.Y.: R. Northway, Jr., 1834), pp. 8–9. Emphasis in original.

9. As quoted in O. Lewis, *Development of American Prisons and Prison Customs*, p. 137. Citing Assembly documents, Lewis credits this statement to mechanics in Geneva, New York.

10. *Proceedings of the State Convention of Mechanics, 1834*, p. 9.

11. New York State Assembly, *Document No. 156*, April 3, 1843, pp. 1–3.

12. Jonathan P. Grossman, "Iron Molders' Struggle against Contract Prison Labor," *New York History* 23 (October 1942), pp. 449–57; Lincoln, *Constitutional History of New York*, vol. 3, p. 273. Apparently Johnson's contract with Sing Sing was not renewed, however.

13. Lincoln, *Constitutional History of New York*, vol. 3, p. 273.

14. *Argus*, February 9, 1867.

15. Ibid., March 14, 1868.

16. Lincoln, *Constitutional History of New York*, vol. 3, p. 273; *Albany Evening Journal*, April 17, 1868; *Argus*, July 29, 1868.

17. *Fincher's Trades Review*, October 7, 1865.

18. Ibid., October 8, 1864.

19. Ibid.

20. Sylvis, *William H. Sylvis*, pp. 413–17. Emphasis in original.

21. See Montgomery, *Beyond Equality*, pp. 368–79.

22. Gildemeister, "Prison Labor and Convict Competition," pp. 236–38; PANY, *Twenty-fifth Annual Report* (Albany: Argus, 1870), pp. 468–69; PANY, *Twenty-sixth Annual Report* (Albany: Argus, 1871), p. 147; New York State Assembly, *Document No. 18,* January 27, 1871, pp. 76–79.

23. Lincoln, *Constitutional History of New York*, vol. 3, p. 275.

24. New York State Bureau of Statistics of Labor, *First Annual Report for the Year 1883* (Albany: Weed, Parsons, 1884), p. 31; *Argus*, February 20, 1877.

25. *Argus*, March 26, 1877.

26. Ibid., May 21, 1877.

27. Gildemeister, "Prison Labor and Convict Competition," p. 181.

28. *Iron Moulders' International Journal*, August 1877.

29. As quoted in Gildemeister, "Prison Labor and Convict Competition," p. 181.

30. See Chapter 7.

31. Albany County, *Journal of the Board of Supervisors for 1878*, pp. 8–11. By a 17–15 vote the joint board also selected John McEwen to replace Louis Pilsbury at the expiration of his term on March 1, 1879. The *Albany Evening Journal*, May 15, 1878, claimed that McEwen was chosen by a vote of the

Democratic majority. The vote on the resolution to end contract labor altogether lost 13–18; the vote for Daly's resolution was 25–3.

32. Albany County, *Journal of the Board of Supervisors for 1879*, pp. 157–58; *Albany Evening Journal*, August 8, September 17, October 9, 1878.

33. Albany County, *Journal of the Board of Supervisors for 1879*, pp. 19–20, and *for 1882*, pp. 22, 33.

34. See Chapter 4.

35. *Argus*, November 26, 1879–December 30, 1880. The *Albany Evening Union* reported twenty-three trade unions in Albany by 1883. See January 8, 1883.

36. *Argus*, January 24, 1882.

37. *Albany Evening Union*, November 20, 1882.

38. Ibid., July 20, 1882. The *Albany Evening Union* believed in peaceful competition within the free labor system. The newspaper proudly engaged in "open-faced, hand-to-hand conflict" as champion of the rights of labor "against the oppression of capital." But it did so on the "solid basis that capital and labor be allies, not enemies." See May 29, 1882.

39. Ibid., October 4, 1882.

40. Lincoln, *Constitutional History of New York*, vol. 3, pp. 276–77.

41. *Albany Evening Union*, September 19, 1882.

42. Ibid., October 5, 6, and 10, 1882.

43. Ibid., October 6, 1882.

44. Ibid., October 13, 1882.

45. Ibid., November 8, 1882.

46. Ibid., January 2 and 8, 1883. Besides Delehanty, two printers, Godfrey Ernst from Buffalo and Daniel Healey from Rochester, were elected to the State Assembly.

47. *Albany Evening Union*, February 15, 1883. The editorial warns organized labor to eliminate the "nihilist element," particularly, the "German Socialist Most," whose utterances "shock the law abiding American workingman." The reference is to Johann Most, a leading anarchist figure of the period.

48. Ibid., March 29, April 23, May 7, 1883.

49. *Albany Evening Journal*, March 23, 1878. See also Chapter 7.

50. *Annual Reports of the Committee of Thirteen of the Citizens' Association*, 2 vols. (Albany, 1881–91); Robert Kerker, "The Committee of Thirteen of

Albany, New York: A Study in the Reaction to Urban Disorder'' (a paper for Professor Steen, State University of New York at Albany, Spring 1971). The Committee of Thirteen was typical of contemporary municipal reform groups; see John G. Sproat, *''The Best Men'': Liberal Reformers in the Gilded Age* (New York: Oxford University Press, 1968), pp. 244–71.

51. *Albany Evening Journal*, March 12, 1883.

52. *Albany Evening Union*, January 15, 1883.

53. Ibid., February 15, 1883.

54. Ibid., March 6, 1883.

55. Ibid., March 29, 1883.

56. Ibid., March 7, 1883. The *Albany Evening Union* claimed that ten thousand persons marched in the parade. The appeal to all interests to unite to abolish prison labor made at this rally echoes the sentiments expressed fifty years earlier at the convention of mechanics in Utica. In 1834, workers had called ''on every citizen of the State, whether mechanic, agriculturist, professional, . . . [to] assist us in the struggle for the destruction of the detestable monopoly of which we complain.'' See *Proceedings of the State Convention of Mechanics, 1834*, p. 11.

57. *Albany Evening Union*, August 17, 1883. This issue reprints Danaher's testimony given on March 20, 1883. Of course, workers initially were aroused against convict labor because of unfair labor competition. Under Perry's first contract, convicts were paid fifty cents per day, whereas molders received almost six times that amount in Albany's foundries.

58. Ibid., March 29, 1883.

59. Ibid., April 18, May 8, 1883.

60. Ibid., May 17, 1883. The *Albany Evening Journal*, April 18, 1883, reported that in the Assembly Democrats voted for the Butts bill and Republicans against it. All four Albany assemblymen voted for the Butts bill. Labor-supported bills that did pass in 1883 created the state Bureau of Statistics of Labor, abolished cigar manufacturing in tenements, and ended hat production at Clinton prison.

61. *Albany Evening Union*, July 23, 1883.

62. Ibid., September 14, 1883.

63. Ibid., July 26, 1883.

64. Ibid., September 24, 1883.

65. Ibid., August 22, 1883. Parr repeatedly attacked those workers who wanted to organize an independent party, calling them the ''visionary element''

and the "striking element"—discontented radicals who cared nothing for workers. See ibid., October 8 and 20, 1883.

66. Ibid., October 31, 1883. Although the *Evening Union* had some reservations, it supported the Democratic candidate for district attorney because his stand on the submission bill showed him to be the workingman's friend.

67. Ibid., September 19, 1883.

68. Ibid., August 1, 1883.

69. Ibid., October 8, 1883.

70. Ibid., October 13, 1883. The interested parties supplied ballots on the submission bill. In voting to provide anti–prison labor ballots, the Democrats were aiding the workers' cause. For their part, Albany workers, to raise money to print ballots, endorsed a State Workingmen's Assembly plan to collect fifteen cents per union member; they also held a fund-raising picnic.

71. Ibid., October 18, 1883.

72. Ibid., November 1, 1883.

73. *Argus*, March 14, 1883.

74. *Albany Evening Journal*, October 23, 1883.

75. Some workers hoped that Delehanty would agree to head an independent labor ticket. The *Albany Evening Union* advised workers against such a move, calling it suicidal; it could only damage the Democrats, the party that was labor's ally in the struggle against contract labor. Delehanty did run as an independent in the Fourth Assembly District, but lost. See the *Albany Evening Union*, October 20, 1883.

76. Ibid., November 10, 1883; Lincoln, *Constitutional History of New York*, vol. 3, p. 279.

77. James Weinstein makes this point about nineteenth-century politics in *Ambiguous Legacy: The Left in American Politics* (New York: New Viewpoints, 1975), p. 140.

78. Lincoln, *Constitutional History of New York*, vol. 3, pp. 280–94. The 1894 amendment took effect on January 1, 1897.

79. The idea of pure-and-simple trade unionism did not, of course, first surface with Gompers. But the newly emerging American Federation of Labor did clearly articulate a pragmatic, job-conscious trade unionism. After supporting Henry George's 1886 New York City mayoral campaign, Gompers abandoned active politics. In contrast to the labor movement in Albany, however, Gompers rejected the notion of mutuality of interests between employers and employees. See Harold C. Livesay, *Samuel Gompers and Organized Labor in America* (Boston: Little, Brown, 1978), pp. 47–48, 58–74.

80. Montgomery, *Beyond Equality*, pp. 7–8.

81. Grange Sard, *Fort Orange Club of Albany, Why and How It Was Organized* (Albany: By the Club, 1902), p. 5. Resident members of the Fort Orange Club paid an entrance fee after age 35 of $420 and annual dues of $412. Junior members and nonresident members also paid high fees. Such charges obviously limited club membership.

82. Rowley, "Albany," pp. 424–25. Two Irish Catholics were founding members of the Fort Orange Club, Mayor Michael Nolan and John H. Farrell, a publisher.

83. Six local assemblies and a district assembly were affiliated with the Knights of Labor in Albany. The Knights made producers' cooperatives an important part of their program. See Howell and Tenney, *Bi-Centennial History of Albany*, p. 723.

Bibliography

Primary Sources

Newspapers and Journals

Albany Daily Evening Times (daily). 1873–77.
Albany Evening Journal (daily). 1844, 1850–84.
Albany Evening Union (daily). 1882–84.
Albany Morning Express (daily). 1874.
Argus (daily). Albany, 1850–84.
Fincher's Trades Review (after March 17, 1866, *National Trades Review*) (weekly). Philadelphia, 1863–66.
Iron Moulders' International Journal (monthly). Cincinnati, 1864–80, 1917.
Metropolitan Record (weekly). New York City, 1860.
Our Work at Home (monthly). Albany, 1875–80.
Workingman's Advocate (weekly). Chicago, 1864–77.

Public Documents and Reports

Albany, New York. Common Council. *Proceedings.* 1859–80.
Albany City Tract and Missionary Society. *Annual Report.* 1851–80.
Albany County. *Annual Report of the Inspectors of the Albany County Penitentiary. . . .* 1850, 1851.
———. *Journal of the Board of Supervisors.* 1862–84.
Albany County Clerk. Certificates of Incorporations. 1836–91. Manuscript.
Albany Directory. 1850–84.
Brief Account of the Albany County Penitentiary. Albany: J. Munsell, 1848.
New York. Albany County. City of Albany. Vol. 4, p. 10, and vol. 10, p. 190. R. G. Dun and Co. Collection. Baker Library. Harvard University Graduate School of Business Administration.
New York State Assembly. *Document No. 156* (April 3, 1843).
———. *Document No. 120* (December 4, 1850).
———. *Document No. 20* (January 7, 1852).

———. *Document No. 18* (January 27, 1871).
———. *Document No. 96* (March 24, 1880).
New York State Bureau of Statistics of Labor. *Annual Report.* 1883–90.
New York State Senate. *Document No. 71* (April 4, 1855).
———. *Document No. 68* (March 14, 1862).
———. *Document No. 51* (May 3, 1883).
Prison Association of New York. *Annual Report.* 1845–88. Various publishers.
Prison Discipline Society (Boston). *Annual Report of the Board of Managers.* 1851, 1854.
United States Census Office. Census of the United States. Census of Industry. Albany County. 1850. Manuscript.
———. *Seventh Census, 1850. Abstract of the Statistics of Manufacturers.* Washington, D.C., 1858.
———. *Eighth Census, 1860. Manufactures in the United States in 1860.* Washington, D.C., 1866.
———. *Ninth Census, 1870. Manufactures in the United States in 1870.* Washington, D.C., 1872.
———.*Ninth Census. Population and Social Statistics.* Washington, D.C., 1872.
———. *Tenth Census, 1880. Report on the Manufactures.* Washington, D.C., 1883.
———. *Twelfth Census, 1900. Manufactures.* Washington, D.C., 1902.
United States Commissioner of Labor. *First Annual Report.* "Industrial Depressions." Washington, D.C., 1886.
———. *Second Annual Report.* "Convict Labor." Washington, D.C., 1887.

Constitutions and Proceedings

Albany Coachmen's Benevolent Union. *Constitution.* Albany: J. Munsell, 1867.
Albany Iron Moulders' Co-operative Association. *Constitution and By-Laws.* Albany: Van Benthuysen, 1865.
American Lodge No. 32, Independent Order of Odd Fellows. *Constitution, By-Laws, and Rules of Order of American Lodge No. 32, of the Independent Order of Odd Fellows of the City of Albany.* Albany: J. Munsell, 1850.
———. *Constitution and By-Laws.* Albany: The Guild Printer, 1882.
Annual Reports of the Committee of Thirteen of the Citizens' Association. 2 vols. Albany, 1881–91.
The Digest of the Grand Lodge, I.O.O.F. of the State of New York, from 1866–1893 Inclusive. New York: John Medole, 1894.
Independent Order of Odd Fellows. *Journal of Proceedings of the Annual Session of the Right Worthy Grand Lodge of New York.* 1846–80. Various publishers.
Iron Moulders' International Union No. 2, of Troy, New York. "Minutes." April 28, 1858–March 29, 1866.
National Convention of Iron Moulders. *Annual Proceedings and Records.* 1859–78.

Proceedings of the State Convention of Mechanics, Held at Utica, August 21st and 22d, 1834, for the Purpose of Taking into Consideration the Effect Produced on the Various Mechanical Trades by the Present System of State Prison Discipline. Utica, N.Y.: R. Northway, Jr., 1834.

Union Lodge No. 8, Independent Order of Odd Fellows. *Constitution and By-Laws of Union Lodge No. 8 of the Independent Order of Odd Fellows.* Albany, n.p., 1845.

Works by Contemporaries

The Albany Hand-Book. A Strangers' Guide and Residents Manual. Compiled by Henry P. Phelps. Albany: Brandon and Barton, 1884.

Bishop, John Leander. *A History of American Manufactures From 1608–1860.* 3rd ed. rev. and enl. New York: Augustus M. Kelley, 1966 [1868].

Brockway, Zebulon Reed. *Fifty Years of Prison Service: An Autobiography.* New York: Charities Publication Committee, 1912.

Conway, Edward C., and Sanford, Edwin W., eds. *Early History of the New York Encampment of Patriarchs No. 1 I.O.O.F. of Albany, N.Y.* Albany: n.p., n.d.

Cook, Ezra. *Five Standard Rituals: Odd-Fellowship Illustrated, Knights of Pythias Illustrated, Good Templars Illustrated, Exposition of the Grange, Ritual of the Grand Army of the Republic, and the Machinists' and Blacksmiths' Union.* Chicago: Ezra Cook, 1880.

Dix, Dorothea. *Remarks on Prisons and Prison Discipline in the United States.* Philadelphia: Kites, 1845.

Dyer, David. *History of the Albany Penitentiary.* Albany: J. Munsell, 1867.

Grosh, Rev. A. B. *The Odd-Fellow's Improved Manual: Containing the History, Defence, Principles and Government of the Order. . . .* New York: Clark and Maynard, 1873.

Howell, George R., and Tenney, Jonathan. *Bi-Centennial History of Albany: History of the County of Albany, New York, from 1609 to 1886.* New York: W. W. Munsell, 1886.

Illustrated History of the Central Federation of Labor Representing the Various Trades Unions of Albany and Vicinity. Albany: Central Federation of Labor, 1898.

The Industries of the City of Albany. Albany: Elstner, 1889.

Littemore, Charles H. W.; Huberty, Peter J.; and Reade, Henry G., eds. *Half-Century Souvenir and First Historical Year-Book of the Albany Typographical Union Number Four.* Albany: J. B. Lyon, 1905.

Louden, M.J., ed. *Catholic Albany: An Illustrated History of the Catholic Churches and Catholic Religious Benevolent and Educational Institutions of the City of Albany.* Albany: Peter Donnelly, 1895.

McCabe, James D. *The History of the Great Riots.* Philadelphia: McCurdy, 1877.

Mayo, A. D. *Symbols of the Capital; or Civilization in New York.* New York: Thatcher and Hutchinson, 1859.

Munsell, Joel, ed. *The Annals of Albany.* 10 vols. Albany: J. Munsell, 1850–59.

———. *Collections on the History of Albany, from Its Discovery to the Present Time.* 4 vols. Albany: J. Munsell, 1865–71.

Parker, Amasa J., ed. *Landmarks of Albany County, New York.* Syracuse, N.Y.: D. Mason, 1897.

Payne, Seth Wilbur. *Behind the Bars: A Book.* New York: Vincent, 1873.

Reynolds, Cuyler, comp. *Albany Chronicles: A History of the City Arranged Chronologically from the Earliest Settlement to the Present Time.* Albany: J. B. Lyon, 1906.

Ridgely, James L. *History of American Odd Fellowship: The First Decade.* Baltimore: By the author, 1878.

———, and Donaldson, Paschal. *The Odd Fellows' Pocket Companion: A Correct Guide in All Matters Relating to Odd-Fellowship.* Cincinnati: W. Carroll, 1867.

Ross, Theodore A. *Odd Fellowship: Its History and Manual.* New York: M. W. Hazen, 1888.

Sard, Grange. *Fort Orange Club of Albany, Why and How It Was Organized.* Albany: By the Club, 1902.

Sprague, Rev. William Buell. "Charter to Which Young Men Should Aspire, to Meet the Demands of the Age." Reprinted in *The American Pulpit* 11 (July 1846).

———. *Hints Designed to Regulate the Intercourse of Christians.* New York: Appleton, 1835.

———. *Religion and Rank: A Sermon Addressed to the Second Presbyterian Congregation in Albany, February 3, 1839, the Sabbath Immediately Succeeding the Funeral of the Honorable Stephen Van Rensselaer.* Albany: Van Benthuysen, 1839.

———. *A Sermon Addressed to the Second Presbyterian Congregation in Albany. . . .* Albany: Van Benthuysen, 1854.

Statutes Relating to the Albany County Penitentiary. Compiled by Nathaniel C. Moak. Albany: J. Munsell, 1872.

Stillson, Henry L., ed. *The Official History and Literature of Odd Fellowship, The Three-Link Fraternity.* Boston: Fraternity Publishing, 1897.

Sylvis, James C., ed. *The Life, Speeches, Labors, and Essays of William H. Sylvis.* New York: Augustus M. Kelley, 1968 [1872].

Tocqueville, Alexis de. *Democracy in America.* 2 vols. New York: Vintage Books, 1945 [1835–40].

Walworth, Ellen H. *Life Sketches of Father Walworth with Notes and Letters.* Albany: J. B. Lyon, 1907.

Secondary Sources

Abell, Aaron I. *American Catholicism and Social Action: A Search for Social Justice, 1865–1950.* Garden City, N.Y.: Doubleday, 1960.

Aronowitz, Stanley. *False Promises: The Shaping of American Working-Class Consciousness.* New York: McGraw-Hill, 1973.

Baker, Robert P. "Labor History, Social Science, and the Concept of the Working Class." *Labor History* 14 (Winter 1973): 98–105.

Banner, Lois W. "Religious Benevolence as Social Control: A Critique of an Interpretation." *Journal of American History* 60 (June 1973): 23–41.

Bates, Harry C. *Bricklayers' Century of Craftsmanship: A History of the Bricklayers', Masons', and Plasterers' International Union of America.* Washington, D.C.: By the union, 1955.

Becker, Martin Joseph. *A History of Catholic Life in the Diocese of Albany, 1609–1864.* United States Catholic Historical Society Monograph Series, No. 31. New York: Catholic Historical Society, 1975.

Bender, Thomas. *Community and Social Change in America.* New Brunswick, N.J.: Rutgers University Press, 1978.

Boyer, Paul. *Urban Masses and Moral Order in America, 1820–1920.* Cambridge, Mass.: Harvard University Press, 1978.

Brown, Thomas N. *Irish-American Nationalism, 1870–1890.* Philadelphia: Lippincott, 1966.

Bruce, Robert V. *1877: Year of Violence.* Chicago: Quadrangle Books, 1970.

Carter, Paul A. "Recent Historiography of the Protestant Churches in America." *Church History* 37 (March 1968): 95–107.

Clark, Dennis. *The Irish in Philadelphia: Ten Generations of Urban Experience.* Philadelphia: Temple University Press, 1973.

Clark, Victor S. *History of Manufactures in the United States, 1607–1860.* 3 vols. New York: McGraw-Hill, 1929.

Commons, John R., et al. *History of Labour in the United States.* 4 vols. New York: Macmillan, 1918–35.

Dawley, Alan. *Class and Community: The Industrial Revolution in Lynn.* Cambridge, Mass.: Harvard University Press, 1976.

———, and Faler, Paul G. "Working-Class Culture and Politics in the Industrial Revolution: Sources of Loyalism and Rebellion." *Journal of Social History* 9 (Summer 1976): 466–80.

DeMille, George E. *A History of the Diocese of Albany, 1704–1923.* Philadelphia: Church Historical Society, 1946.

Derber, Milton. *The American Idea of Industrial Democracy, 1865–1965.* Urbana: University of Illinois Press, 1970.

"Diamond Jubilee Number of the Diocese of Albany, 1847–1922." *Evangelist,* December 22, 1922.

Dillon, John J. *The Historic Story of St. Mary's, Albany, N.Y.* New York: Kennedy, 1933.

Doyle, Don H. "The Social Functions of Voluntary Associations in a Nineteenth-Century American Town." *Social Science History* 1 (Spring 1977): 333–56.

Ehrlich, Richard L. "The Development of Manufacturing in Selected Counties in the Erie Canal Corridor, 1815–1860." Ph.D. diss., State University of New York at Buffalo, 1972.

Ellis, David M. "Albany and Troy—Commercial Rivals." *New York History* 24 (October 1943): 484–511.

Faler, Paul G. *Mechanics and Manufacturers in the Early Industrial Revolution: Lynn, Massachusetts, 1780–1860.* Albany: State University of New York Press, 1981.

Farley, John Cardinal. *The Life of John Cardinal McCloskey, First Prince of the Church in America, 1810–1885.* New York: Longmans, Green, 1918.

Ferguson, Charles W. *Fifty Million Brothers: A Panorama of American Lodges and Clubs.* New York: Farrar and Rinehart, 1937.

Foner, Eric. "The Causes of the Civil War: Recent Interpretations and New Directions." *Civil War History* 20 (September 1974): 197–214.

———. "Class, Ethnicity, and Radicalism in the Gilded Age: The Land League and Irish-America." *Marxist Perspectives* 1 (Summer 1978): 6–55.

———. *Free Soil, Free Labor, Free Men: The Ideology of the Republican Party before the Civil War.* New York: Oxford University Press, 1970.

———. *Tom Paine and Revolutionary America.* New York: Oxford University Press, 1976.

Foster, John. *Class Struggle and the Industrial Revolution: Early Industrial Capitalism in Three English Towns.* New York: St. Martin's Press, 1974.

Garson, G. David. "Radical Issues in the History of the American Working Class." *Politics and Society* 3 (Fall 1972): 25–32.

Genovese, Eugene. "On Antonio Gramsci." In Eugene Genovese, *In Red and Black: Marxian Explorations in Southern and Afro-American History.* New York: Random House, 1971.

Gildemeister, Glen A. "Prison Labor and Convict Competition with Free Workers in Industrializing America, 1840–1890." Ph.D. diss., Northern Illinois University, 1977.

Gist, Noel P. "Secret Societies: A Cultural Study of Fraternalism in the United States." *University of Missouri Studies* 15 (October 1940): 1–184.

Gleason, Philip. "The Crisis of Americanization." In *Catholicism in America,* edited by Philip Gleason. New York: Harper and Row, 1970.

Goodwyn, Lawrence. *Democratic Promise: The Populist Movement in America.* New York: Oxford University Press, 1976.

Gordon, Milton M. *Assimiliation in American Life: The Role of Race, Religion and National Origins.* New York: Oxford University Press, 1964.

Greene, Victor. " 'Becoming American': The Role of Ethnic Leaders—Swedes, Poles, Italians, Jews." In *The Ethnic Frontier: Essays in the History of Group Survival in Chicago and the Midwest,* edited by Melvin G. Holli and Peter d'A. Jones. Grand Rapids, Mich.: Eerdmans, 1977.

Griffen, Clyde. "Occupational Mobility in Nineteenth-Century America: Problems and Possibilities." *Journal of Social History* 5 (Spring 1972): 310–30.

Grossman, Jonathan P. "Co-operative Foundries." *New York History* 24 (April 1943): 196–210.

———. "Iron Molders' Struggle against Contract Prison Labor." *New York History* 23 (October 1942): 449–57.

———. *William Sylvis, Pioneer of American Labor: A Study of the Labor Movement during the Era of the Civil War.* New York: Columbia University Press, 1945.

Guernsey, William D. "A Brief History of Albany Typographical Union No. 4." In *Commemorating the 90th Anniversary of Albany Typographical Union No. 4.* Albany: J. B. Lyon, 1940.

Gutman, Herbert G. *Work, Culture, and Society in Industrializing America: Essays in American Working-Class and Social History.* New York: Vintage Books, 1977.

———. "The Workers' Search for Power." In *The Gilded Age*, edited by H. Wayne Morgan. Syracuse, N.Y.: Syracuse University Press, 1970.

Harrison, J. F. C. *Quest for the New Moral World: Robert Owen and the Owenites in Britain and America.* New York: Scribner's, 1969.

Heale, M. J. "The Formative Years of the New York Prison Association, 1844–1862: A Case Study in Antebellum Reform." *New York Historical Society Quarterly* 59 (October 1975): 320–47.

Hirsch, Susan E. *Roots of the American Working Class: The Industrialization of Crafts in Newark, 1800–1860.* Philadelphia: University of Pennsylvania Press, 1978.

Hobsbawm, Eric J. "From Social History to the History of Society." In *Historical Studies Today*, edited by Felix Gilbert and Stephen R. Graubard. New York: Norton, 1972.

Holden, Matthew, Jr. "Ethnic Accommodation in a Historical Case." *Comparative Studies in Society and History* 8 (January 1966): 168–80.

Horner, Claire Dahlberg. "Producers' Cooperatives in the United States, 1865–1890." Ph.D. diss., University of Pittsburgh, 1978.

Howe, Daniel Walker. *The Political Culture of the American Whigs.* Chicago: University of Chicago Press, 1979.

Hugins, Walter. *Jacksonian Democracy and the Working Class: A Study of the New York Workingmen's Movement, 1829–1837.* Stanford, Calif.: Stanford University Press, 1960.

Johnson, Paul E. *A Shopkeeper's Millennium: Society and Revivals in Rochester, New York, 1815–1837.* New York: Hill and Wang, 1978.

Jones, Gareth Stedman. *Outcast London: A Study in the Relationship between Classes in Victorian Society.* Baltimore: Penguin Books, 1976.

Kleppner, Paul. *The Cross of Culture: A Social Analysis of Midwestern Politics, 1850–1900.* New York: Free Press, 1970.

Lampard, Eric E. "The History of Cities in the Economically Advanced Areas." *Economic Development and Cultural Change* 3 (1954–55): 81–136.

Lang, Ossian. *History of Freemasonry in the State of New York.* New York: Grand Lodge of New York Free and Accepted Masons, 1922.

Lannie, Vincent P. "Catholics, Protestants, and Public Education." In *Catholicism in America*, edited by Philip Gleason. New York: Harper and Row, 1970.

Lasch, Christopher. *The New Radicalism in America, 1889–1963: The Intellectual as a Social Type.* New York: Vintage Books, 1965.

Laurie, Bruce. *Working People of Philadelphia, 1800–1850.* Philadelphia: Temple University Press, 1980.

Leary, Sister Mary Ancilla. *The History of Catholic Education in the Diocese of Albany.* Washington, D.C.: Catholic University of America Press, 1957.

Leggett, John C. *Class, Race, and Labor: Working-Class Consciousness in Detroit.* New York: Oxford University Press, 1968.

Lewis, Orlando F. *The Development of American Prisons and Prison Customs, 1776–1845, with Special Reference to Early Institutions in the State of New York.* Montclair, N.J.: Patterson-Smith, 1967 [1922].

Lewis, W. David. *From Newgate to Dannemora: The Rise of the Penitentiary in New York, 1796–1848.* Ithaca, N.Y.: Cornell University Press, 1965.

Licht, Walter. "Labor and Capital and the American Community." *Journal of Urban History* 7 (February 1981): 219–38.

Lincoln, Charles Z. *The Constitutional History of New York from the Beginning of the Colonial Period to the Year 1905, Showing the Origin, Development, and Judicial Construction of the Constitution.* 5 vols. Rochester: Lawyers Co-operative Publishing, 1894–1906.

Livesay, Harold C. *Samuel Gompers and Organized Labor in America.* Boston: Little, Brown, 1978.

MacDonald, Fergus. *The Catholic Church and the Secret Societies in the United States.* United States Catholic Historical Society Monograph Series, No. 22. New York: Catholic Historical Society, 1946.

McKitrick, Eric L., and Elkins, Stanley. "Institutions in Motion." *American Quarterly* 12 (Summer 1960): 188–97.

McNamara, Robert F. *Historic St. Mary's Church, Albany, New York.* Albany: Published by the parish, 1973.

May, Henry F. *Protestant Churches and Industrial America.* New York: Harper Torchbooks, 1967.

Miller, Douglas T. *Jacksonian Aristocracy: Class and Democracy in New York, 1830–1860.* New York: Oxford University Press, 1967.

Montgomery, David. *Beyond Equality: Labor and the Radical Republicans, 1862–1872.* New York: Knopf, 1967.

———. "Gutman's Nineteenth-Century America." *Labor History* 19 (Summer 1978): 416–29.

———. "To Study the People: The American Working Class." *Labor History* 21 (Fall 1980): 485–512.

———. "The Working Classes of the Pre-Industrial American City, 1780–1830." *Labor History* 9 (Winter 1968): 3–22.

Neu, Irene D. *Erastus Corning: Merchant and Financier, 1794–1872.* Ithaca, N.Y.: Cornell University Press, 1960.

North, Douglass C. *The Economic Growth of the United States, 1790–1860.* New York: Norton, 1966.

———. *Growth and Welfare in the American Past: A New Economic History.* Englewood Cliffs, N.J.: Prentice-Hall, 1966.

Parenti, Michael. "Immigration and Political Life." In *The Age of Industrialism in America: Essays in Social Structure and Cultural Values*, edited by Frederic Cople Jaher. New York: Free Press, 1968.

Pessen, Edward. *Most Uncommon Jacksonians: The Radical Leaders of the Early Labor Movement.* Albany: State University of New York Press, 1970.

Pred, Allan R. *The Spatial Dynamics of United States Urban-Industrial Growth, 1800–1914: Interpretive and Theoretical Essays.* Cambridge, Mass.: M.I.T. Press, 1966.

Purcell, Richard J. "Irish Residents in Albany, 1783–1865." *The Recorder* (Bulletin of the American Irish History Society) 12 (February 1950).

Rayback, Joseph G. *A History of American Labor.* New York: Macmillan, 1959.

Rezneck, Samuel. "Distress, Relief, and Discontent in the United States during the Depression of 1873–78." *Journal of Political Economy* 58 (December 1950): 494–512.

Rodgers, Daniel T. "Tradition, Modernity, and the American Industrial Worker: Reflections and Critique." *Journal of Interdisciplinary History* 7 (Spring 1977): 655–82.

———. *The Work Ethic in Industrial America, 1850–1920.* Chicago: University of Chicago Press, 1974.

Rothman, David J. *The Discovery of the Asylum: Social Order and Disorder in the New Republic.* Boston: Little, Brown, 1971.

Rowley, William E. "Albany: A Tale of Two Cities, 1820–1880." Ph.D. diss., Harvard University, 1967.

———. "The Irish Aristocracy of Albany, 1798–1878." *New York History* 52 (July 1971): 275–304.

Schneider, David M., and Deutsch, Albert. *The History of Public Welfare in New York State, 1867–1940.* Chicago: University of Chicago Press, 1941.

Selections from the Prison Notebooks of Antonio Gramsci. Edited and translated by Quentin Hoare and Geoffrey Nowell Smith. New York: International Publishers, 1971.

Smith-Rosenberg, Carroll. *Religion and the Rise of the American City: The New York City Mission Movement, 1812–1870.* Ithaca, N.Y.: Cornell University Press, 1971.

Stephenson, Charles. "A Gathering of Strangers? Mobility, Social Structure, and Political Participation in the Formation of Nineteenth-Century American Workingclass Culture." In *American Workingclass Culture: Explorations in American Labor and Social History*, edited by Milton Cantor. Westport, Conn.: Greenwood Press, 1979.

Stewart, Ethelbert. "A Documentary History of the Early Organizations of Printers." *Bulletin of the Bureau of Labor* no. 61 (November 1905).

Taylor, George Rogers. *The Transportation Revolution, 1815–1860.* New York: Rinehart, 1951.

Thernstrom, Stephan. *Poverty and Progress: Social Mobility in a Nineteenth-Century City.* New York: Atheneum, 1971.

———. "Working-Class Social Mobility in Industrial America." In *Essays in Theory and History: An Approach to the Social Sciences*, edited by Melvin Richter. Cambridge, Mass.: Harvard University Press, 1970.

———, and Sennett, Richard, eds. *Nineteenth-Century Cities: Essays in New Urban History.* New Haven, Conn.: Yale University Press, 1969.

Thompson, E. P. *The Making of the English Working Class.* New York: Vintage Books, 1963.

———. "The Moral Economy of the English Crowd in the Eighteenth Century." *Past and Present* no. 50 (February 1971): 76–136.

Trachtenberg, Alan. *The Incorporation of America: Culture and Society in the Gilded Age.* New York: Hill and Wang, 1982.

Walkowitz, Daniel J. *Worker City, Company Town: Iron and Cotton Worker Protest in Troy and Cohoes, New York, 1855–1884.* Urbana: University of Illinois Press, 1978.

Ward, David. *Cities and Immigrants: A Geography of Change in Nineteenth-Century America.* New York: Oxford University Press, 1971.

Ware, Norman. *The Industrial Worker, 1840–1860: The Reaction of American Industrial Society to the Advance of the Industrial Revolution.* Chicago: Quadrangle Books, 1964.

Weber, Max. "Class, Status, Party." In *Class, Status, and Power: A Reader in Social Stratification*, edited by Reinhard Bendix and Seymour Martin Lipset. Glencoe, Ill.: Free Press, 1953.

Weisz, Howard. "Irish-American Attitudes and the Americanization of the English-Language Parochial School." *New York History* 53 (April 1972): 157–76.

Wiebe, Robert. *Search for Order, 1877–1920.* New York: Hill and Wang, 1967.

Williams, Gwyn A. "The Concept of 'Egemonia' in the Thought of Antonio Gramsci: Some Notes on Interpretation." *Journal of the History of Ideas* 21 (October-December 1960): 586–99.

Williams, Raymond. "Base and Superstructure in Marxist Cultural Theory." *New Left Review* no. 82 (November-December 1973): 3–16.

Yellowitz, Irwin. *The Position of the Worker in American Society, 1865–1896.* Englewood Cliffs, N.J.: Prentice-Hall, 1969.

Zieger, Robert H. "Workers and Scholars: Recent Trends in American Labor Historiography." *Labor History* 13 (Spring 1972): 245–66.

Index

Agricultural implements and machinery industry, 9–10
Albany, N.Y.: economic growth and decline, 5, 11–19, 69–70, 84, 92–93, 166n.24, 176n.84; population growth, 93, 105, 129
Albany Academy, 132, 135, 137
Albany Burgess Corps (ABC), 71–72
Albany City Lodge No. 385, 93
Albany City Tract and Missionary Society (ACTMS): facilities, 74–75, 125–27, 198n.42, 199nn.43, 59; goals, 124–25, 126, 128; leadership, 127–28; and poor relief, 74, 76, 78, 79, 130. *See also* City Tract Society
Albany Co-operative Foundry, 55, 65
Albany Co-operative Union Store, 54, 174n.56
Albany County Bible Society, 122
Albany County Sunday School Union, 122
Albany Gas Light Company, 75
Albany Guardian Society and Home for Aged Men, 122
Albany Iron Moulders' Union, 36–37, 47; strikes, 5, 36–39, 40 (1859), 172n.12 (1860), 48–50, 54, 172n.10 (1866), 80 (1875-76), 81–82, 121 (1876-77), 82, 150 (1879)
Albany Masonic Relief Association, 72
Albany Orphan Asylum, 122
Albany Penitentiary: architecture, 108–9, 112, 114, 115; governance, 107, 113, 116, 149–50, 190n.30; inmate population, 110, 115–16, 192n.56, 195n.91; middle-class founders, 103, 105, 107, 110, 114, 117; operation, 106, 107–8, 109–10, 111, 112–13; purpose, 103, 104, 107, 108, 111, 112–13, 114, 115, 116–17, 159
Albany Regency, 20, 21, 134
Albany Typographical Union, 34–35, 51–52, 147, 172n.12; newspaper editors on, 39–40, 51–52
Albany Union Lodge No. 8, 95, 97
Albany Workingmen's party, 20–22
Alms House, Albany, 130-31, 133, 138, 181n.42
American Federation of Labor, 159, 208n.79
Antimonopolists, 151
Anti-prison labor convention (Utica, 1834), 145, 146
Argus Company, 154
Auburn Prison, 105, 144, 145
Auburn system, 105, 106, 144

Baltimore and Ohio Railroad, 82–83
Banks, A. Bleecker, 83
Barnard, William H., 177n.100
Barnum, Henry, 147
Beaumont, Gustave Auguste de: on Americans and penitentiaries, 103–4
Bellows, W. B. (company), 18
Bender, C. W., 185n.18
Berkshire system, 36, 37, 81, 170n.38
Beverwyck Brewery, 139
Bloodgood, Francis, 22, 76
Boardmen and Grey and Company: guard corps, 30–31
Board of Supervisors, Albany County, 103, 106, 115, 116, 150
Boot and shoe manufacturing: in Albany, 16, 17, 18, 165n.18; in Lynn, Mass., 1, 10
Boss Builders' Board of Trade, 50, 51, 173n.34
Bowe, John: resolution by, 150

Boyd and Brothers' brewery, 45
Brewing industry, 15, 16–17
Brice, James, 168n.24
Bricklayers', Masons', and Plasterers' Union (BMPU), 50–51
Bricklayers' strike (New York, N.Y.), 58, 59
Brickmaking industry, 165n.18
Building trades industry, 50–51
Busley, James R., 111
Butts bill, 156, 207n.60

Capital Co-operative Foundry Association, 55, 65, 175n.65, 68
Carpenters: 70; employers of, 50
Carpenters' and Joiners' Union, 50–51, 58, 59
Cassidy, DeWitt Clinton, 135, 136
Cassidy, John, 134, 135
Cassidy, Michael, 43, 54, 168n.17
Cassidy, William, 135, 136, 137
Cathedral of the Immaculate Conception, 129, 132
Catholic Church, 120, 128–30; benefit societies, 75, 130; cultural and social societies, 131–32, 159; and Ireland, 136
Catholic Literary Society, 131
Catholic Young Men's Institute, 131
Catholic Young Men's Lyceum, 131
Cattle trade, 15, 19
Champlain Canal, 14, 15
Chase, Nelson H., 138, 139
Chicago, Ill.: Albany compared with, 12, 18–19, 77
Church of the Holy Cross, 129, 131
Cincinnati, Ohio: iron molders' strike in, 49
Citizens' Association, 151, 153, 159
Citizens' Labor party, 151, 152
Citizens' party, 138, 139
Citizens Relief Committee, 76
City Mission Social Society, 127
City Tract Society (CTS), 123, 124, 197n.20, 198n.33. *See also* Albany City Tract and Missionary Society
Civil War, 43, 45
Class, 1, 3, 85, 139
Class consciousness, 1, 2, 4–5, 19–20, 39, 44–45, 53–61, 64–67, 147; dialectic with community consciousness, 40–41, 85, 121, 141
Clinton, Joseph, 32, 33
Coach makers' union, 46–47
Committee of Thirteen. *See* Citizens' Association
Common Council, Albany, 21, 22, 38–39, 75, 76, 77
Commonwealth consciousness, 5, 44–45, 65, 67, 71, 121
Community consciousness, 2, 4–5, 6, 25, 64–65, 159; dialectic with class consciousness, 41, 85, 140
Conspiracy bill, 47, 51
Cooke, Jay, and Company, 69
Cooperation: consumer, 44, 53–54; producer, 44, 53, 54–56, 65, 66, 144
Cooperative foundries, 54–56, 65, 66, 174n.60
Coopers: employers of, 51
Coopers' International Union of North America, 51
Corning, Erastus: as civic leader, 127, 202n.103; and the New York Central Railroad, 14–15, 16, 18, 19, 31, 46, 176n.81
Corning Corps, 30
Costigan, John, 32–33
Craft, Wilson, and Gross, 75
Crawford, J. F., 56
Crime: growth of, in Albany, 2, 103, 105, 107
Croswell, Edwin, 21

Daly, Patrick: resolution by, 149, 150
Danaher, Franklin M., 155
Dawson, Reverend T. R., 108
Delehanty, Joseph, 151, 152, 158, 208n.75
Democratic party: Barnburner-Hunker feud, 135; and ethnic politics, 6, 134, 137, 138–39; leadership. 20, 21, 134; newspapers, 2, 135; and prison contract labor issue, 6, 139, 144, 149, 154, 155–56, 157–58
Democratic-Republican party, 134
Diocese of Albany, 75, 129–30, 200n.66. *See also* Catholic Church
Diocese of New York: Albany parishes, 129

Dix, Dorothea, 105, 106
Doane, Bishop William Croswell, 73
Dodge, M. W. (company), 18
"Dressed beef," 19
Dutch colonists, 14
Dutchess County, N.Y., 115
Dyer, Reverend David, 112, 123, 124, 125, 198n.42

Eagle Furnace, 31, 36, 39
East Albany railroad yards. *See* Harlem and Hudson River Railroad
Eastern State Penitentiary (Pennsylvania), 105. *See also* Pennsylvania system
East New York Boot and Shoe Manufactory, 18
Economic depression (1870s): "Bread or Work" demonstrations, 70, 76, 77, 78, 79, 80; Panic of 1873 and, 5, 69, 71, 121; poor relief, 70, 72–79, 181n.42; public works projects, 76–77, 78, 79; skilled workers during, 70, 77–78, 80; unemployment, 69–70, 71, 80
Editors, newspaper. *See* Middle-class community leaders; Newspapers; Newspapers, workingmen's
Education, 20–21, 130, 131, 132
Eight-hour workday: law covering, 56, 57, 59, 63, 138; movement for, 44, 53, 56–61, 66; newspaper editors on, 3, 62–63
Elections, 21–22 (1830), 5–6, 121, 138–40, 149, 153 (1878), 152 (1882), 158 (1883)
Emery Brothers, 28
Erie Canal, 11, 14, 15, 71
Ethnic benefit societies, 72

Farrell, John H., 209n.81
Feary, John and Thomas, Company, 17
Feary and Sons, 18
Fehrenbatch, John, 60
Fenianism, 136–37
Fenton, Reuben, 57
Fincher, Jonathan, 48, 49
First Reformed (Dutch) Church, 121
Flagg, Azariah C., 21
Fort Orange Club, 159–60, 209n.81
Franklin, Benjamin, 26
Fraternal societies, 72, 89, 90, 94, 99–100. *See also* Masons, Free and Accepted; Odd Fellows, Independent Order of
Free labor order, 4–5, 6, 11, 64–65, 159; events celebrating, 25, 29, 30–31; middle-class spokesmen for, 2, 3, 41, 45, 62, 114, 140; values, 1–2, 22, 26–27, 28, 29, 30, 40, 51, 52–53, 61, 62, 90, 98, 99, 100–1, 144, 160; workers and, 25, 32–33, 35, 39, 41, 44, 53, 57, 65, 71, 84–85, 133, 155, 160, 171n.5
Friends of Ireland, Association of, 134, 136

Gasworks, city, 45
German Colonial Lodge No. 16, 92, 93
German community, 92, 124
Gilbert, Edward: dinner honoring, 25, 26–27, 29
Glen, Cornelius, 95
Gompers, Samuel, 159, 208n.79
Grady, Patrick, 33
Gramsci, Antonio, 6–7
Green, G. B., 47
Greenbackers, 151
Grimes, Edward, 33
Gutman, Herbert, 3–4

Halloran, Cornelius, 176n.86
Harlem and Hudson River Railroad, 18, 57, 58
Hastings, Frederick R., 47
Hastings, H. J., 27
Heffernan, James, 137, 203nn.115, 117
Hegemony, 6–7
Hibernian Provident Society (HPS), 72, 134–35
Hod carriers, 45
Hope Lodge No. 3, 90, 92, 185n.18
Hopkins, John, 77
House of Shelter, 122
Howell, Henry, 75
Hoxie, George W., 75, 76, 181n.36
Hughes, Archbishop John, 129, 131, 132
Hurst, William, 130

Immigrants, 120, 128, 130, 133–34; newspapers on, 29–30
Independent Labor Democratic party, 121, 138, 139, 149
Independent labor politics, 20, 21–22, 59, 79, 144, 148, 151–53, 154; and 1878 election, 5–6, 121, 138, 139–40, 149
Independent Order of Odd Fellows (IOOF). *See* Odd Fellows, Independent Order of
Industrialization: U.S. pattern, 9–12. *See also* Albany, N.Y.: economic growth and decline; *and*, individual industries
Interest-group consciousness, 144, 156, 159, 160
Irish Catholic community, 75, 93, 129, 130, 133, 159; ethnic associations, 133–35, 136–37; ethnic group leaders, 120–21, 133, 134–36, 137, 160; and free labor values, 120–21, 133, 140; politics, 121, 136, 137–38, 139
Iron founders: and iron molders, conflicts with, 35–38, 48–50, 70–71, 80–82, 146, 170n.41
Iron Founders and Stove Manufacturers of the United States, National Organization of the, 48
Iron molders: on convict labor issue, 146, 147, 149; during 1870s' depression, 70, 80, 84; and free labor values, 25, 39; and unionism, 33, 35, 39. *See also* Albany Iron Moulders' Union; Cooperative foundries
Iron Moulders' International Union, 49, 66, 172n.24

Jacksonian labor, 19–20, 34, 145–46
Jagger, Treadwell, and Perry, 36
Jails: Albany County, 22, 104, 105, 112, 113; colonial, 104; Walnut Street, 104–5
Jessup, William, 176n.80
Jogues, Father Isaac, 128
Johnson, G. B., 46
Johnson, I. G., 146
Judson, Edmund L., 75, 76, 77, 78, 80

Kelly, Michael, 77
Kilbourn, James, 33
King, Rufus, 185n.18
Knights of Labor, 151, 160, 209n.83
Knights of Pythias, 94
Knowles, Charles: resolution by, 149–50
Know-Nothing movement, 135

Laborers: on Albany's docks, 45–47, 71; and 1870s' depression, 70, 71, 77, 78, 79–80; on Albany's reservoir, 78, 182n.50; on Albany's waterworks, 25, 32–33
Labor history, new, 3–4
Ladies Industrial Society, 73
Ladies Protestant Union Aid Society, 73–74, 122
Lancaster School, 21, 167n.30
Lew Benedict Post No. 5, 75
Library Association, 131
Littlefield, D. G., 38
Little Sisters of the Poor, 75
Lumber trade, 14
Lynds, Elam, 105

McCloskey, Bishop John, 129–30, 131, 132, 133, 137, 202n.94
McDonald, James, 33
McEwen, John, 205n.31
McNeil, James, 176n.86
McWilliams, Cormac, 173n.34
Maher, James, 134, 135
Mahoney, David, 33
Maloy, John, 83
Masons: employers of, 50. *See also* Bricklayers', Masons', and Plasterers' Union
Masons, Free and Accepted, 72, 90, 94, 185n.12
Mechanics' and Manufacturers' Albany Coopers Union, 51
Microscope, 22
Middle-class community leaders: as free labor spokesmen, 2–3, 41, 45, 62, 114, 140; and support for workers, 32, 33, 76, 78, 83, 154–55
Military guard corps, 30–31, 71, 168n.15
Militia, New York State, 46
Mink, Charles W., 168n.24
Modernization theory, 4

Moore, Ely, 145, 204n.5
Munsell, Joel, 185n.18

Nafew, John, 26
National Labor Union, 172n.20
Nativism, 29, 130, 132, 135–36
Neville, Isaac, 33
Newgate prison, 105
Newspapers: on the Albany Penitentiary, 113–14; on Albany's economy, 14, 16, 19, 69, 84; on the "Alms House Affair," 130; on cooperatives, 61–62, 177n.106; on the eight-hour workday, 3, 62–63; as employers, 3, 51–52; on Fenianism, 137, 203n.116; and free labor ideas, 2–3, 25, 29, 31, 40, 41, 51, 52–53, 61, 62, 64; and nativism, 29–30; as political organs, 2, 135, 138, 139, 153; on poor relief, 30, 71, 74, 78; on prison contract labor, 153–54, 158; on strikes, 39, 40, 52, 60, 62, 63, 83; on the transatlantic cable, 28; on unionism, 39–40, 51; on volunteer corps excursions, 31
Newspapers, workingmen's, 48, 150; on free labor ideas, 147, 206n.38; on prison contract labor, 147, 156; on producer cooperation, 54, 55; on the state's printer, 2, 154; on workers' politics, 152–53, 154, 156–57, 158, 208n.66; on workers' reform goals, 20, 22, 152
New York Central Railroad (NYCRR): and Albany's economy, 14–15, 16, 18–19, 63, 80, 172n.10; Erastus Corning and, 14–15, 16, 18, 19, 31, 46, 176n.81; during 1870s' depression, 70, 71, 84; strikes against, 45–46 (1863), 57–58, 66, 176nn. 81, 85 (1868), 59–60, 61, 63 (1872), 83–84 (1877)
New York State Grand Lodge, 100
New York State legislature, 21, 47, 57, 106, 107, 207n.60; and prison labor issue, 145, 146–47, 148, 150, 156, 158
New York State Workingmen's Assembly, 44, 56, 146, 147, 156, 157, 176n.80
New York Workingmen's party, 22
Noethen, Father, 133
Nolan, Michael N., 6, 138–39, 209n.81

Odd Fellows, Independent Order of (IOOF): American reforms, 94–95, 98–99, 159; degrees, symbols, and rituals, 91, 95, 96–97, 98, 99, 184n.11; free labor values, 90, 98, 99, 100–1; history, 90, 94; membership, 89–90, 91–94; relief benefits, 72, 96, 99–100, 184n.10, 188n.65; structure, 90–91, 98, 99
Olcott, Thomas W., 71–72, 73, 127
Oliver, R. K., 83
Open Door Mission, 122
"Orator Carpenter." *See* Kilbourn, James
Our Work at Home, 125, 199n.48

Parmalee, William, 130
Parr, John, 156–57
Pastor's Association of Albany, 79
Pennsylvania system, 105, 106
Perry, Eli, 27, 28, 38, 46, 78
Perry, John S., 81, 149
Perry and Company, 17, 30, 71, 81; contracts with Sing Sing prison, 82, 84, 143, 149, 155, 183n.77
Perry Volunteers, 30, 168n.20
Pilsbury, Amos, 106, 110, 113, 116, 195n.98; on prison management, 106–7, 108, 109, 111, 112–13, 114–15, 116, 192n.58
Pilsbury, Louis, 106, 116, 148–49, 150, 195n.98
Pilsbury, Moses, 106
Pittsburgh, Pa.: Albany compared with, 12, 166n.24
Plasterers. *See* Bricklayers', Masons', and Plasterers' Union
Police department, 46, 138, 170n.49; and Albany's poor, 71, 76, 78–79
Poor relief, 99–100, 122–28, 130; during 1870s' depression, 70, 72–79, 181n.42
Populism, 65–66
Potter, Alonzo, 108
"Presentations," 31
Printers: and free labor values, 25, 26–27, 35; and unionism, 5, 33, 34–35, 39, 41. *See also* Albany Typographical Union
Printing industry, 17, 34–35, 169n.30

Prison contract labor: 1878 election issue, 84, 138, 139, 140; workers' struggle against, 7, 143–44, 145–46, 147, 149, 150–51, 153, 154–56, 157–58. *See also* Democratic party: and prison contract labor issue; Perry and Company: contracts with Sing Sing prison
Prisons, New York State, 105, 144–45, 146–47, 148–49
Protestant community: benefit societies, 73–75, 119–20, 122–28, 130, 140; churches, 121–22; as civic leaders, 119–20, 123, 128
Pruyn, Robert, 185n.18
Pruyn, Samuel, 103, 106
Pruyn committee, 103, 105, 117
Puttkammer, Reverend A. Von, 124

Quinn, Terence, 137–38, 139, 203nn. 115, 116

Railroad workers: national strikes (1877), 82–84, 121. *See also* New York Central Railroad
Railroad YMCAs, 122, 197n.15
Ransom, Albion, 38–39
Ransom, S. H., and Company, 45; volunteer corps, 30
Rathbone, Joel, 15
Rathbone, Sard, and Company, 80, 81, 82
Rathbone and Sard, 17–18
Rathbone Guards, 28, 30, 168nn. 17, 20
Religious charity societies, 72, 73, 75, 79. *See also* Catholic Church: benefit societies; Protestant community: benefit societies
Rensselaer County, N.Y., 194n.89
Republican Green Rifles, 134
Republican party, 2, 135, 137, 153, 157, 158
Revivalism, 122
Reynolds, Reverend Charles E., 83, 116, 125
Ridgely, James D., 95, 186n.28; on Odd Fellowship, 95, 96, 98–99, 100–1
Rooker, Myron H., 34
St. Agnes Cemetery, 130
St. Andrew's Society, 72, 180n.16
St. George's Benevolent Society of Albany, 72
St. John's Boys Orphan Asylum, 131, 200n.76
St. John's Church, 131
St. Joseph's Church, 131
St. Mary's Church, 128–29, 131, 134
St. Patrick's Church, 129
St. Patrick's Society, 134
St. Peter's Hospital, 130
St. Vincent de Paul, Society of, 75, 130
St. Vincent's Female Orphan Asylum, 131, 200n.76
Seymour, Horatio, 135
Shoe manufacturing. *See* Boot and shoe manufacturing
Shreiber's Band, 58
Sing Sing prison, 5, 144, 146. *See also* Perry and Company: contracts with Sing Sing prison
Slaughtering and meat packing industry. *See* Cattle trade
Smith, Thomas, 177n.100
Social honor, 64
Sovereign Grand Lodge (SGL), 91
Spencerville, N.Y., 15
Sprague, Reverend William Buell, 123
Spuyten Duyvil, N.Y., 146
Stove manufacturing, 15, 16, 17–18, 80
Stove molders. *See* Iron molders
Submission bill, 156, 157; referendum, 158
Sylvis, William, 49, 50, 56, 66, 146, 172n.24; on workers' politics, 148

TenBroeck, Cornelius, 185n.18
Textile workers' strike (Cohoes, N.Y.), 43
Thayer, Walter, 156
Tilden, Samuel, 148
Tin, copper, and sheet-iron workers' union, 47
Tocqueville, Alexis de: on Americans and penitentiaries, 103–4; and religion, 119; and voluntary associations, 89, 90
Townsend, Franklin, 26

Townsend Zoaves, 58
Trades assemblies: Albany, 44, 47, 48, 53, 150, 151, 153, 157; Albany, eight-hour league of, 56, 57; statewide, 48; Troy, 48
Transatlantic telegraph cable: celebration, 25, 27–29
Treadwell, Perry, and Norton, 39
Treadwell and Perry, 39

Union Aid Society. *See* Ladies Protestant Union Aid Society
Union Foundry Association (UFA), 54, 55, 65
United Irishmen of America, 72, 75
Urban growth: U.S., 11–12, 13 (Fig. 1)

Van Benthuysen (company): volunteer corps, 30
Vanderbilt, Commodore, 18, 58
Vanderbilt, William H., 83–84
Van Rensselaer, Stephen, Jr., 21–22
Van Vechtan, Abraham, 185n.18
Voluntary associations, 72, 101, 121, 159; and free labor values, 6, 85, 140
Vose and Company, 54

Walworth, Clarence A., 132–33
Washington County, N.Y., 115
Weaver, George, 197n.15
Weaver, Lyman, 176n.86
Weed, Thurlow, 26
Weed and Parsons, 154
Wells, Robert H., 127
West Albany railroad yards. *See* New York Central Railroad
Wethersfield prison (Connecticut), 106
Wheeler, Melick and Company Nail Works: mechanics' band, 28, 30
Wieskotten, Reverend F. N., 124
Wildey, Thomas, 90, 91
Women's Christian Temperance Union, 122
Working-class culture, 3–4, 7
Workingmen's Assembly. *See* New York State Workingmen's Assembly
Workingmen's Co-operative Association of Albany, 53–54

Young, S., and Server, 31
Young, William A., 138, 139, 153
Young Men's Christian Association (YMCA), 122. *See also* Railroad YMCAs
Young Men's Association for Mutual Improvement (YMA), 135–36, 202n.103